Carleton I

General Editors: Donal

MW01268764

Editorial Advisors:
  J. Douglas Campbell (Carleton)
  Peter Clive (Carleton)
  Louise George Clubb (Harvard)
  Bruno Damiani (Catholic University of America)
  Louise Fothergill-Payne (Calgary)
  Peter Fothergill-Payne (Calgary)
  Amilcare A. Iannucci (Toronto)
  Jean-Marie Maguin (Montpellier)
  Domenico Pietropaolo (Toronto)
  Anthony Raspa (Chicoutimi)
  José Ruano de la Haza (Ottawa)
  Pamela Stewart (McGill)

Carleton Renaissance Plays in Translation offers the student, scholar, and general reader a selection of sixteenth-century masterpieces in modern English translation, most of them for the first time. The texts have been chosen for their intrinsic merits and for their importance in the history of the development of the theatre. Each volume contains a critical and interpretive introduction intended to increase the enjoyment and understanding of the text. Reading notes illuminate particular references, allusions, and topical details. The comedies chosen as the first texts have fast-moving plots filled with intrigues. The characters, though cast in the stock patterns of the genre, are witty and amusing portraits reflecting Renaissance social customs and pretensions. Not only are these plays among the most celebrated of their own epoch, but they directly influenced the development of the comic opera and theatre throughout Europe in subsequent centuries.

In print:

Odet de Turnèbe, *Satisfaction All Around (Les Contens)*
Translated with an Introduction and Notes by Donald Beecher

Annibal Caro, *The Scruffy Scoundrels (Gli Straccioni)*
Translated with an Introduction and Notes by Massimo Ciavolella
and Donald Beecher

Giovan Maria Cecchi, *The Owl (L'Assiuolo)*
Translated with an Introduction and Notes by Konrad Eisenbichler

Jean de La Taille, *The Rivals (Les Corrivaus)*
Translated with an Introduction and Notes by H.P. Clive

Alessandro Piccolomini, *Alessandro (L'Alessandro)*
Translated with an Introduction and Notes by Rita Belladonna

Gian Lorenzo Bernini, *The Impresario (Untitled)*
Translated with an Introduction and Notes by Donald Beecher and
Massimo Ciavolella

Jacques Grévin, *Taken by Surprise (Les Esbahis)*
Translated with an Introduction and Notes by Leanore Lieblein and
Russell McGillivray

Lope de Vega, *The Duchess of Amalfi's Steward (El mayordomo de la
duquesa de Amalfi)*
Translated with an Introduction and Notes by Cynthia Rodriguez-Badendyck

Comparative Critical Approaches to Rennaisance Comedy
Edited by Donald Beecher and Massimo Ciavolella

Pietro Aretino, *The Marescalco (Il Marescalco)*
Translated with an Introduction and Notes by Leonard G. Sbrocchi and
J. Douglas Campbell

Lope de Rueda, *The Interludes*
Translated with an Introduction and Notes by Randall W. Listerman

Girolamo Bargagli, *The Female Pilgrim (La Pellegrina)*
Translated with an Introduction and Notes by Bruno Ferraro

Leone de Sommi, *A Comedy of Betrothal (Tsahoth B'dihutha D'kiddushin)*
Translated with an Introduction and Notes by Alfred S. Golding in
consultation with Reuben Ahroni

*About the Harrowing of Hell: A Seventeenth-Century Ukrainian Play
in Its European Context*
Translated with an Introduction and Notes by Irena R. Makaryk

ABOUT THE HARROWING OF HELL

Carleton Renaissance Plays in Translation

ABOUT THE HARROWING OF HELL
(Slovo o zbureniu pekla)

A Seventeenth-Century Ukrainian Play in its European Context

Translated, with an Introduction and Notes, by

Irena R. Makaryk

Dovehouse Editions Inc.

Ottawa

Canadian Institute of Ukrainian Studies

University of Alberta, Edmonton

1989

Canadian Cataloguing in Publication Data

Makaryk, Irene Rima, 1951–
  About the Harrowing of Hell

(Carleton Renaissance plays in translation; 15)
Includes the English translation and the original
  text of: Slovo o zbureniu pekla.
Bibliography: p.
ISBN 0–919473–89–X

L. Religious drama, Ukrainian. 2. Ukrainian drama—Translations
into English. 3. English drama—Translations from Ukrainian.
4. Religious drama, Ukrainian—History and criticism. 5. Religious
drama, European—History and criticism. I. Canadian Institute
of Ukrainian Studies. II. Title III. Series.

PG3948.S68M34   1988   891.7'921   C88–090234–5

For information on distribution and for ordering write to:
Dovehouse Editions Canada   Canadian Inst. of Ukrainian Studies
32 Glen Ave.   352 Athabasca Hall
Ottawa, Canada   University of Alberta
K1S 2Z7   Edmonton, Alberta, T6G 2E8

For information about the series write to:
The Editors, Carleton Renaissance Plays in Translation
1812 Dunton Tower
Carleton University
Ottawa, Ontario,
K1S 5B6

Typeset by the HUMANITIES PUBLICATION CENTRE, University of Toronto.
Printed in Canada by Imprimerie Gagné Ltée.

This book has been published with the help of a grant from the Canadian Federation for the Humanities, using funds provided by the Social Sciences and Humanities Research Council of Canada.

A page from the manuscript of *Slovo o zbureniu pekla* [*About the Harrowing of Hell*] in the Petrushevych collection. Reprinted from Mykhailo Vozniak, *Istoriia ukrains'koi literatury* [*History of Ukrainian Literature*], III. Lviv: Prosvita, 1924, p. 188.

TABLE OF CONTENTS

Acknowledgements

A translation and edition of the Ukrainian masterpiece *Slovo o zbureniu pekla* [*About the Harrowing of Hell*] is long overdue, for, since Ivan Franko's discovery of the text in the late nineteenth century, it has lingered in obscurity, unknown to all but the Slavic specialist. Unfortunately, it has thus been omitted from all the major Western studies of religious drama.

The work of a scholar involved in editions is often not unlike the travails of a prospector: much silt and many deceptive, glittering grains must be sifted before a miniscule amount of gold may be discovered. In my prospecting I have been fortunate in the assistance of a number of people and institutions. My thanks to the Rector's Fund at the University of Ottawa for a grant which enabled me to travel to three excellent libraries: the Robarts Library of the University of Toronto, the New York Public, and the Library of the University of Illinois. My thanks to all the staff members of these institutions, but particularly to Dr. Dmytro Shtohryn and the Russian and East European Centre of the University of Illinois, where I was a summer research associate. Additional material was found in the Library of Congress, St. Paul's University Library, and the library of the Seminary of the Holy Spirit in Ottawa, access to which was unlimited, thanks to the Rector, Father Joseph Andrijiszyn. Those books which seemed apparently inaccessible were promptly obtained by the Interlibrary Loan Department of the University of Ottawa. Additional advice about the possible location of materials was provided by the Slavic collection librarian, Ms. Oksana Piaseckyj.

I am particularly grateful to those colleagues who patiently read my manuscript in various stages of unreadiness: Professors Harvey Goldblatt, David Jeffrey, Sarah Horrall (all from the University of Ottawa), Paul J. Fenwick (Pontifical Institute of Mediaeval Studies), and Roman Koropeckyj (Harvard). To Professor Paulina Lewin (Harvard), the only living specialist in the drama of the sixteenth and seventeenth centuries, a special thank you for sharing her enthusiasm about the play, as well as for allowing me to observe and briefly study her methods of translation. Particularly difficult passages of the play suddenly gained lucidity with her assistance.

A number of graduate students, both of the English and the Modern Languages and Literatures Departments, assisted me at various times in locating the odd books that I assigned them, and helped proofread the drafts. They are Joseph Bond, Maria Harchun, and Suneeti Phadke. Finally, much gratitude for the patience and good work of the Secretariat of the English Department, which suffered perhaps more than most in the preparation of drafts of this manuscript.

* * * * *

In rendering this play into English, I have abandoned an attempt to reproduce the rhyme (because of its irregularity), and have, instead, concentrated on reproducing each line by itself. The aim of the translation is to produce a reasonably accurate English version of the Ukrainian text. Occasionally, I have decided to err on the side of literalness because of the problematic nature of the text (obscure lines, odd or unlikely word combinations, incomplete lines, and some repetition). I have, however, attempted to maintain both the complex mixture of styles, high and low, and tones in the play—comic and serious, formal and colloquial. Transliteration of all Slavic materials follows a modified Library of Congress System (without diacritical marks). Place names appear either in transliteration or as they are best known.

I. R. M.

Cover photo: Nelson Pau, Applied Photography, Toronto.

Icon: "Descent into Hell," St. Nicholas Ukrainian Catholic Church, Toronto.

Preface

The harrowing of hell is a fascinating theme for literary scholar, theologian, and layman alike. The story of Christ's Descent into Hell during the three-day period when His Body lay in the sepulchre, and His battle with the Prince of Darkness is a dramatic tale of cosmic magnitude. An archetypal war of titans with echoes from ancient folklore and myth, the harrowing also dramatizes the mediaeval theme *par excellence*: the redemption of the human race by the Messiah.

This celebrated apocryphal theme was first officially recognized in 359 and 360 at the Arian Synods of Sirmium in Pannonia, Nicaea in Thrace, and Constantinople. Scriptural references, both from the Old and the New Testaments, and a long tradition since Apostolic times, gave the Descent of Christ into Hell its foundation, while the whole apocryphal story was recorded by a zealous believer in the fourth or fifth century and was later named the *Gospel of Nicodemus*.

From its Byzantine source, the story of the destruction of hell was rapidly dispersed throughout Central, Eastern and Western Europe, where it took root in many forms—as the subject of theological disputes, poetry, drama, sermons and art. In literature this theme became known as the harrowing of hell.

Often the dramatic focal point of religious play cycles, the harrowing of hell play offers many opportunities for the spectacular and the awesome, as well as the farcical. The gaping hellmouth, the comic blustering of Satan, the solemn entrance of Christ with his warrior angels, the confusion of the devils and the joy of the liberated patriarchs—all these offer splendid scenes of good theatre at the same time as they dramatize important theological concepts.

In Western Europe, the harrowing plays are among the best of extant mediaeval dramas. In Slavic lands, which felt the reverberations of the Middle Ages, the Renaissance, the Reformation and the Counter-Reformation almost all at once, the drama is both numerically and qualitatively more slight. One outstanding and unusual example is the

Ukrainian play entitled *Slovo o zbureniu pekla* [*About the Harrowing of Hell*], probably an early seventeenth-century play.

This study has two aims: to make *Slovo o zbureniu pekla* available in English translation for English-speaking scholars with a limited background in Eastern European studies, and to examine the context in which *Slovo* was formed: the sources, influences, and analogues, the problematic aspects of its composition, and its relation to other harrowing plays in Eastern and Western Europe. Much of the information presented here—a survey of Ukrainian drama and its origins, the text of the Ukrainian harrowing play—will already be familiar to scholars of Ukrainian literature; other aspects of the study (the survey of Western harrowing plays), while familiar to Western mediaevalists, may not be well-known by Slavic scholars. Its value lies primarily in its synthesis; these are materials never before gathered together in one place.

Little work has been done on Ukrainian religious drama since the early part of this century. What has been done with few exceptions is general in nature, and often merely reiterates the findings of nineteenth-century scholars. *Slovo o zbureniu pekla* has been recognized as a dramatic masterpiece of seventeenth-century Ukrainian literature; yet few scholars have ventured beyond a rephrasing of this now commonplace notion and into an investigation of the nature of the play's uniqueness. An examination of its Western and Central European context in part answers that question.

A remarkable dramatic achievement, and probably the last manifestation of this genre anywhere in Europe, *Slovo o zbureniu pekla* forms a nexus between Western and Eastern dramatic traditions.

The Text

Editions of the play

Slovo o zbureniu pekla [*About the Harrowing of Hell*] was first discovered and published by Dr. Ivan Franko, whose scholarly achievements and unflagging interest in apocrypha and legends are often obscured by his fame as poet, writer, and dramatist. *Slovo* first appeared in *Kievskaia starina* [*Kievan Antiquity*] in 1896 with an introduction to the play by Franko, writing under the pseudonym of "Myron".[1] Yet this text soon proved to be only one version of a harrowing of hell play. Franko had received a copy of the play in 1894, when, as he writes, he was given a manuscript by Osyp Rozdols'kyi (who later became a renowned collector of ethnographic material). This manuscript was written in a contemporary cursive by Toma Kyshka (or Kishka), a peasant from Mostych in the province of Kalush. Without mentioning its origins, Kyshka had originally presented the MS to a seminarian, an acquaintance of Rozdols'kyi. Once the text was in Franko's possession, he immediately recognized its age and literary value; obviously, Kyshka could not possibly have been its true author. Franko's later meeting with the peasant established very little about the play's provenance. Kyshka would only admit that he had copied the text from an unspecified source into his notebook, which included various materials transcribed from old documents that interested him.

Trying another tack, Franko, with the assistance of Dr. Ivan Kurovets', a resident of Kalush, later became acquainted with a very old peasant named Iakovyna, who possessed those old books from which Kyshka so liked to copy. From Iakovyna, Franko finally obtained a copy of the Paschal drama (as he calls it), a copy considerably more reliable than the Kyshka text.

In comparing the two versions, Franko discovered that Kyshka had apparently copied Iakovyna's text and then added various elements from other, unknown sources. According to Franko, the Kyshka manuscript contains fifty-four pages of a quarto text. The first sixteen pages contain the tale [*kazka*] "*Premudryi mladenets*" [*Clever Youth*]. *Slovo* begins on page seventeen and ends on thirty-nine. The verse stanzas are printed without separation. Following *Slovo* in this manuscript are "*Chudo sviatytelia Khrystova Nykolaia*" [*The Miracle of St. Nicholas*] (pp. 39–44); a short apophthegem; a poem, "*Bida iz bidoiu*" [*Trouble with Trouble*] (pp. 45–46); a tale entitled "*Hospodar i perepelytsia*" [*The Landlord and the Quail*]; conversations between the peasant Hryts' Okovytka and the Jew Mortko Piavkes (pp. 49–51); and a poem, "*Po bytvi pid Pevnoii*" [*After the Battle at Pevna*]. After some more detective work, Franko republished *Slovo* in 1908, this time "reconstructing" a full work from the various dramatic fragments he had discovered since publishing Kyshka's text in 1896.[2] In his attempt to "reconstruct" the work, Franko uses the following texts:

1) A1: Lviv, Narodnyi Dim Library, Manuscript 181 (pre-World War I, present location unknown), written either in the early or mid-eighteenth century in a clear, round Ruthenian cursive graphically similar to a printed Cyrillic text. A1 is the primary source for Franko's edition of the play, despite the fact that it is not uniformly authoritative (according to Franko) when compared with the other texts.[3]

2) A2: Four excerpts, probably older in origin than A1, but in general very close to A1, they formed the book covers of MS. 212 of the Narodnyi Dim Library.

3) A3: Two excerpts, severely damaged, printed on a leaf in chant-like format. Besides providing some alternate readings for a number of words, they offer very little for a reconstruction of the play.

4) B: The Iakovyna MS, 18 pages of rather thin paper, printed in quarto. The last page is slightly damaged at the top. The MS is written entirely in one hand, probably, hazards Franko, by a cantor or a cantor-teacher in the first half of the nineteenth century.

5) The Kyshka text, a nineteenth century MS, published in *Kievskaia starina*, which Franko does not use in his reconstruction, but which I will call B1.

In his detailed comparison of the texts A1, A2, A3 and B, Franko notes many similarities, but also numerous differences. Of the four texts, B generally appears to be a later, more popular version, that is, one closer to the vernacular. Franko observes that while the copies clearly stem from a protograph, they obviously endured many redactions before they came to their present state. This, he claims, is especially true of the Iakovyna (B) text; but is true, although to a lesser extent, of the group A texts. Franko also dates these manuscripts no later than the mid-eighteenth century. B text then appears to be considerably (at least 50 years) later.[4]

Even a cursory examination of Kyshka's (B1) or Iakovyna's text (B) will reveal some unnecessary repetition; perhaps the scribe was reconstructing the work from memory and therefore could not recall the exact order of certain lines. Other problems include unlikely word combinations, incomplete phrases (which may find their completion in another text), and uneven line lengths. Franko lists two hundred variant readings, and thirteen repetitions or redundancies in his 1908 version. Yet, for some unexplained reason, Franko does not include in his reconstruction a large segment from Kyshka's text (included here as lines 425–464).

M. Vozniak, in an article entitled "Znadibky do ukrains'koi velykodnoi dramy [Research Towards a Ukrainian Easter Drama]"[5] takes issue with Franko's reconstruction, arguing that Franko should have first published a diplomatic edition of A1 (Franko's primary text), a task with which Vozniak completes his article. On the basis of Sventsitskyi's description of the manuscript (*Opys rukopysiv Narodnoho domu z kolektsii Antona Petrushevycha* [*A Description of the Manuscripts of the Narodnyi Dim from the Collection of Antin Petrushevych*] Part II, *Ukrains'ko-rus'kyi Archyv*. VI. Lviv: 1911, pp. 194–200), Vozniak claims that this MS was written not in the mid-eighteenth century, as Franko believed, but rather in the last quarter of the eighteenth century.[6] Vozniak reproduces this text without changes, additions or deletions: only the spelling has been modernized to facilitate printing.

Despite Vozniak's critical view of Franko's version of the play, there are few important substantive differences (these I have drawn attention to in the notes following the translation). The essential difference between Franko and Vozniak's editions is that Vozniak's fragment breaks off after 380 (line 464 in my text), that is, after Christ's first speech.

Vozniak also draws the reader's attention to another MS which has been ignored by scholars, but which is, he claims, probably one of the earliest versions of *Slovo*. It, too, is a "defective" version, that is, apparently a fragment which formed part of an eighteenth-century menologion. The fact that a version of the *Slovo* play was discovered in a menologion suggests that it was theologically sound enough to be included with other religious material.

F. Dobrians'kii's 1882 description of this manuscript in *Opisanie rukopisei Vilenskoi Publichnoi Biblioteki, tserkovno-slovianskikh i russkikh* [*An Inventory of the Manuscripts of the Vilnius Public Library, Church Slavonic and Russian*] (Vilnius: 1882), pp. 279–280, reveals that *Slovo o zbureniu pekla* was included with a variety of apocryphal, eschatological material, including another well-known Slavic work, *Khozhdenie Bogoroditsi po mukam* [*The Journey of the Birth-giver of God Through the Torments of Hell*, often translated as *The Descent of the Virgin to Hell*, or *The Virgin's Visit to Hell*]; a tale about the condition of the soul after death; a description of the Passion of Christ; various prayers; and the litany of Lauds at Pentecost. Unfortunately, queries about this manuscript have failed to elicit a reply from the libraries of the Lithuanian S.S.R.; its present location is therefore unknown.

Yaroslav Hordyns'kyi also published an edition of *Slovo* from yet another version of the work. His article, *"Slovo pro zburenne pekla po Staruns'komu rukopysu XVIII v.* [*About the Harrowing of Hell in an XVIII Century Manuscript from Starunii*]," appeared in *Zapysky Naukovoho Tovarystva im. T.H. Shevchenka*, 97 (1910), 155–174. But Hordyns'kyi's claims that his was an eighteenth-century manuscript were later confidently refuted by Vozniak, who conclusively proved the Staruns'kyi text a nineteenth-century product in his article "Znadibky do ukrains'koi velykodn'oi dramy."[7]

This text was discovered in the village of Starunii (Bohorodchasnyi district) by Hordyns'kyi's student Vasyl' Lazoriv. The play forms part of a small quarto, written all in one hand in Roman (with a small sprinkling of Cyrillic) letters. The text is, like the others, defective; it is missing the first twenty-nine lines of the play, and has many incomplete lines, as well as numerous scribal errors which appear to have occurred during the transliteration from one alphabet to another.[8]

The greater bulk of the text is close to Franko's reconstructed edition of the play, but it is generally more concise; Hordnys'kyi's text consists of 415 lines; he calculates that approximately 30 lines were lost, making a total of 450 (as compared with Franko's 486). As were all the other extant manuscripts, so also, affirms Hordyns'kyi, was this text copied down in the mountainous region of Galicia; to support this claim, he draws attention to various dialectical forms peculiar to Galicia. There are many variants of individual words in Hordyns'kyi's version; they are too numerous to list and do not gravely affect the interpretation of the play; however, a number of important substantive differences must be noted:

a) The names of the demonical commanders appear as Benera instead of Venera (obviously a scribal error, the letter "B" is read as "V" in Cyrillic) and Frubliak (used once to complete a rhyming couplet) or Frub(e)l.[9]

b) Christ appears dignified and solemn; he offers no solace or comfort whatsoever to Lucifer.

c) Lucifer's speech comforting Hades (ll. 220–225) is missing in Hordyns'kyi's text.

d) Lucifer blames the Baptist, not the "King of glory," for the mess in which he finds himself. He does not understand how God, who is in heaven, could be on earth.

e) Lucifer urges his servants into battle, telling them not to fear Christ. The servants reply that they warned Lucifer many times of Christ's strength.

f) Christ's lines 475–476 are missing, as is the reference to the Holy Spirit in the stage directions which follow.

g) Solomon's concluding song of praise is intact, although it is presented second-hand—that is, it is related by the devils who attribute the song to Solomon.

h) Some minor differences include the following omitted references: Lazarus' status as a "secret participant" or "cult follower" (*Slovo*, l. 108), Judas' name (*Slovo*, l. 125); the torture of drinking infernal *kvass* [rye-beer] (*Slovo*, l. 261, l. 280); and Hades' "passion" (*Slovo*, l. 203, l. 205). Hordyns'kyi's text adds a new item to the description of Christ's Passion: the Third Messenger tells his listeners that Christ was spat upon.

Two other editions must be mentioned. V. Rezanov's composite recension, "*Slovo o zbureniu pekla* [*About the Harrowing of Hell*]," in *Drama ukrains'ka* [*Ukrainian Drama*], I (Kiev: Ukrains'ka Akademiia Nauk, 1926), pp. 142–163, follows Franko's 1908 version ll. 1–421, correcting printer's errors only, and adding the concluding lines of the play from Franko's earlier, 1896 version. A more recent edition has been published by O.I. Bilets'kyi as "*Slovo o zbureniu pekla* [*About the Harrowing of Hell*]" in *Khrestomatiia davn'oi ukrains'koi literatury* [*Anthology of Ancient Ukrainian Literature*] (Kiev: Radians'ka shkola, 1967), pp. 220–232. Bilets'kyi reprints Rezanov's text, but modernizes the spelling, and omits all references to the Jews, which appear in all of the extant fragments.

Since it has proved impossible to locate the above manuscripts, this edition and translation of *Slovo* is based upon the easily accessible Rezanov text, which in turn follows Franko's 1896 and 1908 transcriptions.

Author, Place, and Date

The identity of the *Slovo* writer, like that of the creators of most religious plays and, certainly, of Eastern religious art as a whole, remains a mystery. At most, we may postulate that he was a learned polyglot, probably a cleric, with a highly inventive imagination, able to assimilate and combine many traditions.

The question of authorship in relation to Eastern religious texts is a particularly problematic one, for Slavdom, as Riccardo Picchio argues, conceived of an author "only in the primeval, etymological sense of our Latin word (*auctor* from *augeo* 'to augment, to increase'). He [the author] was supposed to record factual or spiritual truths as they were revealed to him by any aspect of the phenomenological experience of human life."[10] It is not surprising that one extant version of *Slovo* survived in a menologion, since literature was conceived of as an "open book."[11] The Bible was at the core of all literature; it was the supreme model to which additional material could be included only if it were inspired. Many eschatological, apocryphal stories were constructed with no clear beginning or ending so that they might be included in larger compositions, such as chronicles, collections, or menologia. Thus individual works were not important in themselves; they were significant as part of a corpus of works which glorified the True Faith.[12] *Slovo* seems to follow in this Slavic tradition. Its inclusion in a menologion attests to its basic orthodox beliefs, in spite of the broad humour and license that seems to be taken by the author.

The place where *Slovo* may have first been written is equally difficult to establish. Oral and written traces of the play survived at the two opposite ends of Ukraine—in the Iziums'kyi and Pulians'kyi regions (Kharkiv province), and in Galicia. Both variants of the play, as well as prose narratives taken from its episodes (especially the episodes concerning the wisdom or cleverness of Solomon in successfully escaping hell), were transcribed from peasants' oral accounts. Oral evidence of the play was also discovered in Transcarpathia. Only in Central Ukraine have vestiges of the play failed to materialize.

According to Franko, the play probably originated in Western Ukraine (either in Volynia or Galicia), and was carried to the East when Sloboda Ukraine was being colonized. If this is the case, says Franko, then the date of the text must be moved back to the early seventeenth century, a theory apparently supported by the language of the play.[13] (See below, *Language*.)

Franko's theory is an attractive one, since many scholars agree that Western Ukraine was the cradle of Ukrainian drama; it was the first to receive the influence of the West by way of Poland. Most likely the puppet theatre (*vertep*) also developed here. (See below, *Ukrainian Drama*.)

Like Franko, O.I. Bilets'kyi also puts the date of the play in the first half of the seventeenth century. He believes that it is a popular drama rather than a school play, in part because it contains no act or scene division.[14] V. Rezanov, who also concurs with Franko's dating, draws attention to *Slovo*'s links with Western European mystery plays. He notes the strong Western influence *via* Poland, which was felt particularly strongly in Galicia, where the Poles controlled many schools.[15] It is interesting, however, that *Slovo* does share some features with Western models of harrowing plays but (with a few small exceptions), bears no resemblance to Polish vernacular models. (See below, *Slovo and the Harrowing Play in Western and Central Europe*.)

Rezanov draws our attention to the fact that in *Slovo* Christ himself appears on stage (as he does in Western European models), but in Eastern plays he is represented by allegorical personages such as God's Grace. Rezanov makes the important observation that *Slovo* appears to be a self-contained play, not part of a cycle, since the whole Passion sequence (represented in Western European plays) is here narrated by messengers who rush on stage announcing news from the world above.[16] In effect, then, *Slovo* is both a harrowing of hell and a Passion play.

Rezanov draws attention to the fact that the harrowing itself, the destruction of the devil's domain and the leading out of the saints, is not clearly indicated in the play. He believes that the *Slovo* which Franko discovered (here Rezanov is speaking of the 1896 text, B1) must be a defective original that is missing a few leaves. According to Rezanov, we learn of these lacunae through Hell's words after Christ's exit: "My eternal palaces are ruined," and see further proof in the Easter poem which employs *Slovo* as its source.[17] Although Rezanov may be correct in his assumptions, none of the extant versions of the play contains a hint of these "missing lines." It may be that dialogue was not necessary in such a dramatic scene of battle, and that Christ's inevitable victory over the hellish army was simply enacted, not narrated. Thus perhaps only a stage direction is missing.

N. Petrov is alone in arguing that the prototype of *Slovo* is a so-called "school" drama written by someone in the Kievan Academy; from here monks and seminarians could easily have taken the play to other parts of the country, where it subsequently may have undergone revision or change.[18] It is a tantalizing thesis, because it hints at the possibility of a more direct Western influence. Many of the instructors and students of the Kievan Collegium (later Academy) were educated in the West; France (the Sorbonne) was particularly popular. The founder of the Academy, Petro Mohyla, studied there. Others pursued studies in Italy (Bologna, Padua, Milan), Czechoslovakia (Prague), Germany, and even England (Oxford and Cambridge).[19]

Yet many facts argue against Petrov. Extant plays written in the Kievan Academy are of an entirely different character. More didactic and solemn that *Slovo*, Kievan plays never represent Christ directly, but rather obliquely, by personifying His attributes. This hesitancy to represent God is particularly common in the Eastern Orthodox tradition. The allegorical form of representation, however, was probably also influenced by the Jesuit-Polish dramatic style which, in this instance, coincided with the Orthodox attitude.[20]

While Petrov seems to be wrong in his attribution, it is also very difficult conclusively to prove or disprove Franko or Bilets'kyi's theories on the origins of the play. Evidence is scanty. It seems, however, safe to assume that this is a seventeenth, perhaps even an early seventeenth-century drama.[21]

Language

Slovo o zbureniu pekla is very much a product of the atmosphere of the new period of the Counter-Reformation. Reaching Ukraine *via* Poland, the Counter-Reformation ushered in a disparate variety of influences. Without renouncing their Byzantine heritage, spiritual leaders looked to the West for invigoration and Europeanization, particularly of their educational system. Because of Ukraine's close links with Poland, Western religious orders including Jesuits, Dominicans and Piarists penetrated especially the Western lands of Ukraine and established a network of schools based upon Western European, particularly Polish, models.

The Kievan Collegium (later Academy), founded in 1632 by Metropolitan Petro Mohyla, offers the clearest example of Western-inspired education in Ukraine. The founder and the faculty were themselves products of Western universities and colleges (especially Jesuit colleges).[22] Its multilingual faculty commanded Church Slavonic, Latin, Polish, Italian, and Ukrainian.

Such an overt interest in Western educational models resulted in the increased popularity and influence of Latin, as the profusion of Latin proverbs, motifs and classical figures in Ukrainian literary works show.[23] Under these changed circumstances, drama prospered, particularly in the schools. Yet because the cultural and intellectual elite was, for the most part, the clergy, drama (especially serious drama) was limited to religious subjects and moral themes.

Knowledge of Greek was still a necessity in the sixteenth century because of closer ties with Greek hierarchs, with whom correspondence was carried out in their native language.[24] In the Lviv Orthodox Brotherhood schools, Greek was studied very thoroughly, as the 1637 inventory of the Stavropighian library indicates: it includes an extensive collection of Greek books, including the Church Fathers, Hesiod, Plato, Aristotle, and various apocrypha.[25]

Closer to Greek than Latin in its construction,[26] Church Slavonic remained the domain of Orthodox Slavs, who published numerous lexicons, dictionaries, and grammar handbooks at this time. The end of the sixteenth century, the late period of Church Slavonic, brought with it a "radical new turn," in part as a response to Polish attempts to Catholicize Ukraine, and, consequently, discredit Slavonic as a language of culture and scholarship. Ukrainians began to standardize Church Slavonic in order to affirm the opposite—its worthiness. Slavonic thus came to have that relation to the vernacular that Latin and Greek had in relation to the vernaculars of Europe.[27]

Middle Ukrainian is full of Slavonic influences, although Polish and Czech elements, Latinisms, and German loan words are also in evidence. Through the influence of the Counter-Reformation, the vernacular was raised to a new level of respectability, and thus aided in Ukrainian national and cultural revival.[28]

The language of *Slovo o zbureniu pekla*, lively vernacular with traces of a more academic Slavonic influence, Polish borrowings, and Galician dialectical changes, place the play firmly in the seventeenth century.[29] The proximity of its verse to *dumy* (lyrical epics based upon historical events in the Cossack Ukraine, performed in recitative to the accompaniment of the *kobza*, or lute) with its uneven line lengths, frequent use of double synonyms and epithets, a definite rhythm and rhyme (especially of seventeenth-century verbs) suggest that *Slovo* may date from the early part of the seventeenth century.[30]

Genre

Recent work in mediaeval studies by such scholars as Alan Knight, Henrik Birnbaum, Igor Eremin, Dmitry Likhachev, Riccardo Picchio, and Hans Robert Jauss has drawn attention to the false division of mediaeval drama into comedy and tragedy, or for that matter, into any of the traditionally accepted genres applied to post-Renaissance works.[31] Picchio and Birnbaum both stress the interrelatedness, rather than separation, of forms for the mediaeval writer and audience. Picchio, for example, argues that such writers considered their work only "imperfect images of higher iconic messages," and would therefore be unlikely to "believe in the absolute significance of technical categories such as 'genre,' which depended on a merely historical level of meaning."[32] Birnbaum goes further by stressing the connections between literature, painting, and music, which he believes can be perceived as "interrelated manifestations of an overall religiously inspired concept of art."[33] The development of a common "language," which served art, music, and literature is discussed by Konrad Onasch.[34] In another article, Picchio opines that the equation of chronicles, sermons, and hagiography with "genres" leads to the loss of viewing interconnections of themes and forms.[35] Likhachev, on the other hand, emphasizes the absence of clear boundaries between various works, a matter related to the question of authorship (see above). While twentieth century anthologies present us with separate works, the originals were always seen within their own context (that is, in large collections), where individual achievement meant nothing except as it added to the magnificence of the whole.[36]

Such recent scholarly work stresses the importance of the ecclesiastical culture which both shaped artistic creation, and was responsible for any "theory of literature."[37] The work of Alan Knight in French drama coincides with the findings of Slavic scholars. Attempting to place mediaeval works in their proper context, Knight argues that in production mediaeval plays were "addressed to God in a para-liturgical act of praise, petition, or thanksgiving."[38] Drama, like the Mass, is directed toward God (the Mass proper) and toward man (the homily). Episodic and sequential, linear or processional, mediaeval drama is opposed to the usual structure of comedy and tragedy, which takes on a "crisis" shape. According to Knight, the distinguishing feature of mediaeval drama, like that of Old Comedy, is the agon. In mediaeval drama we have the constantly opposed forces of good and evil, God and Lucifer, vices and virtues. In such a schema, characters appear and disappear, as they do in history or biography, but not in the way required by rigorously plotted drama.[39] Misunderstandings about the form of mediaeval drama may also be responsible for our difficulty in grasping the way the comic and even grotesque are permitted along with the pious and serious.[40]

In addition to these general problems associated with the form of mediaeval works, *Slovo o zbureniu pekla* contains a specific problem of genre manifested by its full title, *Slovo o zbureniu pekla kohda Khrystos s mertvykh vstavshy peklo zburyl* [*A Word about the Harrowing of Hell, When Christ, Having Risen from the Dead, Harrowed Hell*]. The word *slovo* literally means "word." However, to translate the harrowing play as "A Word About the Harrowing of Hell" seems, in English, to imply an offhandedness not at all present in the original title. Instead, we should consider *slovo* as the equivalent of *logos*. In his study of *Slovo o polku Igoreve* (usually translated as *The Tale of Igor's Campaign*, or *The Lay of Igor*), Igor Eremin examines *slovo* as a type of epideictic literature, which follows the rules of the epideictic category of oratory. Mediaeval Slavic literature is full of works called *slovo*, as, for example, *Slovo o zakone i blagodati* [*Sermon on Grace and Law*], and *Slovo o pogibeli russkyja zemli* [*Discourse on the Ruin of the Land of Rus'*]. *Slovo* may thus more aptly be translated as the "Narrative" or "Discourse about the Harrowing of Hell."

The orthodoxy of our play, *Slovo o zbureniu pekla*, becomes apparent in such a context. *Slovo* clearly partakes of the mediaeval traditions of Orthodox Slavdom, which lasted, according to most scholars, into the early eighteenth century. Since *Slovo o zbureniu pekla* is, however, a seventeenth-century product, it both arises from its mediaeval tradition, and, in some respects (as a product of the Counter-Reformation), departs from it. (See below, *The Period: Baroque*.)

The epideictic category of oratory (in praise or blame of something, for the pleasure and edification of the audience) stands, as Eremin points out, opposed to the strictly didactic.[41] Taken over by Kievan Rus' in the eleventh and twelfth centuries, the category of *slovo* clearly has a long tradition. It is not surprising that the popular Scaliger, one of the essential theorists taught in Ukrainian educational institutions, includes rules for the types of epideictic poetry in his *Poetices libri septem* (1561), rules which differ little from those presented in the third century B.C. by Menander in his *Peri epideiktikon* (*On Epideictic Poetry*). (See below, *Poetical and Rhetorical Theory*.)

Eremin's examination of types of *slovo* shows that a prologue always opens the work. It prepares the reader or listener and sets out the goals of the orator. Customarily, such an introduction begins with effective sententiae or with a direct appeal to the audience, as well as with praise of the person who is the subject of the text. The topic is then briefly sketched, and the prologue concludes with the orator's request for forgiveness of his audacity. Alternately, a rhetorical appeal or praise brings the prologue to an end.[42] The epideictic work, often in praise of a hero-warrior, makes frequent use of rhetorical devices: formulaic anaphora, repetition, a distinct rhythm. The work typically ends with the word *slava* (glory), and with "amen" (in the Old Rus' Church formula of epideictic works).[43]

It is not difficult to see the parallels in form between Eremin's study of *The Tale of Igor's Campaign*, and the structure of *Slovo o zbureniu pekla*. The Ukrainian harrowing play clearly celebrates Christ as warrior, and partakes of what Knight calls the para-liturgical act of praise. While Christ does not appear in the text until the last third of the play, His presence is evident in every minute of the action, as the devils try to come to terms with His nature and prepare to do battle with Him. Lucifer, who opens the play in a long monologue, seems to carry the function of the prologue. While he does not praise Christ, the devil's ignorance, and his incomprehension of Christ's identity indirectly cause the audience to glorify Him.

Lucifer's reciting of the history of creation in his opening monologue coincides with Dmitry Likhachev's notion that the mediaeval Slavic writer "never forgets about the course of history on a world scale."[44] He cites *The Life and Death of SS. Boris and Gleb* and the more secular *The Tale of Woe-Misfortune* as beginning their stories literally "from Adam."[45] Similarly, Lucifer leads us through a history of the world up until the present moment, the imminent arrival of Christ. The comic blusterer thus both sets out the grand plan of creation (a task usually performed by virtuous characters, or even by whole plays), and prepares us for what is to come. His gloating at the Fall of man, and at the successful peopling of hell is immediately undercut by the audience's superior knowledge of the events to follow. Lucifer's prologue thus effectively introduces the comic dramatic irony which underlies the whole play up until Christ's entry, and also reveals the devil for what he really is: a posturer, and a braggart, but not a real adversary of God.

The text of the play itself, as previous commentators (such as

Franko) noted, is full of repetitions. But if Eremin is correct, these are not necessarily errors in transcription, but rather functional devices deliberately deployed by the author. The most frequently encountered type of repetition is anaphora, most especially found in longer speeches (such as Lucifer's opening sequence: for example, ll. 36–38, 43–44, 73–75, 81–82).

The play's conclusion returns the action to a para-liturgical context. Christ appears both as mighty warrior and as priest. He sprinkles the darkness of hell with holy water, exorcising the evil spirits. While the devils speak colloquially, Christ does not stray very far from the solemn, formulaic pattern of the twenty-fourth Psalm. Finally, the play ends with a hymn from the All-Night Vigil Service (still sung today) in praise of the Virgin as Birth-Giver of God (*Bohorodytsia*), again placing the action of the play in its wider, cosmic context.[46]

Poetical and Rhetorical Theory

Since H. Syvokin''s 1960 study of poetical and rhetorical theory of the seventeenth and eighteenth centuries,[47] both Soviet and Western scholars have turned in greater numbers to this formerly little studied area.[48] Their findings have conclusively shown a strong influence of rhetoric on the drama. The links between *Slovo o zbureniu pekla* and the tradition of epideictic works has already been noted. (See above, *Genre*.) To round out the picture of the context of the play, a brief look should be taken at rhetorical and poetic studies within the framework of the educational curriculum.

During the seventeenth and eighteenth centuries, courses in rhetoric and poetics—part of the humanistic training of the seven liberal arts—were taught in Latin, while examples and exercises were given in Church Slavonic, Polish, the vernacular, and Latin.[49] As D.S. Nalyvaiko has pointed out, new traditions of genre and style were being formulated at this time[50] that incorporated the influence of new cultural currents: humanism, the Counter-Reformation, and the Baroque. As a transitional period, the sixteenth, seventeenth, and eighteenth centuries sponsored the development of novel structures, transforming and rebuilding literary techniques and characteristics according to Western European models.[51]

In the nineteenth century, lectures on poetics from the Kievan Academy and from other Ukrainian educational institutions were rediscovered and reprinted.[52] From these works we may see that both aesthetic ideas in general, and the normative poetics in particular, of

Western Europe were introduced into Ukraine by way of Poland.[53] Scaliger, Pontanus and Vida were the most important and most influential theorists, along with Aristotle and Horace.[54] The practical side of rhetoric and poetics, examples for emulation, acquainted students with the great authors of classical antiquity, as well as with classical mythology and with contemporary writers. These provided the students with a storehouse of images, narratives, metaphors and metrical patterns.

Not easily separated from poetics, rhetoric had the same goals and aims. It is significant that in at least one extant treatise on poetics, *Liber artis poeticae* (1637), the poet is described as being closest to an orator.[55] Poets, like orators, had a triple responsibility: to teach, to entertain, and to move—the last reflects the particular interest of the Baroque. A complex of meanings was associated with the word "rhetoric": an art of eloquence; a theory of styles; a literary composition; and an art of persuasion. Eloquence was important because it was thought to help develop the intellect of the students and raise their moral standards.[56]

Theatrical training was also an essential part of the humanistic programme and a practical result of a study of poetics and rhetoric. Declamations, a series of poems on a single theme, were spoken by various students on the occasion of visiting eminent guests.[57] These were much more than simple readings of poems, involving, as they did, pantomime, dramatization and audience participation.[58] The month of May, the end of term, was designated a type of celebration of poetry, during which time dialogues, declamations, and dramas were performed out of doors.[59] These involved both professors and students, and showed off their mastery of their subjects, as well as entertained the local intellectual elite who came to observe the performances.

While the drama of the seventeenth and eighteenth centuries is religious in subject matter, the poetics taught in the academies and schools was secular. The genres, for example, are defined in the traditional Renaissance fashion as comedy, tragedy, and epic, although some treatises also designate and define tragicomedy,[60] and yet another even further refines this list to include "comedotragedy" (depending upon the mixture of elements in the work).[61] A dramatic work was to be constructed of five parts (*prologus, protasis, epitasis, catastasis, catastrophe*), and was to have three, four, or five acts, with each act containing at least four scenes.[62] A chorus was to appear after each act to present the moral teaching.[63] While of great interest from many perspectives, the treatises are not helpful in understanding or making aesthetic judgements about the religious drama, such as *Slovo o zbureniu pekla*.

However, normative school poetics also indicated that *intermedia*—short comedies about the quotidian—were to be included between the acts of serious dramas. Derived from the Jesuit schools by way of the Polish-Lithuanian Commonwealth, *intermedia* took on local forms and patterns. Involving the audience through direct address and physical movement (the stage and auditorium "served as a common playground"),[64] the characters from everyday life included Polish and Ukrainian gentlemen, peasants, clergymen, wives, gypsies, and Jews. Later, *intermedia* were easily transferred from the school to the popular stage. *Slovo o zbureniu pekla*, with the direct address of Lucifer, the bustling activity of the characters, the references to everyday life (such as the drinking of *kvass*, and the concerns of Hades about his properties), the absence of act and scene division, and the disregard for the generic types may be seen to spring from this tradition.

An understanding of the nature of the irregular verse of *Slovo o zbureniu pekla* may be heightened by the recent studies of V.P. Kolosova, who examines the structure and models of poetry. Her work on *Slovo o polku Igoreve* [*The Lay of Igor's Campaign*] may, by analogy, be extended both to other Kievan Rus' works, and to the much later *Slovo o zbureniu pekla*. Placing rhythm as the central organizational principle of mediaeval poetry, Kolosova examines hymnography as its model, especially the *kondakion*, which formed part of menologia and other holy books. The *kondakion* is marked by the absence of rhyme; it contains five to sixteen syllables with two to four stresses.[65] Perhaps a variant of the free non-syllabic poetry of byzantine and, ultimately, of biblical poetry, the *kondakion* is characterized by a system of rhythmic signals at marked positions (usually at the beginning of lines); syntactic parallellism or syntactic inversion; anaphora; alliteration (and other sound devices); and a flexible rhythm.[66] This type of poetry has ties to native, oral folk poetry.

The translated literature of hymnography provided structures of versification, as well as sources of images, epithets, and metaphors.[67] Kolosova's study suggests a continuum may be established between the works produced in Kievan Rus' and what is usually considered the period of the "origins" of Ukrainian versification in the sixteenth century.[68]

Slovo o zbureniu pekla is full of the devices found in *kondakions*. Alliteration, repetition, syntactical parallelism and inversion may be

amply illustrated by reference to the play. The inclusion of the harrowing play, at least in one version, in a menologion suggests not only
that its message is orthodox, but also that it may possess wider, possibly poetic, connections with the other materials in such a religious
compendium. The hymnography of Kievan Rus', with its prayers to
God, the Virgin, and the Holy Spirit, may thus be yet another influence
on *Slovo o zbureniu pekla*. The concluding song of the play, taken
from the All-Night Vigil Service, acts as a type of closing invocation,
a specifically Christian responsibility of the poet strongly advocated by
the writers of poetical and rhetorical treatises.[69]

NOTES

1 Myron [I. Franko], "Iuzhnorusskaia Paskhal'naia drama [South-Russian Pascal Drama]," *Kievskaia starina*, 53 (1896), 380–412.

2 I. Franko, "*Slovo pro zburene pekla*; Ukrains'ka pasiina drama [*About the Harrowing of Hell*; A Ukrainian Passion Play]," *Zapysky Naukovoho Tovarystva im. T.H. Shevchenka (ZNTSh)*, 81 (1908), 5–50.

3 Franko, "*Slovo pro zburene pekla*," p. 11. Since this book went to press, another edition of *Slovo o zbureniu pekla* appeared in the anthology *Ukrains'ka literatura XVII st.* [*Ukrainian Literature of the XVII Century*], ed. O. V. Myshanych, compiled, with an introduction and notes, by V. I. Krekoten' (Kiev: Naukova Dumka, 1987), pp. 364–374. This edition in contemporary Ukrainian orthography is based upon Al (Franko's 1908 version, taken from the Petrushevych collection). The editor lists the present location of the manuscript as Lviv, Naukova biblioteka im. Vasylia Stefanyka, Akademiia Nauk.

4 This summary of the description of the manuscripts is taken from Franko's 1908 article, "*Slovo pro zburene pekla*," pp. 10–13.

5 M. Vozniak, "Znadibky do ukrains'koi velykodn'oi dramy [Research Toward a Ukrainian Easter Drama]," *ZNTSh*, 146 (1927), 119–153.

6 Vozniak, p. 143.

7 Vozniak, p. 142.

8 Yaroslav Hordyns'kyi, "*Slovo pro zburenne pekla* po Staruns'komu rukopysu XVIII v. [*About the Harrowing of Hell* in an XVIII Century Manuscript from Starunii]," *ZNTSh*, 97 (1910), 168–169.

9 Hordyns'kyi, p. 174. Since the names of Benarii and Trubarii appear in the poem on the subject of the harrowing, Hordyns'kyi argues against the use of the name Venera in favour of Benera.

10 Riccardo Picchio, "Models and Patterns in the Literary Tradition of Medieval Orthodox Slavdom," in *American Contributions to the Seventh International Congress of Slavists. Warsaw, August, 1973*, ed. Victor Terras (The Hague, Paris: Mouton, 1973), p. 447.

11 Picchio, p. 447.

12 Picchio, pp. 446–449.

13 Franko, "*Slovo pro zburene pekla*," pp. 49–50.

14 O. Bilets'kyi, ed., *Khrestomatiia davn'oi ukrains'koi literatury* [*Anthology of Ancient Ukrainian Literature*] (Kiev: Radians'ka shkola, 1967), pp. 199–200. The categories of "native" or "popular," and "school" or "academic" plays are generally accepted terms, not meant to be mutually exclusive. "School" plays are as native as "native" drama.

15 V. Rezanov, ed., *Drama ukrains' ka* [*Ukrainian Drama*], I (Kiev: Ukrains'ka Akademiia Nauk, 1926), p. 39.

16 Rezanov, p. 39.

17 Rezanov, pp. 43–44. Franko reprints this poem twice, in his 1896 article

(pp. 381–384), and then again in his 1908 article (pp. 6–9). In the first study (*Kievskaia starina*, 1896), he analyses in great detail the similarities and differences between the poem and the *Slovo* play.

18 N. Petrov, *Ocherki iz istorii ukrainskoi literatury XVII i XVIII vekov* [*Outline of the History of Ukrainian Literature in the XVII and XVIII Centuries*] (Kiev: Petr Barskii, 1911), pp. 110–112.

19 Hryhorii Nud'ha, "Pershi mahistry i doktory; ukrains'ki studenty v universytetakh Evropy XIV-XVIII stolit' [The First Magisters and Doctors; Ukrainian Students in the Universities of Europe XIV-XVIII Centuries]," *Zhovten'*, 7, No. 3 (1982), 89–100. See, especially, pp. 91–93. Also, see Ia. D. Isaievych, *Dzherela z istorii ukrains'koi kul'tury doby feodalizmu XVI-XVIII st.* [*Sources of the History of Ukrainian Culture in the Period of Feudalism*, XVI-XVIII Centuries] (Kiev: Naukova Dumka, 1972), pp. 101–102.

20 M. Vozniak, *Istoriia ukrains'koi literatury* [*History of Ukrainian Literature*], III (Lviv: Prosvita, 1924), p. 163f.

21 For a related discussion of dating, see below, *The Puppet Theatre: Vertep and Raiok.*

22 See, for example, Alexander Sydorenko's full-length study, *The Kievan Academy in the Seventeenth Century* (Ottawa: Ottawa University Press, 1977), *passim*, and Paulina Lewin, "Polish-Ukrainian-Russian Literary Relations of the Sixteenth-Eighteenth Centuries: New Approaches," *The Slavic and East European Journal*, 24, No. 3 (1980), 256–269. Also, see Lewin's *Wykłady poetyki w uczelniach Rosyjskich XVIII w. (1722–1774) a tradycje polskie* [*Lectures in Poetics in the Educational Institutions of XVIII Century Russia (1722–1774) and Polish Tradition*] (Wroclaw: Polska Akademiia Nauk, 1972), pp. 6–7.

23 Constantine Bida, "Vestiges of Antiquity in Ukrainian Baroque Literature," in *Canadian Contributions to the VIII International Congress of Slavists. Zagreb-Ljublijana 1978. Tradition and Innovation in Slavic Literatures, Linguistics, and Stylistics,* ed. Zbigniew Folejewski *et al.* (Ottawa: Canadian Association of Slavists, 1978), pp. 25–28.

24 Rezanov, p. 22.

25 Konstantin Vasil'ievich Kharlampovich, *Zapadnorusskiia pravoslavnyia shkoly XVI i nachala XVII veka* [*West Russian Orthodox Schools of the XVI and Early XVII centuries*] (Kazan: n.p., 1898), p. 287f.

26 P. Zhytets'kyi, *Narysy literaturnoi istorii ukrains'koi movy XVII v.* [*Outline of the Literary History of the Ukrainian Language in the XVII Century*] (Lviv: Ukrains'ke vydavnytstvo, 1941), p. 3.

27 Riccardo Picchio, "Guidelines for a Comparative Study of the Language Question Among the Slavs," in *Aspects of the Slavic Language Question*, I, ed. Riccardo Picchio and Harvey Goldblatt (New Haven: Yale Concilium on International and Area Studies, 1984), especially pp. 61–62.

On Slavic "language questions," among others, also see Harvey Gold-blatt, "The Language Question and the Emergence of Slavic National Languages," in *The Emergence of National Languages*, ed. A. Scaglione (Ravenna: Longo Editore, 1984), pp. 107–156, and Riccardo Picchio, "Church Slavonic," in *The Slavic Literary Languages: Formation and Development*, Yale Russian and East European Publications, I, ed. A. Schenker and E. Stankiewicz (New Haven: Yale University Press, 1980), pp. 28–32.

28 On the emergence of a national consciousness and the Ukrainian language see, for example, Teresa Chynczewska-Hennel, "The National Consciousness of Ukrainian Nobles and Cossacks from the End of the Sixteenth to the Mid-Seventeenth Century," *Harvard Ukrainian Studies*, Special Issue, 10, No. 3/4 (Dec., 1986), 377–92, and Bohdan A. Struminsky, "The Language Question in the Ukrainian Lands Before the Nineteenth Century," in *Aspects of the Slavic Language Question*, II, ed. Riccardo Picchio and Harvey Goldblatt, pp. 9–48.

29 Dmytro Čyževs'kyj, *A History of Ukrainian Literature*, trans. by Dolly Ferguson *et al.*, (Littleton, Colorado: Ukrainian Academic Press, 1975), p. 278, notes the Slavonic language's tendency to absorb a large number of elements of the vernacular at this time. Deviations toward Polish and the vernacular are common, toward Russian, rare.

30 Some scholars detect a similarity in verse between *Slovo* and *dumy*. See, for example, Franko, "*Slovo pro zburene pekla*," pp. 49–50; he is supported by Rezanov, p. 47. But dating the play is a risky and uncertain business, particularly because the extant manuscripts stem from a later period.

31 Alan E. Knight, *Aspects of Genre in Late Medieval French Drama* (Manchester: Manchester University Press, 1983); Henrik Birnbaum, *On Medieval and Renaissance Slavic Writing: Selected Essays* (The Hague, Paris: Mouton, 1974); I. Eremin, "Zhanrovaia priroda 'Slovo o polku Igoreve' [The Generic Nature of *The Tale of Igor's Campaign*]," in *Literatura drevnei Rusi [The Literature of Old Rus']*, ed. D.S. Likhachev (Leningrad: Nauka, 1966), pp. 144–163; Dmitry Likhachov (*sic*), *The Great Heritage; the Classical Literature of Old Rus'* (Moscow: Progress Publishers, 1981); and numerous articles by Riccardo Picchio, including, "The Impact of Ecclesiastical Culture on Old Russian Literary Techniques," in *Medieval Russian Culture*, ed. Henrik Birnbaum and Michael S. Flier (Berkeley: University of California Press, 1984), pp. 247–279; Riccardo Picchio, "Levels of Meaning in Old Russian Literature," in *American Contributions to the Ninth International Congress of Slavists. Kiev 1983*, II, ed. Paul Debreczeny (Columbus, Ohio: Slavica, 1983), pp. 357–370; Riccardo Picchio, "Models and Patterns in the Literary Tradition of Medieval Orthodox Slavdom," in *American Contributions to the*

Seventh International Congress of Slavists. Warsaw 1973, ed. Victor Terras (The Hague, Paris: Mouton, 1973), pp. 439–467; Riccardo Picchio, "Guidelines for a Comparative Study of the Language Question among the Slavs," in *Aspects of the Slavic Language Question*, I, ed. Riccardo Picchio and Harvey Goldblatt (New Haven: Yale Concilium on International and Area Studies, 1984), pp. 1–42; Hans Robert Jauss, "Littérature médiévale et théorie des genres," *Poétique*, 1 (1970), 79–101.

32 Picchio, "Levels of Meaning," p. 368.

33 Birnbaum, *On Medieval and Renaissance Slavic Writing*, p. 32.

34 Konrad Onasch, "Identity Models of Old Russian Sacred Art," in *Medieval Russian Culture*, pp. 176–177.

35 Picchio, "Ecclesiastical Culture," p. 265.

36 Likhachov (*sic*), *The Great Heritage*, p. 14.

37 Picchio, "Ecclesiastical Culture," p. 252.

38 Knight, p. 16.

39 Knight, p. 31.

40 Knight, p. 13.

41 Eremin, p. 150.

42 Eremin, p. 151.

43 Eremin, pp. 157–162.

44 Likhachov (*sic*), *The Great Heritage*, p. 13.

45 Likhachov (*sic*), *The Great Heritage*, p. 13.

46 For an English translation of this hymn see Isabel Florence Hapgood, trans. and comp., *Service Book of the Holy Orthodox-Catholic Apostolic Church* (Englewood, N. J.: Antiochian Orthodox Christian Archdiocese, 1975), p. 34.

47 H.M. Syvokin', *Davni ukrains'ki poetyky* [*Ancient Ukrainian Poetics*] (Kharkiv: Kharkivs'koho ordena trudovoho chervonoho prapora Derzhavnoho universytetu im. O.M. Hor'koho, 1960).

48 See, for example, Ryszard Łużny, *Pisarze kręgu Akademiji Kijowsko-Mohylańskiej a literatura polska* [*Writers of the Kievan-Mohyla Academy Circle and Polish Literature*] (Cracow: Zeszyty Naukowe Universytetu Jagiellońskiego 142, 1966); Paulina Lewin, *Wykłady poetyki*; M.M. Sulyma, *Ukrains'ke virshuvannia XVI—pochatku XVII st.* [*Ukrainian Versification XVI—Beginning of the XVII Century*] (Kiev: Naukova Dumka, 1985); O.V. Myshanych, ed., *Literaturna spadshchyna Kyivs'koi Rusi i ukrains'ka literatura XVI-XVIII st.* [*The Literary Heritage of Kievan Rus' and Ukrainian Literature of the XVI-XVIII Centuries*] (Kiev: Naukova Dumka, 1981).

49 Syvokin', p. 5.

50 D.S. Nalyvaiko, "Kyivs'ki poetyky XVII-pochatku XVIII st. v konteksti evropeis'koho literaturnoho protsesu [*Kievan Poetics of the XVI—Beginning of the XVIII Centuries in the Context of the European Literary*

Process]," in O.V. Myshanych, pp. 157–158.

51 Nalyvaiko, p. 102.

52 M.I. Petrov, "O slovesnykh naukakh i literaturnykh zaniatiiakh v Kievskoi akademii ot nachala ee do preobrazovaniia v 1819 godu [About Literary Studies and Literary Activities in the Kievan Academy from its Beginnings to its Reorganization in 1819]," *Trudy Kievskoi dukhovnoi akademii* (*TKDA*), 7, 11, 12 (1866); 1 (1867); 3 (1868).

53 See Łużny and Lewin (especially *Wykłady poetyki*) on the role of Poland on the formation and evolution of Ukrainian theoretical views and literary practice.

54 Syvokin', p. 103.

55 V.I. Krekoten', "Kyivs'ka poetyka 1637r. [Kievan Poetics of 1637]," in Myshanych, p. 127.

56 Ia. D. Isaievych, *Bratstva ta ikh rol' v rozvytku ukrains'koi kul'tury XVI–XVIII st.* [*Brotherhoods and Their Role in the Development of Ukrainian Culture in the XVI–XVIII Centuries*] (Kiev: Naukova Dumka, 1966), p. 160.

57 See Lewin, "Early Ukrainian Theatre," *Nationalities Papers*, 8, No. 2 (1980), pp. 223–224 on Berynda's declamations.

58 See Lewin's "Early Ukrainian Theatre," *passim*.

59 D. Antonovych, *Trysta rokiv ukrains'koho teatru 1619–1919* [*Three Hundred Years of Ukrainian Theatre 1619–1919*] (Prague: Ukrains'kyi hromads'kyi vydavnychyi fond, 1925), p. 31.

60 As, for example, in the *Liber artis poeticae*, cited by Krekoten', p. 132.

61 Nalyvaiko, p. 190.

62 The treatise entitled *Lira* (1696) extensively treats of drama. See Syvokin', p. 91f.

63 Syvokin', p. 90.

64 Lewin, "Early Ukrainian Theatre," p. 227.

65 V.P. Kolosova, "Tradytsiii literatury Kyivs'koi Rusi i Ukrains'ka poeziia XVI-XVIII st. [*Kievan Rus' Traditions of Literature and Ukrainian Poetry, XVI–XVIII Centuries*]," in Myshanych, p. 94.

66 Also, see Sulyma's full-length study of versification on some of these same points.

67 Kolosova, p. 92.

68 Kolosova, p. 99.

69 Syvokin', p. 88.

The Period: Baroque

Although shorter-lived, the controversy surrounding the term "Baroque" is not unlike the contentiousness of the debate about Romanticism. Like Romanticism, "Baroque," as Werner Friederich observes, "can serve as a useful general label, though it covers a multitude of aspects and is capable of an imposing number of definitions."[1] Originally a lapidary term referring to stones that were "irregular, uncouth, not polished, not perfect,"[2] Baroque became a popular term in the eighteenth century, and was subsequently adopted by art historians, particularly by Wölfflin, who passed it into the sphere of literary criticism. In Slavic literature it has also had a stormy past. Championed by Dmytro Chyzhevs'kyi, who, as George Grabowicz notes, defended the Baroque both from populist, "vulgar-Marxist" criticism, and from those scholars who questioned the value of this religious literature,[3] the Baroque now seems to be a generally accepted term.[4]

While frequently employed, the term Baroque still carries a variety of meanings, the basic two of which are Baroque as style and Baroque as period. Baroque as style has been identified as a single, consistent style characterized by the recurrence of particular devices, concerns, and ideas.[5] More cautiously, but more accurately, Baroque has been defined as "a complex of related styles constituting a distinct period in European literary history."[6] The later definition shades into the notion of Baroque as period only, a point of view vigorously propounded in a recent book by José Antonio Maravall.[7]

According to Maravall, the Baroque lasted from 1600 to 1675, and had as its centre of greatest intensity the period 1605–1650.[8] Miroslav John Hanak concurs that by 1600 the Baroque was felt everywhere.[9] In Eastern Europe, especially in Ukraine, the Baroque was an especially "long-lived phenomenon, lasting for the better part of two centuries,"[10] from the late sixteenth to the late eighteenth.

Central to any description of the Baroque art form is the notion of exaggeration, extremity and exuberance. Historians and literary critics have located the source of these characteristics in the series of upheavals Western and Eastern Europe faced at the time.[11] Religious especially, but also intellectual, political, social and economic crises brought about a Counter-Renaissance. In contrast to the synthesis, harmony, and optimism of Renaissance art, the Baroque ushered in a sense of conflict. Revolting against Renaissance belief in the perfectibility of man, deeply aware of man's mortality, the mutability and flux of all things, and the vanity of all human wishes,[12] Baroque art nonetheless needed to make little man appear significant; this was achieved through overstatement. Artists, remarks Friederich, "worked with shrill colors and double and triple adornments, as though nothing less would do to help them assert themselves in the midst of this tragically ephemeral world of ours."[13]

At the basis of the violent, the terrifying, and the exaggerated in Baroque art is the "pessimistic conception of the human being and of the world."[14] This view is reflected in the subject matter, stylistic devices, and themes of Baroque.[15] Often occupying Renaissance forms, Baroque concerns seem to stretch the old forms "to the point of explosion, which accounts for the fundamental distortion of the baroque."[16] The beholder is moved, even terrified by the work of art, which brings him face to face with death, the horrors of the afterlife, and with an awareness of his own smallness. Man is then ready to make the leap of faith, ready to be persuaded of the truth.[17] The art of the Baroque is the art of the metaphysical, of the "titanic struggle between reason and faith."[18] "Never before or since has man been so obsessed with reaching the absolute through such desperately elated interiorization of his existence."[19]

Such a worldview is at the basis of the Baroque preoccupation with the macabre, morbid, and fantastical. One of the dominant themes of the period is that of the four ultimate things of man: death, doomsday, heaven, and hell. A Ukrainian *Book of Death* (1626), the popularity of *Khozhdenie Bogoroditsi po mukam* [*The Journey of the Birth-Giver of God Through the Torments of Hell*] and the graphic description of war in chronicles, among many other works, attest to this interest.[20]

The Baroque art form *par excellence*,[21] the theatre, perhaps more than any other, is most capable of dealing with the theme of illusion and reality. And, as Maravall observes, "an illusion made real is the most efficient testimony to the illusory character of reality."[22] The world as theatre *topos* captured the imagination of the seventeenth century.[23] One of the most popular type of plays in this period is the martyr play, "with its emphasis on pessimism, on the vanity of all human endeavors, on the frightfulness of hell-fire, and with its belief that life was only a dream . . . or, worse, a nightmare."[24]

Despite its exaggerated forms, the Baroque reflects the needs of a conservative culture which attempted to restore an order and the values of an earlier time. This, claims Maravall, accounts for the many mediaeval elements in architecture and art.[25] The Baroque yearned for authority, certainty, and order, and tried to stave off the disruptive, skeptical, relative, and anarchic. Art was perceived as one effective means of controlling human conduct. But whereas the mediaeval and Renaissance cultures sought to subdue the passions, the Baroque encouraged and made use of them. In fact, the aim of the artist was to affect, awaken, and move the passions. Aristotle's *Rhetoric*, rather than his *Poetics*, was a much-studied book because of the importance of the art of persuasion.[26] The Spanish painter Francisco Pacheco advised his colleagues to "seek to have his figures move psyches, some figures disturbing them, others making them happy, others inclining them to piety, others to disdain, according to the quality of the stories. And if he fails in that, may he realize that he has done nothing."[27]

At war between spiritualism and sensualism, Christ and Venus, Baroque works appear to be distorted, exaggerated, irrational—particularly when a classical measuring rod is employed in judging these works.[28] Baroque style has come to mean an art heavily ornate, variegated and disconnected, exalted in expression (although also prone to mix both high and low styles), given to opacity (a love of riddles, symbols, hieroglyphics, allusions), paradox, oxymorons, the unexpected, the novel, the extreme.[29] The difficult was preferred to the simple, the "artificial" to the natural, the miraculous, the fantastic, and the outlandish to the rational and ordinary. The preference for antonymic pairs and for paradox and oxymoron seem to be particularly pronounced in the Baroque, perhaps because, as Rosalie Colie suggests, these envelop rather than develop; they reach out to the beholder and reader "appealing across conventional limits between 'art' and 'reality.' "[30] Also, as Maravall argues, such devices as antitheses articulate the tension in the human experience felt particularly strongly by the Baroque culture.[31]

East Slavic Baroque, although longer-lived, reflects these same tensions. The subjects of Slavic Baroque works frequently harken back to the Middle Ages. Even the clear theocentrism appears to suggest that these are works more properly belonging to an earlier age. Yet the influence of the Renaissance is equally present, particularly in classical allusions, but also in Renaissance forms. The so-called Cossack or

Ukrainian Baroque (seventeenth–eighteenth centuries), more properly a term applied to architecture, is an amalgam of various traditions: from Polish-Latin and other Western influences to native, folk-oral roots. This amalgam of mediaeval and Renaissance, Orthodox and Catholic strains naturally resulted in a style which strove for bold combinations, paradox, the grotesque, turbulence, and excitation. Because of the tension between various struggling influences, antithesis was a popular rhetorical device. The marriage of humour with seriousness in all forms of literature, even in the most dignified, is a good indication of this tendency.[32]

A time of ecclectic borrowing from and translations of various works and periods—Church Fathers, myth, folklore, apocrypha, contemporary writings—the Slavic Baroque's obsession with form, especially with ornamentation, may be clearly seen in the rhetorical arabesques of Ukrainian sermons of the period whose heavy moral and theological overtones are graced by elaborate stylistic flights of fancy.[33]

East Slavic theatre was typical of its time. Moving the audience by wit, erudition and verbal gymnastics, the Baroque school theatre constantly attempted to amaze, not through intrigue, but through effects—conceptual, verbal, theatrical.[34] It is thus perhaps not surprising that Seneca was the best known and studied of the classical dramatists.[35]

Slovo o zbureniu pekla seems to be just such a distinctive product of the Baroque. In subject matter, it deals with a spectacular eschatological theme: the harrowing of hell. The hero of the play is not only a martyr, but Christ the Lord Himself. The triumphant victory over the forces of evil, probably a splendid theatrical effect in the literal vanquishing of darkness by the forces of light, conforms to the Baroque artist's desire to amaze, astonish, and move. The beholder would surely perceive the orthodox message: all is dross save faith in Christ. He alone gives meaning to all.[36]

The constantly opposed pairs, Archangel Michael and Commander Venera, Christ and Lucifer, heaven and hell, good and evil in their different variations, remind the audience of the only proper conduct for a Christian. The consequences of not following in Christ's path are indicated by Christ's promise to Lucifer: on Judgement Day hell will once more be filled to the brim with souls. The audience is thus called upon to contemplate not only the mystery of the Resurrection and the glory of the harrowing, but is also reminded of the Apocalypse, and, indirectly, of its own part in it. *Slovo*, like other Baroque works, thus deals with the four ultimate things of man.

Slovo terrifies, but it also delights, for it draws upon both apocryphal themes (the *Gospel of Nicodemus*), and folkloric traditions. It is the latter which are responsible for much of the comedy, and for the low style of many segments of the play. Like any Baroque work of art, *Slovo o zbureniu pekla* contains a mixture of styles. The devils, for the most part, speak in a colloquial, vernacular comic, low style. Lucifer is occasionally an exception, as for example, in the opening monologue, where he serves the purpose of a prologue and recounts the history of creation to the point of the Resurrection. In most other instances, however, he speaks in a familiar, even domestic, tone. St. John the Baptist and Christ, however, speak in a high style, deriving their rhythms and patterns from Church Slavonic Scripture.

Ukrainian Drama: Origins and Tradition

When, in England, Shakespeare was writing his last plays, in East Slavic lands drama was only beginning to flourish. The first reference to a specific production in Ukraine is the recording of Ukrainian interludes performed in the entr'acts of a Polish drama, *Tragedia albo wizerunek śmierci przeświętego Jana Chrzciciela, przesłanca Bożego* [*The Tragedy or Picture of the Death of St. John the Baptist, the Messenger of God*], on August 29, 1619 in the marketplace of the town of Kaminets' Strumylovyi, not far from Lviv.[37]

Few documents indicate a continuous dramatic tradition in Ukraine before 1619. The frescoes of St. Sophia in Kiev (eleventh century) suggest that drama was kept alive by *skomorokhy* (probably from the Greek *skommarkhos*, the leader of a play-game). Ministrels, players, and (according to recent research by Russell Zguta)[38] possibly even high priests of the old pagan faith, *skomorokhy*, like their mediaeval English counterparts the minstrel-players, also included comedy, puppet shows and recitations of serious heroic verse in their wide-ranging repertoire of entertainment. Humorous and satirical sketches, fantasy, and type characters were part of their standard fare.

Although only fragments of such entertainments survive in verse form and no dramatic texts are extant before the seventeenth century, various chronicle and especially clerical writers from the eleventh century onward refer disparagingly to and warningly about *skomorokhy*, playing, games, clowns, masquerades and other forms of dramatic endeavours.[39] This criticism, which is itself an indication of a surviving tradition of drama, culminates in the oft-cited fulminations of the ascetic monk of Athos Ivan Vyshens'kyi who, writing at the end of the sixteenth century, condemns the staging of comedies and "masquerades" in Ukrainian churches.[40] Despite the constant outcries of the clergy, pagan rites and games (including seasonal rituals and theatrical wedding play ceremonies) survived, some almost to the present day.[41]

The Byzantine liturgy itself, colourful and extremely theatrical, probably satisfied some of the natural desire of Ukrainians for drama. Separated from the parishioners by the *iconostasis* (a screen hung with icons) and serving the Divine Liturgy on a raised platform, the priest was not unlike an actor framed by a proscenium arch, and strictly separated from his audience. The church curtain and the gates through which the priest entered, the sacristy, all have secular parallels in the theatre.[42] Of all the services, the Resurrection service (*Voskresna utrenia*) in particular is a deliberately theatrical service meant to evoke the emotions of surprise and joy at Christ's Resurrection and his defeat of the forces of darkness and death.

Almost unknown to the Orthodox Slavic world, liturgical drama was, in western Europe, the source of many theatrical forms. The Orthodox Slavs, however, with the exception of Galicians (who maintained a close link with Polish culture from the earliest of times), "knew no mature, well-developed liturgical drama."[43] Instead, extant para-theatrical forms (such as dialogues and declamations) suggest that they followed Byzantine tradition. For example, the para-theatrical *Christos Paschon*, once attributed to Gregory of Nazianzus (but variously dated from the fourth to the twelfth century),[44] was known in Galicia at least from 1630, when it was freely adopted as *Virshi s tragedii Khrystos Paskhon* [*Verses from the Tragedy Christos Paschon*] by Andrii Skul'ski. A hint in the text suggests that probably the first part was performed in a Lviv church on Good Friday.

Much controversy still clouds the origins of Ukrainian drama. I. Steshenko argues that Western drama was transferred bodily to Ukraine, which possessed no native dramatic tradition. N. Petrov believes that Ukrainian drama began as religious drama tied to church services; and M. Drahomanov tentatively suggests the possible Germanic origin of Ukrainian theatre, fostered by a large German colony living in Lviv.[45] Hryhor Luzhnyts'kyi, on the other hand, claims that the origins of Ukrainian drama should be sought in folk music, especially in ballads, but also in *hahilky* (pagan in origin, first spring, then later Easter ritual songs, games and dances).[46] More recently, Paulina Lewin suggests that a history of Ukrainian drama must begin much later, with performances in schools.[47]

Whatever its exact origins, the development of drama is unquestionably due to the impulses of the Counter-Reformation in Ukraine. Two specific events pushed Ukraine toward closer contact with the West. The Union of Lublin, 1569, which caused "Ruthenian" (Ukrainian and Belorussiasn) territories to fall under the direct administration of the Polish Crown, and the Church Union declared at Brest (Berestia) in 1596 (which, in matters of faith, subordinated Ruthenians to the Holy See), magnified the influence of Polish culture and the Latin tradition. A competetive, later a confrontational, atmosphere was born. It was on this "tense borderline between Catholicism and Orthodoxy," Western European and Eastern Slavic cultures, that Ukrainian drama developed.[48]

School Drama

Through Poland (more accurately, the Polish-Lithuanian Commonwealth), Ukraine gained access almost simultaneously to Western European traditions of the miracle, morality, and mystery plays, as well as to the plays of Seneca, Terence, Plautus, and even to the contemporary plays of Corneille and Racine. In Poland, drama began and followed the evolutionary line already traced in the West from its liturgical origins in Easter tropes. The earliest reference in Polish is to nativity scenes staged by Bernardins in 1470 in the city of Lviv.[49] Also from the fifteenth century survive references concerning the representation of Passion plays.[50]

In the sixteenth century, Passions—called dialogues—were staged in a Cracow monastery by Dominicans; the plays included allegorical personages such as Mercy and Sorrow.[51] To the sixteenth century belongs perhaps the most famous of Polish Passion plays, Mikołaj of Wilkowiecko's *Historyja o Chwalebnym Zmartwychwstaniu Pańskim* [*History of the Glorious Resurrection of Our Lord*]. Well-known in Ukraine, it was a very popular play which was frequently reprinted. (See below, *Poland*.) Indications also exist which show that lay people staged Passion plays (including short harrowings).[52] In 1603, the Cracow primate, Bernard Maciejowski, banned the staging of mysteries in churches. In the second half of the sixteenth century, the Jesuits, now entrenched in Poland, developed drama by allowing students to stage plays in schools, in churches, and later in town squares. Public presentations were made on the occasion of school, church or other holidays. It was the Jesuits who were responsible for the remarkable number of twenty-nine theatres organized from 1571 to 1773 in Poland and Western Ukraine.[53] The Jesuits firmly placed drama in their school curriculum, and it served them as an educational and propagandistic tool. It trained "youth in diction and proper manners, and [educated] them in the arts, literature, church history, music, dance and Latin. The productions served also to support political ideas and to criticize social behaviour."[54] Jesuit Polish plays of the seventeenth century in particular served to promote both Catholicism and Polonization. Thus the Polish gentry or *szlachta* is lauded and the Cossacks are defamed, while Ukrainian subservience to Poland is advocated.[55] The Polish challenge initiated a type of war of theatres, for, in turn, the Orthodox took up the weapon they earlier despised, and employed drama in the struggle against the Polonization of Ukraine, Ukrainian culture and spirituality. In Ukrainian plays, Cossacks are idealized and ties with Poland and Moscow are condemned.[56] Often, the main character of these plays is Ukraine personified; just as a hundred years earlier, in Tudor plays such as *Gorboduc*, audiences clearly understood that England was the central, albeit absent, character.

The forms of Jesuit drama included occasional plays and panegyrics; church plays for Easter, Christmas, Corpus Christi and other holy days; and festival plays. Didactic, tendentious, moralizing, and allegorical, these plays conformed to set patterns, including a prologue, epilogue and three to five acts. Because of Ukraine's close links with Poland, Western religious orders penetrated especially the western lands of Ukraine and established a network of schools and academies based upon Western European, particularly Polish, models.[57] Spiritual leaders hoped to Westernize, Europeanize, and invigorate the East without renouncing their Byzantine heritage. The best example of Western influence on education is the Kievan Collegium (Academy), whose founder and faculty were themselves products of Western universities and colleges (especially Jesuit colleges). The Academy's faculty, which commanded Church Slavonic, Latin, Polish, Italian, and Ukrainian, openly competed with colleagues at the Jesuit Academy at Zamość (Poland), itself modelled upon the Universities of Padua and Cracow.[58]

In the Kievan Academy, the paradigm and model of all Ukrainian schools, drama was compulsory in classes of poetics and rhetoric. (See above, *Poetical and Rhetorical Theory*.) Serious drama was usually written in Church Slavonic[59] with lively interludes (*intermedia*) in Ukrainian representing scenes from everyday life, peopled with stock

national and social types, and liberally filled with broad humour and
farce. While the "serious" plays were written by academics who were
limited in their subject matter, the interludes were often written by talented students of poetics, a fact which made the *intermedia* all the more
interesting. In 1630–1631 in the Stavropighian Brotherhood School
Church in Lviv, the first Passion scenes known to us were presented:
Ioannykyi Volkovych's play, *Rozmyshlanie o mutsy Khrysta Spasytelia*
[*Meditations Upon the Passion of Christ the Saviour*].[60]

Students and professors played a major role in propagating drama
in Ukraine and later in Russia, where many graduates of the Kievan
Academy became professors.[61] Ukrainian instructors, often educated in
the West, followed Polish example by assigning the writing of verses
and drama to their students. Monthly readings of students' work, May
recreations and declamations developed in the students a good dramatic
sense which received considerable exercise in the summer months.
During their holidays, students travelled in groups performing plays
and declaming verses in town and country, marketplace, tavern and
lord's house. Donations were used to help them finance their next
academic year. Instructors also assisted in this dissemination process;
they were called upon to write occasional plays, especially for the May
recreations to which the clerical and lay leaders as well as townsfolk
were invited.

Designed to be a practical application of courses in poetics and
rhetoric, school plays imitated classical forms and verse, including a
prologue and epilogue, act and scene division. The rhetorical influence
is seen in the declamatory character of the plays, in the extensive use
(or abuse) of formal laments (sometimes alternated with song), and long
monologues. The richness of sound effects was particularly stressed.[62]

Mystery Plays

At the same time as Jesuit school drama was altering and shaping
Ukrainian drama, mediaeval mysteries also exerted a strong force. Still
well-known in Poland in the sixteenth century, but not deemed appropriate to Jesuit needs, was the mystery play. Its influence is most
clearly found in *Slovo o zbureniu pekla*, which has little of the stodgy
academic drama play about it. (See below, *Slovo and the Harrowing
Play in Western and Central Europe*.) Without a formal prologue, epilogue, act or scene division, and lacking allegorical personages, *Slovo*
seems clearly outside the Jesuit tradition.[63] *Slovo* is, in fact, the only
extant early Ukrainian drama which does not have the veneer of aca-

demic drama. This observation seems to confirm the date of the play
as the late sixteenth or early seventeenth century.

Staging and Delivery, Audience and Actors

Written by professors, or by professors and their students, Ukrainian
plays were also acted by talented, often upper-class students. As
rhetoricians, they would undoubtedly deliver their lines in a declamatory, rather than a naturalistic, style; moreover, they would also be
used to reciting verses and "dialogues." This may be seen in the comments of an active scholar and important teacher at the Brotherhood
schools in Lviv and Vilnius, Kyril Tranquillion Stavrovets'kyi, who
refers to himself as a "composer, or compositor [skladach] of verses,"
and advises that his works be read or sung.[64] It is useful to know that
one of the first practical results of the students' learning was to read
from holy books and assist during the serving of the Divine Liturgy,
where a melodic recitative is frequently employed. We may thus obtain a glimpse into the style of seventeenth-century dramatic delivery
by observing today's method of reading from the Acts of the Apostles and the Scriptures in Eastern churches (where little has changed in
hundreds of years).[65]

The staging of Ukrainian plays from the sixteenth to the eighteenth
centuries probably varied, depending upon the place of the play's presentation. If school plays were performed at their institution, they were
often made part of school festivities, as well as course curriculum pre-
requisites. Large schools perhaps could well afford expensive, complex
sets. Travelling student plays would certainly not have these resources
available to them. Staging would have been very simple, and the play's
performance may have been enhanced by the use of costumes, or possibly masks, which were not unknown, especially for the characters of
Christ, angels, and saints.

The stage directions of many plays demand sophisticated machinery, including flying machines. (Peretts observes that heaven is always
present in settings of the plays.[66]) Slovo demands a complex set, including the fortress of Hades with a drawbridge and gates, which need
machinery to cause them to collapse when Christ appears with his
banners. Artificial lighting was probably used with great effect, since
Christ's presence suddenly illuminates all parts of hell.

The exigencies of the stage must have demanded a fortress-like
setting for most harrowing of hell plays, since the climax of the drama
involved Christ breaking down the doors of hell. Donald Clive Stuart

and A.M. Nagler remark upon the great variety of representations of hell—from simple cauldrons to elaborate hellmouths and strongholds.[67] The variety of representations depended upon the dramatic necessities of the play. The stronghold notion, so central to the harrowing plays, was already conceived of in thirteenth-century France, as suggested by a Parisian miniature in which hell is "pictured as a stronghold with towers from which devils defend the place."[68] The absence of a reference to a hellmouth, argues Stuart, means that there is none on the stage.[69]

In a more recent book, Peter Meredith and John E. Tailby reprint a great number of mediaeval references to the construction and description of hellmouths. A production in Rouen in 1474, for example, includes the following description of hell:

Hell made like a a great mouth (*guelle*) opening and closing as is needful. The Limbo of the Patriarchs made like a prison and they were only visible above the waist (*du haut du corps*).[70]

An earlier production (1437) in Metz seemed calculated to frighten and awe its spectators:

The gateway and mouth of Hell in this play was very well made, for by a device (*engin*) it opened and closed of its own accord when the devils wanted to go in or come out of it. And this great head (*hure*) had two great steel eyes which glittered wonderfully.[71]

While all of Meredith and Tailby's references are to Western European productions, we should not assume that Central and Eastern European dramatists were unacquainted with at least some of these models; they may even have used similar machinery to create special effects. Here we must bear in mind the international network of the Jesuits, as well as the fact that many Eastern European scholars studied abroad.[72]

Slovo's dual emphasis on hellmouth and stronghold suggests that the setting could well be like the Metz hell described in Meredith and Tailby's book. It is a description which is also curiously similar to a depiction of hell on the south portal of the eleventh-century Chapelle de Perse et Espalion. There, a dragon's head forms the entrance to hell, behind which Lucifer appears enthroned; the whole scene is open to view.[73] The stage of a *Slovo* production may have employed a hellmouth almost as a proscenium arch through which the audience would be able to observe the action. The hell gates, then, would lie somewhere behind the "arch," perhaps in the centre rear part of the stage so that all eyes would be on the triumphant entry of Christ.

In speculating about the staging of the play, it is useful to know that in seventeenth-century Ukraine there was still a tradition of staging plays in churches.[74] Excerpts from *Christos Paschon* were probably staged by students of the Brotherhood School in the newly-built church in Lviv in 1630 on Good Friday and Easter Sunday. Considering its orthodox message, *Slovo* could also have been staged in a church, where use could be made of liturgical vestments (for Christ), as well as of other accessories (gonfalons, censers, and so on).[75] However, since the extant versions of *Slovo* afford only minimal stage directions, and since there are no available records of performances of the play, observations on the staging must remain in the realm of speculation only.

The Puppet Theatre: Vertep and Raiok

It is interesting to speculate that, despite the erudition apparent in *Slovo o zbureniu pekla*, it may also be linked to that very popular form of puppet theatre, *vertep*, which survived well into the twentieth century. *Vertep* (the ancient Ukrainian word for "cave") was essentially a two-tiered wooden box resembling a two-storey house, measuring one and a half metres in height and width, and approximately fifty centimetres in depth. A single puppeteer would sit behind the box, speaking in different voices, and manipulating the wooden dolls on the small box stage in front of him.[76]

In subject matter, *vertep* carried over from religious and academic drama the theme of the Birth and the Resurrection of Christ. But, while academic plays were arranged for and attended by a minority composed essentially of intellectual and spiritual leaders, *vertep* was intended for a much wider, more popular audience. During the Christmas festivities, it was carried from house to house, where the performances would take place. Yet extant versions of the texts of *vertep* (the earliest surviving texts date from the eighteenth century) reveal a mixture of "bookish" and popular elements, as well as unquestionable links to Western European mystery plays.[77]

The origins of the puppet theatre are murky. Kievan Rus' documents refer to games and dolls (*kukli*) as part of the usual fare offered by the *skomorokhy* (minstrels). Later documents attest to the native tradition of "walking" with dolls.[78] Although the first certain allusion to *vertep* comes from 1586, most scholars argue that *vertep* was not developed until the seventeenth century, basing their belief on a reference to expenditures made on July 14, 1666 at the Stavropighian Brotherhood School for the building and decoration of a *vertep*; no text is mentioned.[79] Henryk Jurkowski further speculates that *vertep* may have become popular at the end of the sixteenth century as an alternative to mystery plays. The *intermedia* (the comic interludes only tenuously, if at all, linked to the main action) did not become a part of *vertep* until the seventeenth century.[80]

The extant texts indicate that *vertep* traditionally represented the birth of Christ on the top "storey" of the box. Here Mary, Joseph, the angels, and the animals appeared, as did the Ukrainian shepherds Hryts'ko and Pryts'ko, who danced and sang carols. On the lower level, scenes took place involving Herod, who was later carried to hell by a devil. Here, also, various scenes with folkloric characters, national and social types were presented; characters such as the *did* and *baba* (old man and old woman), the Gypsy, Pole, Jew, Hungarian, the Student, and others. One of the characteristics of the *vertep* play is the grouping of characters by pairs—a device obviously intended to lighten the burden for the puppeteer. In the extant Sokryns'kyi text,[81] two of these pairs include two devils (nameless) and two angels, as well as Death with a scythe who, in his assurance of bringing all men down, and in his gleeful boasting of power over the whole world, resembles at once both Hades and Lucifer of the *Slovo* play.

A variant of the two-storey *vertep* is the more rare, but apparently not unusual, three-level *vertep*.[82] Here, the action on the top level showed paradise, the expulsion of Adam and Eve, icons of Christ, the characters of St. John the Baptist, and the Virgin. On the middle level the cave where Christ was born was shown, as were the shepherd scenes. Finally, on the lower, Herod's palace, other scenes set on earth, and comic folk scenes were portrayed.

This variant type of *vertep* has been the object of Franko's speculation on another type of play of which only fragments survive—the *raiok* or Paradise play. These, Franko is certain, were puppet plays about the redemption of man. They were set, or began, in paradise with a scene of the Fall.[83] The climactic conclusion of the action was the scene of Christ's (the second Adam's) delivery of mankind from sin and darkness.[84] The extant fragment from the seventeenth century entitled "Antiprologue," Rezanov explains, is a scene which allegorically describes the action to come.[85] The dialogue between Adam and Eve is thus a synecdoche for the play about paradise lost and then later regained. A second fragment appears to be from the conclusion of the play, where an angel announces the Resurrection and Descent. The *raiok* seems to come closest to Western cycle plays in its subject matter, although, of course, it differs greatly in form. Rezanov even suggests that these fragments indicate that Ukraine possessed as broad a range of religious plays as did the West; the difference is that evidence of the drama did not survive.[86]

Common to all *vertep* plays are humour, satire, stock characters, folk traditions, and extensive use of monologue. In the secular scenes played on the lower level, the main role is frequently taken by a Cossack who is victorious in numerous circumstances; he verbally defeats a boastful Polish lord, he catches the devil by his tail, and carries out other comic-heroic deeds.

Slovo o zbureniu pekla may be said to be constructed as a diptych, or *vertep*, one half of which we actually see: the comic action which takes place in hell. Peopled by Lucifer and Hades who recall the puppet theatre's stereotypes of *senex* and ambitious braggart, as well as by paired devilish commanders, *Slovo* is a type of Paradise play which ends with its characters going to heaven. The lively dialogue and comic action of *Slovo* appears to have much more in common with *vertep* than with academic drama. But, unfortunately, the links between the *vertep* and *Slovo o zbureniu pekla* are only tantalizing possibilities, which, at present, cannot be substantiated.

NOTES

1 Werner Friederich, "Late Renaissance, Baroque or Counter-Renaissance?"
   Journal of English and Germanic Philology, 46 (1947), 132.
2 Friederich, p. 138.
3 George Grabowicz, *Toward A History of Ukrainian Literature* (Cambridge:
   Harvard Ukrainian Research Institute, 1981), p. 15. See Gordana Vulović-
   Stanchfield, *Russian Baroque: A.D. Kantemir* (Ann Arbor: Xerox University Microfilms, 1977), *passim* for a good survey of the debate about
   the Baroque among Slavic scholars. Dmytro Chyzhevs'kyi (Čižévsky,
   Čyževsky) wrote many books and articles on the Baroque. See, for example, *Comparative History of Slavic Literatures* (Nashville: n.p., 1971);
   A History of Ukrainian Literature, trans. Dolly Ferguson *et al.* (Littleton,
   Colorado: Ukrainian Academic Press, 1975); and *Ukrains'kyi literaturnyi
   barok* [*The Ukrainian Literary Baroque*] (Prague: Ukrains'ke istorychno-
   filologichne tovarystvo v Prazi, 1941), III.
4 Since Chyzhevs'kyi, scholars such as C. Bida, P. Lewin, I.V. Ivan'o,
   T. Klanitsai, and D.S. Nalivaiko, among many others, have written on
   the Baroque. Yet there seems to have been a remnant of opposition
   to the term in the Soviet Union. In the recently published *Ukrains'ke
   literaturne barokko* [*Ukrainian Literary Baroque*], ed. O.V. Myshanych
   (Kiev: Naukova Dumka, 1987) a number of contributors felt obliged to
   defend the use of this term. See, for example, I.V. Ivan'o's introductory
   essay, "Pro ukrains'ke literaturne barokko [About the Ukrainian Literary
   Baroque]," pp. 3–18.
5 See, for example, Wylie Sypher, *Four Stages of Renaissance Style: Trans-
   formations in Art and Literature, 1400–1700* (N.Y.: Doubleday-Anchor,
   1956), and Jean Rousset, *Circé et Paon: La littérature de l'âge baroque
   en France* (Paris: José Corti, 1954).
6 Frank Warnke, *Versions of Baroque: European Literature in the Seventeenth Century* (New Haven, Conn.: Yale University Press, 1972), p. 4.
7 José Antonio Maravall, *Culture of the Baroque: Analysis of a Historical
   Structure*, trans. Terry Cochran, Theory and History of Literature, 25
   (Minneapolis: University of Minnesota, 1986).
8 Maravall, p. 4.
9 Miroslav John Hanak, "The Emergence of Baroque Mentality and Its
   Cultural Impact on Western Europe after 1550," *Journal of Aesthetics
   and Art Criticism*, 28, No. 3 (Spring, 1970), 318.
10 Grabowicz, p. 33.
11 This is the thesis presented in Maravall's book. Also, see Iu. B. Vipper,
   "O 'semnadtsatom veke' kak osoboi epokhe v istorii zapadnoevropeskikh
   literatur [About the 'Seventeenth Century' as a Separate Epoch in the
   History of Western European Literature]," in *XVII vek v mirovom literaturnom razvitii* [*The Seventeenth Century in the Context of the Devel-*

opment of World Literature], ed. Iu. B. Vipper *et al.* (Moscow: Nauka, 1969), pp. 11–60.

12 The use of the term Counter-Renaissance was popularized by Hiram Collins Haydn, *The Counter-Renaissance* (Gloucester, Mass: P. Smith, 1966), who studied especially the intellectual currents of the period.

13 Friederich, p. 139.

14 Maravall, p. 162.

15 Warnke, pp. 17–18.

16 Hanak, p. 315.

17 Maravall, pp. 67–68.

18 Hanak, p. 325.

19 Hanak, p. 325.

20 Chyzhevs'kyi, *Comparative History*, p. 95.

21 Maravall, p. 216.

22 Maravall, p. 200.

23 See Ernst R. Curtius, *European Literature and the Latin Middle Ages*, trans. W.R. Trask (Princeton: Princeton University Press, 1953), pp. 138–144, for a detailed history of this *topos*.

24 Friederich, p. 135.

25 Maravall, p. 144.

26 Maravall, p. 74. An examination of any seventeenth-century lectures in poetics, especially in East Slavic lands, will bear this out. See, for example, H.M. Syvokin', *Davni ukrains'ki poetyky* [*Ancient Ukrainian Poetics*] (Kharkiv: Kharkivs'kyi orden Trudovoho chervonoho prapora Derzhavnoho universytetu im. O.M. Horkoho, 1960).

27 *Arte de la pintura*, I, p. 387, cited in Maravall, p. 76, note 94.

28 Hanak, p. 316.

29 See chapter VII of Gordana Vulović-Stanchfield for a very complete list of commonly accepted features attributed to the Baroque.

30 Rosalie Colie, *Paradoxia Epidemica: The Renaissance Tradition of Paradox* (Princeton: Princeton University Press, 1966), p. 519.

31 Maravall, p. 210.

32 Chyzhevs'kyi, *Ukrains'kyi literaturnyi barok*, p. 58.

33 *Rozvidky Mykhaila Drahomanova pro ukrains'ku slovesnist' i pys'menstvo* [*The Research of Mykhailo Drahomanov about Ukrainian Oral and Written Literature*], I (Lviv: Naukove Tovarystvo im. T.H. Shevchenka, 1899), p. 16.

34 Paulina Lewin, "The Ukrainian School Theatre in the Seventeenth and Eighteenth Centuries: An Expression of the Baroque," *Harvard Ukrainian Studies*, 5, No. 1 (March, 1981), 62.

35 Alojzy Sajkowski, *Barok* [*Baroque*] (Warsaw: Państwowe Zakłady Wydawnictw Szkolnych, 1972), pp. 111–12, and W. Weintraub, "Teatr Seneki a Struktura 'Odprawy posłow greckich' [The Theatre of Seneca and the

Structure of *The Dismissal of the Greek Ambassadors*]," in *Kultura i Literatura Dawnej Polski* [*Culture and Literature of Ancient Poland*] (Warsaw: Państwowe Wydawnictwo Naukowe, 1968), p. 95.

36 The use of apocryphal themes does not necessarily put into question the orthodoxy of *Slovo*. As Harvey Goldblatt, "Apocrypha," *Handbook of Russian Literature*, ed. Victor Terras (New Haven: Yale University Press, 1985), p. 24 points out, "The widespread diffusion of Apocrypha suggests . . . that they might not have been viewed as contrary to Orthodox teachings. Indeed, some Apocrypha apparently were regarded and used as anti-heretical documents."

37 D. Antonovych, *Trysta rokiv ukrains'koho teatru 1619–1919* [*Three Hundred Years of Ukrainian Theatre 1619–1919*] (Prague: Ukrains'kyi hromads'kyi vydavnychyi fond, 1925), p. 7.

38 Russell Zguta, *Russian Minstrels: A History of the Skomorokhi* (Philadelphia: University of Pennsylvania Press, 1978). Also, Henryk Jurkowski, "Teatr lalek w dawnej Polsce; Próba Zarysu historycznego [Puppet Theatre in Ancient Poland; An Attempt at an Historical Outline]," in *O Dawnym Dramacie i teatrze; Studia do syntezy* [*About the Ancient Drama and Theatre: Studies Toward A Synthesis*] (Wroclaw, Warsaw, Cracow, Gdansk: Wydawnictwo Polskiej Akademii Nauk, 1971), p. 15, argues that *skomorokhy* may have been the successors of Byzantine mime artists.

39 As, for example, the monk Nestor writing in his twelfth century chronicle *Povest' vremennykh let* [*Chronicle of Bygone Years*], ed. V.P. Adrianova-Peretts, trans. D.S. Likhachev and B.A. Romanov (Moscow-Leningrad: Akademiia Nauk SSR, 1950), p. 314.

40 Oleksander Barvins'kyi, *Istoriia ukrains'koi literatury* [*History of Ukrainian Literature*], I (Lviv: Naukove Tovarystvo im. T.H. Shevchenka, 1920), p. 216.

41 O. Bilets'kyi, *Vid davnyny do suchasnosty* [*From Ancient to Contemporary Times*], I (Kiev: Khudozhna literatura, 1960), p. 152.

42 Karl Holl, "Die Entstehung der Bildwand in der griechischen Kirche [The Origin of the Icon Screen in the Greek Church]," *Archiv für Religionswissenschaft*, 9 (1906), 365–384, even argues that the altar screen (*iconostasis*) in Greek churches derives from the façade of the Hellenistic theatre.

43 Paulina Lewin, "Early Ukrainian Theatre and Drama," *Nationalities Papers*, 8, No. 2 (1980), 221.

44 Sandro Sticca, "The *Christos Paschon* and the Byzantine Theatre," *Comparative Drama*, 8, No. 1 (1974), 13–44.

45 I. Steshenko, "Istoriia ukrains'koi dramy [*History of Ukrainian Drama*]," *Ukraina* (Kiev, 1907), I, 102; N. Petrov, *Ocherki iz istorii ukrains'koi literatury XVII i XVIII vv* [*Sketches from a History of Ukrainian Literature of the XVII and XVIII Centuries*] (Kiev: Petr Barskii, 1911); *Rozvidky Mykhaila Drahomanova pro ukrains'ku slovesnist' i pys'menstvo,*

pp. 128–155.
46 Hryhor Luzhnyts'kyi, "Istoriia ukrains'koho teatru [History of the Ukrain-
    ian Theatre]," *ZNTSh*, 171 (1961), 135–190.
    Luzhnyts'kyi cites the in-
    teresting example of *Vorotar* (gatekeeper) as an incipient drama: here the
    dancers construct two rows. One row forms a "gate" through which the
    second proceeds. Dividing the complex ritual into acts and scenes, Luzh-
    nyts'kyi then claims that this is clearly a ritual influenced by Christianity,
    and that the *vorotar* is really *volodar* (ruler), a reference to the Christ
    child. If this is so, it may both suggest Christ's enfranchisement from the
    womb, and the harrowing of hell; both events were typologically linked
    with gates. See, for example, George Ferguson, *Signs and Symbols in
    Christian Art* (N.Y.: Oxford University Press, 1961), p. 107.
47 Paulina Lewin, "Polish-Ukrainian-Russian Literary Relations of the Six-
    teenth-Eighteenth Centuries: New Approaches," *The Slavic and East Eu-
    ropean Journal*, 24, No. 3 (1980), 265.
48 Lewin, "Early Ukrainian Theatre," 221.
49 Bilets'kyi, *Vid davnyny*, p. 153.
50 Bilets'kyi, *Vid davnyny*, p. 153.
51 Bilets'kyi, *Vid davnyny*, p. 153.
52 Bilets'kyi, *Vid davnyny*, p. 154.
53 Stanislaw Windakiewicz, *Teatr Kollegjów Jesuickich w Dawnej Polsce
    [The Jesuit Academic Theatre in Ancient Poland]* (Cracow: Polska Aka-
    demja Umejętności, 1922), p. 3.
54 Ronald G. Engle, "Jesuit Educational Theatre," *North Dakota Quarterly*,
    41, No. 3 (1973), 38.
55 Antonovych, pp. 9–10.
56 Antonovych, p. 10.
57 Alexander Sydorenko, *The Kievan Academy in the Seventeenth Century*
    (Ottawa: Ottawa University Press, 1977), *passim*.
58 Sydorenko, p. 63.
59 Lewin, "Polish-Ukrainian-Russian Literary Relations," 265.
60 There is some controversy surrounding the date and place of the stag-
    ing of these passion scenes. V. Rezanov, *Drama ukrains'ka [Ukrainian
    Drama]*, I (Kiev: Ukrains'ka Akademiia Nauk, 1926), p. 25, points out
    that the church was not consecrated until 1631. Possibly, the play was
    performed in St. Onufrius, another church belonging to the Brotherhood.
    It is important to note that the Orthodox Brotherhoods were very ac-
    tive, enlightened societies resembling guilds. Among the various tasks in
    which they were involved was the establishment of schools and printing
    houses. The first of these Brotherhood schools was established in Lviv
    in 1586 by the Assumption (later Stavropighian) Brotherhood.
61 See Sydorenko, pp. 120–21, for a discussion of drama in the Kievan-
    Mohyla Academy. Also, see the introduction and notes of Vitallii Masliuk

et al. to *Apollonova lutnia* [*Apollo's Lute*] (Kiev: Molod', 1982), especially pp. 16–17 on the May recreations, a type of holiday "consecrated" to poetry.

62 V. Peretts, "Teatral'nye effekty na shkolnoi stsene v Kieve i Moskve XVII i nachala XVIII veka [Theatrical Effects on the School Stage of Kiev and Moscow 17 and Early 18 Centuries]" in *Starinnyi spektakl v Rossii* [*Ancient Theatre in Russia*] (Leningrad: Akademiia, 1928), p. 92.

63 Bilets'kyi, *Vid davnyny*, p. 163.

64 V. Masliuk, *Apollonova lutnia*, p. 17.

65 Antonovych, p. 27.

66 V. Adrianova-Peretts, "Stsena i priemy v russkom shkol'nom teatre XVII-XVIII v. [The Stage and Staging Techniques in Russian School Drama of the XVII-XVIII Centuries]," in *Starinnyi spektakl*, p. 23. Also see Paulina Lewin, "The Staging of Plays at the Kiev Mohyla Academy in the Seventeenth and Eighteenth Centuries," *Harvard Ukrainian Studies*, 5, No. 3 (1981), 320–334.

67 Donald Clive Stuart, "The Stage Setting of Hell and the Iconography of the Middle Ages," *Romanic Review*, 4 (1913), 342, and A.M. Nagler, *The Medieval Religious Stage: Shapes and Phantoms* (New Haven: Yale University Press, 1976), *passim*. Nagler is very skeptical of evidence drawn from pictorial documentation of the mediaeval stage. He argues that both art and theatre drew upon a common literary heritage, but that their developments, while parallel, were not synchronized.

68 Stuart, p. 335.

69 Stuart, p. 340.

70 Meredith and Tailby, p. 90.

71 Meredith and Tailby, p. 90.

72 See, for example, Ia. D. Isaievych, *Dzherela z istorii ukrains'koi kul'tury doby feodalizmy XVI-XVIII st.* [*Sources from the History of Ukrainian Culture in the Period of Feudalism XVI-XVIII Centuries*] (Kiev: Naukova Dumka, 1972), pp. 101–102. Also see Paulina Lewin, *Wykłady poetyki w uczelniach Rosyjskich XVIII w. (1722–1774) a tradycje polskie.* [*Lectures in Poetics in the Educational Institutions of XVIII Century Russia (1722–1774) and Polish Tradition*], pp. 6–7.

73 Stuart, p. 339. Also, George R. Kernodle, *From Art to Theatre* (Chicago: University of Chicago Press, 1944; rpt. 1970), p. 80, notes that "In medieval painting the hell-mouth is often the entrance to a fortress town."

74 Antonovych, p. 34.

75 Ivan Franko, "Iuzhnorusskaia paskhalnaia drama [South Russian Drama]," *Kievskaia starina* [*Kievan Antiquity*], 53 (1896), 412.

76 For a detailed study of *vertep*, including the extant texts, see Ievhen Markovs'kyi, *Ukrains'kyi vertep* [*Ukrainian Puppet Theatre*] (Kiev: Akademiia Nauk URSR, 1929). For more recent findings see I. Iu. Fedas,

Ukrains'kyi narodnyi vertep [*Ukrainian Folk Puppet Theatre*] (Kiev: Naukova Dumka, 1987).

77 Markovs'kyi, p. iii.

78 L.E. Makhnovets', *Vertepna drama* [*Puppet Drama*], in *Istoriia ukrains'koi literatury* [*The History of Ukrainian Literature*], II, ed. E.S. Shabliovs'kyi (Kiev: Naukova Dumka, 1967), p. 81. Also see Russell Zguta, *Russian Minstrels*, p. xi, 111, and *passim*. Zguta argues that the puppet tradition is an ancient one and that it certainly formed an integral part of the *skomorokh* entertainment.

79 Such as I. Franko, "Novi materialy do istorii ukrains'koho vertepa [New Materials Toward a History of Ukrainian Puppet Theatre]," *ZNTSh*, 82 (1908), 30–52.

80 Henryk Jurkowski, p. 15.

81 Reprinted by Markovs'kyi. See p. 6ff.

82 Markovs'kyi, p. 4.

83 Franko, "Novi materialy," p. 30f, examines the fragment entitled "Antiprologue," which begins with a scene of the Fall and the expulsion from paradise, and ends with an angel urging Adam to leave hell because Christ has risen.

84 Franko, "Novi materialy," pp. 31–34.

85 Rezanov, *Ukrains'ka drama*, p. 48.

86 Rezanov, *Ukrains'ka drama*, p. 48.

Origins : Biblical, Liturgical, Apocryphal Sources and Analogues

The harrowing play probably has no connection with the Easter *Quem quaeritis* trope, that trope which forms the germ of most mediaeval drama. Instead, its origins appear to be liturgical—the *Elevatio Crucis* with the *Attolite portas* antiphon as its nucleus, and the Holy Saturday services which give this theme a prominent place.[1] Since the days of Epiphanius, Holy Saturday has been traditionally commemorated as the day on which the harrowing took place, and homilies in defense of this doctrine were read then.

Psalm 24 (23)

The belief in Christ's Descent into Hell, a commonplace since the earliest of Christian times,[2] has "wide and intricate connections."[3] Among the many Biblical allusions (both Old and New Testament) to this belief are the following: Psalms: 24: 7-12; 30: 3; 107: 13-16; Isaiah: 25: 8; 26: 19; Hosea: 13, 14; Matthew: 12: 40; 27: 52-57; I Corinthians: 15: 20-22, 55-57: Hebrews: 2: 14-16; 1 Peter: 3: 18, 19;[4] Revelation: 1: 18-19; Acts: 2: 27: Ephesians: 4: 9-10.

Psalm 24 (23) is perhaps the most important, as well as the oldest, of these references. It also forms the core of all harrowing of hell plays: the words of the Psalm (*Attolite portas*) are echoed when Christ approaches the gates of hell and commands them to open.[5]

Psalm 24 (23): 7-10:

Lift up your gates, O you princes, and be lifted up, O eternal gates, and the King of Glory shall enter in. Who is this King of Glory?
—The Lord who is strong and mighty, the Lord mighty in battle. Lift up your gates, O you princes, and be lifted up, O eternal gates, and the King of Glory shall enter in.
Who is the King of Glory?
—The Lord who is strong and mighty, the Lord mighty in battle.

Who is the King of Glory?
—The Lord of Hosts, He is the King of Glory.[6]

Already in use on Sunday in Jewish synagogue worship during the period of the early church,[7] Psalm 24 has a very long connection with the day of Resurrection. Allen Cabaniss argues that "the early Christian Church was using the twenty-fourth Psalm liturgically to commemorate the Lord's victorious conquest of Hades and death" probably "long before the preparation of the *descensus* section of the Gospel of Nicodemus."[8] A. Rose, studying the early uses of the Psalm, notes that the Psalm was associated with three entries of the Son of God. The oldest linked the Psalm with Christ's Ascension into Heaven; a second, with Christ's Descent into Hell; and a third with Christ's entrance into this world through the Incarnation.[9] Robert Taft suggests that Psalm 24 was probably the early Constantinopolitan Great Entrance Psalm, and that the Great Entrance itself signifies the triumphal entry of Christ into Jerusalem.[10]

The oldest use of Psalm 24 in relation to the Ascension is found in the *Apocalypse of Peter*: "The angels crowd around, so that the word of Scripture may be fulfilled: 'Open your gates, O princes'."[11] Believing the Psalms to be prophecies of the Ascension, the early Church therefore incorporated them into the liturgy.[12]

In addition to its liturgical use, Psalm 24 also appears in the dedication ceremony of a church. Generally accepted as ultimately of Byzantine origin,[13] the Ceremonial Dedication of a Church also has suggestions of a triumphal entry (such as Christ's entry into Jerusalem on Palm Sunday, Christ's entry into hell, and the Ascension). Mediaeval thinkers noted the relationship of the entrance ceremony to exorcism, or, "at least, as a ritual preparatory to initiation into the faith."[14] (And baptism had a fixed rapport with the Descensus, since baptism was given on Easter Sunday. Baptism and redemption were parallel actions, for "Redemption is understood as being the victory of Christ over the demon, the victory by which humanity is set free. It is this liberation that Baptism applies to each Christian."[15]) More recent scholars, such as Daniel Sheerin, have remarked upon the baptismal character of the dedication of a church, a "replication for the church building of the rites of Christian initiation imparted to individuals."[16]

The harrowing of hell is alluded to in the entrance ceremony by both the dramatic action and the use of Psalm 24. The cleric utters the challenge (*Quis est iste rex gloriae?*) while hidden in the church, and then flees when the doors are opened, like the devils of mediaeval drama who challenge, then vainly attempt to flee from Christ when He destroys their gates. The purifying of the church is also associated with Christ's subsequent purifying of hell, and His leading the righteous out of the darkness of hell into the light of heaven.[17]

In his detailed study of *The Liturgical Elements in the Earliest Forms of Medieval Drama*, Paul Edward Kretzmann examines the origins and development of the use of the *rex gloriae* antiphon (which, together with the *Attolite portas* and the *Advenisti desiderabilis* came to dominate the *Elevatio Crucis*). Arguing that the antiphon is an ancient response based upon a pseudo-Augustinian homily,[18] Kretzmann reconstructs the type form in the following fashion:

OFFICIATOR: Tollite portas, principes vestras, et elevamini, portae eternales.
CHORUS: Et introibit rex gloriae.
DIACONUS (IN FIGURA DIABOLI): Quis est iste rex gloriae?
CHORUS: Dominus virtutum ipse rex gloriae (fortis et potens).
CHORUS: Cum rex gloriae infernum debellaturus intraret
Et chorus angelicus ante faciem eius portas principum
tolle praeciperet;
Sanctorum populus qui tenebatur in morte captivus voce
lacrimabili clamaverat:
ANIMAE: Advenisti desiderabilis, quem expectabamus in tenebris,
ut educeres hac nocte vinculatos de claustris.
Te nostra vocabunt suspiria,
Te larga requirebant tormenta.
Tu facta es spes desperatis, magna consolatio in
tormentis.[19]

Mid-way between liturgical, apocryphal usage and the full realization of a harrowing of hell play is the earliest example of a liturgical drama found in the ninth-century section of the Book of Cerne. This harrowing text may, in fact, be considerably older—perhaps from the early eighth century.[20] It, too, shows the influence of the pseudo-Augustine homily 160. (See below.)

Summing up the connections between liturgy and drama, Kretzmann writes:

Under the influence of the Descensus doctrine, whose public confession was fixed for the Great Sabbath, a liturgy with expressed dramatic character was collated for that day. This liturgy and the sermons upon which it was based were the source of the Latin plays of the Descensus and furnished the material for them. If there was no special Descensus play, the material of the liturgy was apparently used as an introduction to Easter plays. . . . There is something in all vernacular plays, except the Cornish, that points to liturgical source or influence.[21]

Like its Western counterparts, *Slovo o zbureniu pekla* also reveals clear links with the liturgy and creatively manipulates the stanzas of Psalm 24 (cf. *Slovo* ll. 460-463, 468-470, 475-476).

The Harrowing in the Eastern Liturgy

Mass: The Divine Liturgy of St. Basil the Great (used during Holy Week on Holy Thursday and Holy Saturday); the Divine Liturgy of St. John Chrysostom (used on weekdays and Sundays, including Easter Sunday).

Text of the Canonical Office: In the Eastern Church, the Holy Saturday Office is dedicated to the retracing of Christ's Passion, Entombment, Descent into Hell to save the souls of the righteous, and opening the gates of heaven. Every Sunday is a "little Easter" in recollecting the events of the Resurrection. Unlike the Western Church, the Eastern includes Resurrection hymns in every Sunday service.

The eight offices of the liturgical year, contained in the *oktoekhos*, hold numerous allusions to the harrowing of hell, which is frequently mentioned together with the Crucifixion, Resurrection, and Ascension. *The Holy Saturday Office* is a meditation on Christ's Entombment and Descent into Hell.[22] It includes special hymns addressed to the Mother of God, because through her God became incarnate, hell was vanquished, and the curse abolished.

Light symbolism is central to the Eastern Holy Saturday service. The priest holds an unlit candle in his left hand, incenses the four corners of the holy table, the icons and the congregation, and then begins the Prayer for the New Light, addressed to "Lord Jesus Christ, our God, our Source of Life and Immortality, Eternal Light born of Eternal Light."[23] Christ is exhorted to "grant spiritual and physical light to our minds and hearts that had been blinded with worldly errors. . . . Since you have raised us up and delivered us from the stain of our sins and the darkness of our transgressions, make us worthy in your loving kindness to kindle our lamps with today's light, the symbol of your radiant and glorious resurrection."[24] Similarly, *Slovo* calls for Christ to illuminate hell "with his bright rays" and to sanctify "all infernal places" (l.476f). The Blessing of the New Light dramatically narrates the effects of the harrowing: "Today Hades tearfully sighs: 'Would that I had not received Him who was born of Mary, for He came to me and destroyed my power; He broke my bronze gates, and being God, delivered the souls I had been holding captive. . . . Today, Hades groans: 'My power has vanished. I received One who died as mortals die, but I could not hold Him. . . .'"[25]

The Easter Sunday service also develops the theme of the liberation of the souls. Thus, for example, the Sixth Ode of Easter Sunday; "O Christ, when You went down into the deepest abyss of the earth, You broke the indestructible chains that kept souls prisoners in Hades, and on the third day You rose from the tomb, as did Jonah from the belly of the whale." [26]

Psalm 24 is sung as part of the Sunday service, and the Resurrection *troparion*[27] is frequently repeated: "Christ is risen from the dead, conquering death by His death, and bestowing life upon those in the tomb." The Resurrection homily, attributed to John Chrysostom, further recalls Christ's Descent into Hell, Isaiah's prophecy, and the harrowing itself: "Hades is angered because frustrated, it is angered because it has been mocked, it is angered because it has been destroyed, it is angered because it has been reduced to naught, it is angered because it is now captive. It seized a body, and, lo! it discovered God; it seized earth, and, behold! it encountered heaven; it seized the visible, and was overcome by the invisible. O death, where is your sting? O Hades, where is your victory."[28]

Slovo echoes all of these and the intermingling images of hellmouth, chasm, and fortress reiterated in the Resurrection Canon. In particular, Solomon's concluding words in the play (ll. 509-519) are taken almost verbatim from the Great Doxology, Holy Saturday Office. (See below, note to ll. 509-519 for full text.)

In the Byzantine Ukrainian Resurrection matins, the priest and his congregation march three times in a procession around the church. Then, singing "Christ is risen!" the priest strikes the main doors with the cross and enters, followed by the entire congregation. The resemblance to the Descent into Hell and the harrowing is unmistakable.

In addition to the Holy Saturday and Easter Sunday offices, the Order of the Funeral of the Dead (*panakhyda*) frequently alludes to the theme of Christ's Descent into Hell: "O God of all spirits and of all flesh. . . . [You] have destroyed death, overcome the devil, and have given life to the world."[29] And, as in the Western, so in the Eastern Church Psalm 24 appears in the liturgy of the Ascension as a command by the Holy Spirit to all the angels to open the heavens: "Lift up your gates, O you princes."[30]

Passions

Since the sixteenth century, the tradition of reading the Passions of Christ during Lent and Holy Week in Ukrainian churches contributed to the popularity of apocryphal material related to the harrowing. This tradition, apparently ritualized by Metropolitan Petro Mohyla in the seventeenth century, involved reading from the canonical Gospels and then providing an exegesis and commentary in the vernacular. This meant that priests could embellish their homilies with material from legends and apocrypha. Theatricality (and, in particular, the convention of several readers) is a notable feature of the Eastern Church's homilies.[31]

The introduction of this ritual, according to V. Rezanov, was a clear indication of the Catholic liturgical Passion play, and led to the creation of Ukrainian liturgical drama.[32] More probably, Mohyla introduced into the East a fairly recently established Western tradition. Although at least as early as the fifth century the four canonical accounts of the last days of Christ were intoned during the Mass by a single deacon, it was not until the fifteenth century that they were given a more dramatic presentation. These passages, which became known as *Passions* (*Strasti* in Ukrainian) were then distributed among three readers, each with a different vocal range. The tradition rapidly caught on in Poland in the fifteenth and sixteenth centuries.[33] It is more likely that Mohyla looked to this liturgical precent, rather than to an example from drama when creating his Eastern ritual.[34]

The *Gospel of Nicodemus*

The obvious, although distant, source of *Slovo o zbureniu pekla* is the apocryphal *Acts of Pilate*, a supposed account of Christ's trial, crucifixion, and burial. The second part of the *Acts* (later known as the *Gospel of Nicodemus*[35]) is an older text written possibly two or three centuries earlier,[36] which was first appended to the *Acts* not before the fifth century,[37] that is, soon after the Synods of Sirmium in Pannonia and Nicaea in Thrace, in 359 and 360, respectively. As Jean Monnier has demonstrated, the idea of the Descent was already well established by the time the Gospel was written. Although the Gospel did not introduce any new material,[38] it became extremely popular and was "widely held to be a sacred document, almost equal in authority to the canonical Gospels."[39] It is this second part which deals with Christ's Descent into Hell.

The *Gospel*'s story is narrated by two eye-witnesses, Leucius and Karinus, raised from the dead. The Descensus proper deals with the righteous who perceive a light in the midst of hell's darkness. They begin to rejoice because this is a sign of Christ's promised coming. St. John the Baptist confirms this news and tells of Christ's baptism. Adam urges his son Seth to tell the saints about Archangel Michael's promise to deliver the oil of mercy to him only when 5,500 years have passed, and when Christ comes to raise up the dead.

At the same time as the saints rejoice, Satan and Hell prepare to receive Jesus. Once Hell learns from Satan that this is the same Jesus who took Lazarus away from him, he becomes fearful and is certain that only a god could have such mighty powers. A voice like thunder interrupts the devils with a command to "Remove, O princes, your gates, and be ye lift up ye doors of hell, and the King of glory shall come in."[40] While the saints shout to the devils that the gates may be opened, David and Isaiah remind them of their prophecies about the raising of the dead. When the mighty voice rings out the command a second time, David recognizes it as the voice of the King of glory. Christ then appears as a man and fills the darkness of hell with his light. The bonds of the saints are loosened, death is trampled underfoot, and Satan is delivered into the power of hell. Christ stretches out his hand to Adam, and leads him and the other saints out of hell. David and the saints sing praises to the Lord.

The *Acts of Pilate* are extant in four versions: form A, a Greek text, c. A.D. 600, containing part I only, that is, no harrowing; form B, an Early Latin text; form C, a loose Greek paraphrase of Latin B; and form D, a Late Latin recension, containing both parts of the text.[41] Greek copies are very rare; the text appears to have flourished chiefly in Latin. The Slavic text is closest to type D of the *Gospel*, the best example of which is the *Codex Einsidlensis*.[42]

After the baptism of Rus'-Ukraine in 988, numerous translations were made from the Greek into Church Slavonic. Among these, we know that the New Testament in its entirety, most of the Bible, the works of the Church Fathers and many apocrypha were made available. Apocrypha were especially popular;[43] although in theory there was a distinction between the canon of Scripture and apocrypha and pseudepigrapha, in practice there was not.[44] The Old Slavonic translation of the *Gospel of Nicodemus* appears to have been made not from the Greek, but from the Latin longer version, or even possibly, Ivan Franko laconically suggests, from the German.[45] André Vaillant, in his study of the Slavic translation of the Nicodemus Gospel, argues for its origin in a Benedictine monastery in Dalmatia in the tenth century.[46] M. Speranskii and Ivan Franko, by contrast, suggest the eleventh, or even the twelfth century.[47]

There are two versions of the *Gospel* in Slavic. A "short" version translated from the Greek (corresponding to form A), that is, only Part I. Speranskii reprints this version from a thirteenth-century manuscript, followed by Epiphanius' homily which is connected to the office of Holy Saturday.[48] The "long" version translated from the Latin has both parts, and is found in many later manuscripts, the best one of which comes from St. Sophia in Novgorod (fourteenth-fifteenth centuries). Ivan Franko published a seventeenth-century version in his *Apokryfy i lehendy* [*Apocrypha and Legends*].[49] That the Slavs were very familiar with the harrowing story is confirmed by the evidence provided by icons, oral legends, and various chronicles, indices of prohibited books, and other documents, such as the menologia,[50] to say nothing of the 184 Slavic extant manuscripts of the *Gospel of Nicodemus*.[51] That the oldest fragment of *Slovo o zbureniu pekla* survived in an eighteenth-century menologion suggests the continuing popularity of this legend and its possible use in conjunction with liturgical purposes.

Slovo dispenses with the oil of mercy story and with the opening scene of the saints in favour of a more dramatic alternative: Lucifer proudly recounting the history of the creation of his realm, yet anxiously awaiting information about this mysterious Christ who claims to be the Son of God. The drama then roughly follows the *Gospel* in setting up the opposition between the joy of the righteous (as exemplified by John the Baptist in *Slovo*) and the contentiousness and dawning fear of the devils. Satan (Lucifer in the Ukrainian play) and Hell (*Ad*, or Hades, in the Ukrainian) argue about the identity of Christ and the need to bring Him to their realm. *Slovo* follows the *Gospel of Nicodemus* in making Hell-Hades the more fearful of the two devilish princes. While the *Gospel* includes Adam, Seth, Eve (Latin B only), John the Baptist, Jeremiah, Abraham (Greek), David, and others, *Slovo* provides only John the Baptist and Solomon (not present in the *Gospel*) with speaking parts. *Slovo*'s comic conclusion, of course, also radically differs from the *Gospel of Nicodemus*.

The Homiletic Tradition: Eusebius of Alexandria and Epiphanius of Cyprus

In addition to the Bible and the apocrypha, hundreds of sermons were translated in the period of the Kievan Rus'. Of these, over twenty per-cent are devoted to eschatology.[52] Complete collections of the homilies of Gregory the Great, Gregory of Nazianzus, and a large collection of the sermons of Ephraim Syrus came to the Slavic lands.[53] The most widely read Church Father was John Chrysostomus; over 300 works of his were wholly or partly translated.[54] Basil of Caesarea, Cyril of Alexandria, Athanasius of Alexandria,[55] Gregory of Nyssa, John of Damascus, Athanasius of Alexandria, Andrew of Crete, John of Dam-ascus, Cyril of Jerusalem, and Eusebius of Alexandria were among the many translated Fathers. The Descent theme figures prominently in many of their works.[56]

Slavs, including Ukrainians, knew the harrowing story best from a homily which may have originated independently of the *Gospel of Nicodemus*,[57] and seems to have been written roughly in the same period.[58] Entitled "Oratio de adventu et annuntiatione Joannis (Bap-tistae) apud inferos" in its non-Slavic versions, the Eusebian homily is a direct and dramatic retelling of the Descent story,[59] consisting of three basic scenes: the first and second are "choral" scenes explaining the present action, the "death" of Christ, the trembling of Hades, and the preparation of the prophets for Christ's coming; the third scene presents the actual Descent and the liberation of the righteous.

The homily is extant in ninety-nine manuscripts, four of which are in Ukrainian texts from the sixteenth and seventeenth centuries.[60] Three are in Kievan collections (two in *sborniks*, and the third in a menalogion), the fourth in a Lviv manuscript reprinted by Franko.[61] Variously attributed to Eusebius of Alexandria, Eusebius of Samosata, and John Chrysostom,[62] the Ukrainian manuscripts all identify the au-thor as Eusebius. (For the sake of convenience only, the homily will be referred to as Eusebian.) Probably translated into Slavic at about the same time as the *Gospel of Nicodemus*,[63] the homily came to replace it. Vaillant argues that the brilliance of this version of the Descent story in part explains the disappearance in Greek and Coptic of the second part of the *Gospel of Nicodemus*.[64]

An imaginative and greatly elaborated adaptation of Eusebius' homily,[65] a Ukrainian version entitled *Slovo o shestvii Ioanna Predtecha v ad* [*The Descent of St. John the Baptist into Hades*] begins with a scene of the descent of John the Baptist, whose arrival in Hades initiates a discussion about the arrival of Christ. Some of the righteous are anxious that Christ will not take on the terrible Passion, which they themselves have prophesied. Eight Old Testament characters speak in turn, recalling their prophecies of the coming of Christ. Among the prophets and patriarchs is Solomon, who appears in no other source. The prophets then rejoice and make merry at the arrival of John the Baptist. Hearing the noise, Hades wishes to know the cause. The Devil, addressing Hades as "brother," briefly recapitulates the work of John on earth as baptiser of Christ and as His forerunner. Warning the devils to carefully guard John, the Devil then hurries to his "friends," the Jews, and in particular to his "dear friend," Judas Iscariot, in order to initiate the action of the Passion. Overhearing Christ's remarks, "My soul is sad even unto death," the Devil delightedly believes that Christ fears mortality.

Returning to hell, the Devil tells Hades to prepare a hard place for Christ who will soon be with them. He then begins a lengthy complaint about the great injustices Christ has committed against him. While comic, his lamentations serve a serious purpose: they remind the reader of Christ's many miracles. The Devil complains, for example, that Christ has made it impossible for the Devil to dwell anywhere on earth. When the Devil decided to enter pigs, he found that he, "poor thing," was not safe even there. In colloquial dialogue, the Devil exclaims that he "really got angry then,"[66] but was afraid to do anything about it. The Devil then entered a young girl, and delighted himself by doing much evil there. But Christ gave the girl's mother His strength, and the Devil is much ashamed because a woman drove him out.

After hearing the recitation of all the miracles, Hades, having listened attentively, inquires whether this is the same Christ who enfranchised Lazarus by calling him out of the tomb. When the Devil responds in the affirmative, Hades quakes and tells the Devil to be merciful; it is certain that they will lose all their prisoners if he continues in his actions. The Devil, however, says he does not fear Christ, and urges Hades to remain firm, because he has incited Judas and the Jews against Christ. Hades continues to warn the Devil about the possibility of Christ's victory. But the Devil does not heed Hades' advice. He goes to the Jews once more and stirs their hearts. Then follows a summary of the events of the Last Supper and Good Friday. In a curious addition to the Eusebian homily, the Ukrainian scribe adds a scene of the Devil flying to Christ while He is on the cross. Mocking the Lord, the Devil claims that he is very sorry for Him in His suffering. But upon arriving in hell, the Devil finds for the first time that he feels afraid. It is, of course, too late.

While he unsuccessfully pleads with Hades for assistance, and attempts to lock and bolt all entrances to hell, Christ sends one division to guard the sepulchre, while another descends with Him. The angels cry, "Open the gates, infernal princes! Open, eternal ones, let the King of glory enter."[67] The evil spirits ask, who is the King of glory? And the angels reply in the formulaic manner. Hades asks why Christ comes here, and whether it is not enough that He has a kingdom in heaven? The angels reply that it is necessary, for Christ will tie up the Devil and deliver him to Hades, and will lead out the righteous from hell. Hades then upbraids the devil (called Beelzebub for the first time) and laments. The Devil begins to cry and begs Hades for help in keeping the gates locked. But the angels begin to sing, "Lift up, the gates, o princes, and open the infernal gates." Hades trembles. David reminds him of his prophecy, and asks, "O death, where is thy sting?" Then Christ enters like the sun. The scribe remarks that Christ's arrival occurs exactly as depicted by John of Damascus, and then quotes from the Resurrection Canon. Christ then approaches the gates, calls out that He is resurrected, and that all who hate Him should flee from His sight. The chains crumble, a terrible noise is heard. Christ enters hell, and the angels begin to beat the devils. They tie up Beelzebub[68] for a thousand years until the Last Judgement. Then David begins to sing. All join in, and so rejoicing they go to heaven.

The Ukrainian version of the Greek text is not only a very free translation, but also a rather colloquial one. While the passages involving the Biblical characters are dignified, the exchanges between Hades and the Devil (only once referred to as Beelzebub) are informal, even chatty in tone. The Ukrainian text includes a new scene, not found in any of the homilies, that of the Devil speaking with Christ on the cross.

Slovo o zbureniu pekla may be seen to follow in rough outlines the Ukrainian version of the pseudo-Eusebian homily. St. John the Baptist takes a prominent role in the harrowing play, and is, in fact, the only New Testament character to speak. While *Slovo o zbureniu pekla* does not give speaking parts to Abel, Noah, Abraham, Isaac, Jacob, Joseph and the numerous other Old Testament figures of the homily, it does provide Solomon (who is absent from the *Gospel of Nicodemus*, and other well-known versions of the Descent story) with a prominent role. The Leucius and Karinus narrators, the Seth story, and the Enoch-Elijah and robbers scene are absent in both *Slovo* and in the homily, but the play does include a reference both to Adam and to Eve (as in form B of the *Gospel of Nicodemus*). The colloquial tone of the homily's dialogue involving the devils is also echoed and considerably developed in the play.

There are, however, also many differences between the homily and the harrowing play. *Slovo o zbureniu pekla* takes place entirely in hell, rather than alternating scenes on earth with those in the infernal regions. Most probably for ease of presentation, the playwright instead uses the device of messengers to bring news of the Passion of Christ from the earthly realm. The heightened activity of the play's action serves to make it more dramatic, and contrasts with the solemnity and marked change of pace which takes place with the arrival of Christ. Rather than giving speaking parts to all the righteous (as is found in the homily), the playwright condenses the prophecies and allows John the Baptist to speak for all. This prevents the repetitiousness, and even dullness, evident in some other harrowing plays. It is also a decision which seems to reveal a true sense of drama: the construction of scenes with a view to conflict, dramatic irony, and variations in pace. The busy actions of the numerous devils contrast with the calm certitude and the strength of the single prophet.

There are other differences between the homily and the play. The Devil, unlike *Slovo*'s Lucifer, is well aware of Christ's true identity. He wants the Son of God's soul in hell in part out of revenge, since He has been undoing the Devil's work on earth by healing the sick and by bringing the dead to life. Hades, on the other hand, is fearful not only of losing his kingdom and its prisoners, but also of initiating a titanic war. The tension between old Hades and the Devil recalls the play, but it is a tension of a different order. Eusebius' Devil is a proud overreacher who aims to undo God himself, while Hades almost seems to be in league with God. *Slovo o zbureniu pekla*'s Lucifer is not in full possession of the facts; he is perturbed throughout the play by Christ's incognito status; and his ambitious hopes are constantly undercut by dramatic irony.

It seems most likely that the Eusebian homily was an important influence on the *Slovo* playwright; in particular, it may have suggested the use of Solomon. The fact that the homily was recommended reading in the place of the Passions[69] certainly points to its basically orthodox message, as well as to its general popularity. However, the playwright's deviations from the homily also suggest that he may have looked elsewhere to flesh out his drama.

Epiphanius's Holy Saturday homily presents another version of the harrowing.[70] A very long homily, it lays particular stress on the rescue of Adam and Eve (only Eve figures in form B of the *Gospel of Nicodemus*). Unlike the *Gospel of Nicodemus*, which presents the Descent story from the point of view of Hades and Satan, the Epiphanian homily avoids personifying the infernal powers, and instead peoples a very gloomy hell with nameless demons. St. Michael and Gabriel alternate speaking the various parts of the *Attolite portas* formula. Drawing upon the tradition of Christ preaching in hell, Epiphanius' Christ concludes the homily with a very long speech directed especially to Adam and Eve. MacCulloch, in his study of the Descent, finds traces of the homilies of Eusebius and possibly Ephraim Syrus in Epiphanius's sermon. He also notes some parallels to passages in the *Odes of Solomon*.[71]

Epiphanius's homily directly influenced two homilies of the Ukrainian Orthodox theologian Kyril Tranquillion Stavrovets'kyi—the homily for Holy Saturday, and for the Feast Day of St. Lazarus (1619).[72] Although based upon the *Gospel*, Epiphanius and Eusebius' homilies are much more elaborate accounts of Christ's Descent, and, in particular, of Satan's and Hell's conversations.

Several other homilies, discussed by J.A. MacCulloch,[73] deal with the harrowing theme. One concerns John the Baptist's question to Christ, "Are you He who should come?" The second is a brief dialogue between the Devil and Hades, and the third is an account of the betrayal, arrest, trial, and scourging. The latter two homilies closely resemble scenes in the *Gospel of Nicodemus*, and were later conflated into one sermon entitled *Sermo de Confusione Diaboli*. As MacCulloch observes, all the homilies contain notable omissions: the Adam, Seth, and tree of life story, and the emphasis on the rescue of Adam.[74] Unlike the concise, "well-balanced" *Gospel of Nicodemus*, the homilies are diffuse, "rhetorical addresses."[75]

Sermo de Confusione Diaboli

E.K. Rand reprints the *Sermo de Confusione Diaboli*, a Latin ninth-century translation of two fifth- or sixth-century Greek homilies, which, Rand argues, may be ascribed to Eusebius of Alexandria, one for Maundy Thursday, the other for Good Friday, later (probably in the sixth century) combined into a single narrative.[76] Rand's text, which closely follows the chronology of events set out in the *Gospel of Nicodemus*, although in a much elaborated fashion, suggests yet another instance of the influence and popularity of the harrowing story.

As in *Slovo o zbureniu pekla*, so here only two of the dead have speaking parts: John the Baptist and David (*cf. Slovo*'s John and Solomon). The procession of the prophets is extremely brief, and Adam is not mentioned by name. The scene in paradise centres on the good thief, rather than on Enoch and Elijah (as it does in the *Gospel of Nicodemus*). Although no Slavic translation of the *Sermo* has been noted by scholars, its Greek "originals" were well known in a Slavic version attributed to Eusebius. (See above.) It is curious, however, that certain structural features present in the *Sermo* (such as the use of only two speaking characters, and the brevity of the procession), but in no other source, find a parallel in *Slovo*. While this may suggest that the *Slovo* playwright knew the Latin text, it may also merely indicate that the rich subject of the Descent was capable of generating many related, yet different treatments, each in its own way an independent, new work. Certainly homilies were a very important influence on the *Slovo* writer, since in the Eastern Church the sermon assumed the form of a work of rhetorical art, particularly in the period in which *Slovo* was written.[77]

Odes of Solomon

Of the forty-two apocryphal *Odes* from the second century attributed to Solomon, two (numbers 17 and 42) allude to Christ's Descent into Hades. "I opened the doors that were closed, and brake in pieces the bars of iron . . ." (Ode 17), and

Sheol saw me and was made miserable: Death cast me up and many along with me. I was gall and bitterness to him and I went down with him to the utmost of his depths . . . and those who had died ran towards me: and they cried and said, Son of God, have pity on us . . . and bring us out from the bonds of darkness: and open to us the door by which we shall come out to thee. . . . And I heard their voice; and my name I sealed upon their heads. (Ode 42)[78]

According to J.H. Bernard, the *Odes* are of Palestinian or Syrian origin, sacramental in intention, and almost liturgical in character. Well-known in the East (they are extant in Greek, Syriac, and Coptic), there is no evidence to prove that they were known in the West. Bernard

argues that the *Odes* are baptismal hymns, sung during the Lenten season and employed ritually in the initiation of catechumens in the period
that precedes the Easter baptism.[79] Rendel Harris and Alphonse Min-
gaga, however, refute Bernard's suppositions, and, in turn, contend that
any references to baptism are "merely occasional and not structural,"
although they agree that St. Cyril of Jerusalem employs them in his
lectures to the candidates for baptism in the year 348.[80] Both Cyril and
the *Odes* enjoin the catechumens to "Guard the mystery," the mystery
of the rite of baptism, suggesting that the Christian teachers' attitude
at that time was that of a *disciplina arcani*.[81]

MacCulloch adds further evidence to the link between baptism
and the harrowing: "the effect of baptism is . . . often made parallel to
the effect of the Descent . . . baptism took place on Easter Eve." Mac-
Culloch draws attention to the tradition that Christ not only preached in
Hades, but that he also baptized, since baptism was thought to be abso-
lutely necessary to salvation. He further notes that baptism was known
in the early Church as "illumination."[82] The fixed association between
baptism and the Descent is studied by Per Lundberg, Jean Daniélou,
and by Bo Reicke,[83] who underscore the parallelism of baptism and
redemption. Both are victories of Christ over the devil.

The *Slovo* writer may have been familiar with this connection between Solomon and the rites of baptism, a connection underscored by
St. Cyril of Jerusalem in his *Catechetical Lectures*, where he notes that
Solomon, as cited by Ecclesiastes, prefigures baptismal grace.[84] He is
given an unusually prominent place in the last few moments of *Slovo o
zbureniu pekla*, a place traditionally held by David in other harrowing
of hell plays (or by Mary Magdalene in Polish Passion plays). Solomon
usually forms a pair with King David in the Eastern icons of the Descent, but it is unlikely that the *Slovo* writer simply confused the two
kings. Solomon was a very popular figure in Eastern legends, and numerous apocrypha were attributed to him.[85] His apocryphal works (the
Psalms, and Wisdom) were widely read. Folklore turned Solomon into
a clever, wily type with some resemblance to both Ulysses and Oedi-
pus in the emphasis on his riddle-making and answering ability, and
in his mental agility as a whole (particularly as it served to help him
wriggle out of difficult situations). The *Slovo* writer's use of Solomon
thus appears in part to be a calculated effort to employ a familiar folk
hero much admired by audiences.

Solomon also had attributed to him authority over demoniacal
powers of evil; originally a Jewish belief, it lingered long in Christian-

ity.[86] Thus the *Slovo* playwright's choice of Solomon as the concluding figure of the play is understandable: an Old Testament King who
prefigured baptismal grace, and who supposedly alluded to the first
harrowing of hell in his *Odes* is also made to prophesy the second
harrowing. Conversely, Christ, as the embodiment of Wisdom-Sofia
(in his role as wise judge), and as the vanquisher of evil, was often
regarded as a second Solomon.

Harris and Mingana's views about the notion of Christianity as
a secret cult seem explicit in Hades' words in the play: "He [Christ]
chose him [Lazarus] for a secret participant, and pulled him from my
sharp teeth" (*Slovo*, ll. 108-109). The meaning becomes clear if the
lines are interpreted as a reference to the early Church's cult status.
They would then suggest the practice of the Church's teachers to give
full instruction in the mysteries only to the baptized.

If this is the case, that is, if the *Slovo* playwright deliberately used
Solomon to conclude his play because of the *Odes'*—or of Solomon's—
apparent connection with the rites of baptism, and hence alluded to
Christianity as a *disciplina arcani*, then a further mystery would be
solved, namely the stage direction at the end of the harrowing which
reads: "And while He [Christ] makes the sign of the cross three times,
then the gates and the chains disintegrate, and Christ enters hell, and
illuminates it with His bright rays, and blesses all infernal places, and
He sprinkles holy water [imbuing hell] with the Holy Spirit" (*Slovo*,
l. 476f).

In this stage direction the Ukrainian text is once again unlike all
other harrowing plays. Usually, Christ causes the gates of hell to open
and, holding a cross or a standard, leads the righteous out of hell and
into paradise. In the Ukrainian play, Christ causes the gates to crumble,
and then not only makes the sign of the cross, but also sprinkles hell
with both holy water and the Holy Spirit. If the playwright was thinking
of baptismal customs and rites, he may have found this stage direction
particularly fitting, for it certainly seems to allude to the parallel action
of baptism and Resurrection. Baptism conveys the gift of the Holy
Spirit.[87] The sacrament of the water frees the catechumen from the
Sea of Death, and the cross transforms the water of baptism to the
water of redemption.[88] As in baptism, so in redemption, "the demon is
conquered, again man is saved, and this is accomplished by the sign
of water."[89]

In the Byzantine Liturgy of the Presanctified, usually celebrated on
the three days of the Holy Week, a prayer addressed to the catechumens

enjoins them to "go out" and "be illuminated . . . with the light of knowledge and piety. . . . That He may make them born again of water and the Holy Spirit." The choir responds, "Truly the King of glory enters. . . ."[90] The rite of baptism includes an exorcism of Satan (by prayer, laying on of hands, and breathing upon the catechumen), and a renunciation of the devil. In the child's name, the godparents face the West (sunset, symbol of darkness, hence the realm of Satan), and then turn toward the East (sunrise, light, Christ).

In the Eastern Church, Christ is "only known in the Holy Spirit," and He always appears triumphant: "even in His Passion; even in the Tomb. . . . He descends as a conqueror into Hades and destroys for ever the power of the enemy."[91] Completely foreign to Eastern tradition is the cult of the humanity of Christ.[92] "The consciousness of the fullness of the Holy Spirit, given to each member of the Church, . . . banishes the shades of death, . . . [and] makes of the paschal night 'a banquet of faith'. . . ."[93]

In addition to the possible link with baptism, the Solomon episode was unquestionably influenced by a popular legend discovered in all areas of Ukraine: "Iak Solomon iz pekla vymydryvsia [How Solomon Wriggled Out of Hell]." Ivan Franko reprinted this legend from the seventeenth-century manuscript of Father Stefan Teslevs'kyi.[94] The legend begins with an unhappy King David who notices that Christ, after leading out the righteous, has forgotten his son Solomon. But Christ consoles David and promises that Solomon's cleverness will get him out of hell. Indeed, Solomon begins to sing the Resurrection Canon in hell. Curious, the devils ask why Solomon has remained behind. He replies that Christ will come a second time, at which point He will retrieve the king. Frightened by Christ's first harrowing, the devils summarily thrust Solomon out of hell. Observing the action, Christ turns to David, and remarks, "I told you that your son Solomon would escape by means of his wisdom."[95]

M. Drahomanov attributes this joker-prankster figure of Solomon to the influence of the German *Eulenspiegel* of the fourteenth and fifteenth centuries, which he believes was taken up by Ukrainian folk drama.[96]

Eusebius of Caesarea

One of the leading representatives of ecclesiastical conservatism of the fourth century, Eusebius of Caesarea wrote the *Demonstratio Evangelica* [*The Proof of the Gospel*] in twenty books, only ten of which remain.[97] Intended as a guide to strengthen the faithful, the *Demonstratio*, c. 314-318, deals with various aspects of the life of Christ. Seven Greek texts are extant, as well as a Latin translation of 1498, which was reprinted five times in the sixteenth century.[98] If the knowledgeable *Slovo* writer knew this popular work, he would probably be familiar with the Greek or Latin versions, since no Slavic translations are extant. Book VIII, chapter 1 of the *Demonstratio* in particular deals with the traditional elements of the harrowing of hell, and develops the battle imagery so vividly represented in *Slovo*:

... He went to the place of His enemies, having life in Himself, to loose death, and the powers arrayed against Him, which perhaps at first conceived that he was an ordinary man and like all men, and so encircled Him and attacked Him as they would any one else, but when they knew that He was superhuman and divine, they turned their backs and fled from Him. . . .[99]

This description bears some resemblance to Satan's proposed battle strategy, which the devils vainly attempt to carry out until they are overwhelmed by their terror before Christ. (See *Slovo*, ll. 335-355.)

The *Gospel (Questions) of St. Bartholomew*

In original form a third-century document attributed to Bartholomew, and referred to as a *Gospel*, or as *Questions*, it is extant in three languages: Greek, Latin, and Slavonic. M.R. James dates the Greek text at circa A.D. 5. The Latin text is extant in two forms, 1 a fragment of two leaves from the ninth century, and form 2, complete, from the sixth or seventh century. James does not date the Slavonic text, despite the fact that he employs the Slavonic and Greek as the basis of his version of the *Questions*.[100] According to Santos Otero, the Slavic text was known by the title *Bartholomew's Questions to the Mother of God*. The five extant Slavic manuscripts present a problem of dating, since (in contradiction to the dissemination of the work), each text is known only from the fourteenth century onwards.[101]

The *Questions* are set in the days following the Resurrection. St. Bartholomew boldly asks Christ where He went from the cross, since the disciple saw Christ's body disappear at the moment of darkness. Jesus responds, "For when I vanished away from the cross, then went I down into Hades that I might bring up Adam and all them that were with him, according to the supplication of Michael the archangel."[102] The time of Christ's Descent is significant; it occurs while He is on the cross, not after the entombment, hence suggesting that not only Christ's

soul, but also His body descends into hell. Christ then proceeds to
narrate the events of the Descent, especially the tremblings of Hades.
The devil (Satan) tries to comfort Hades who, in the Greek version
has "gripes in [his] belly and [his] entrails rumble" (*cf. Slovo*'s Hades,
ll. 205-208). Suspense clearly builds as Christ describes his Descent,
five hundred steps at a time. The two Slavonic versions have Hades
say to Satan, "I was created before you," a phrase which suggests that
Satan is a relative newcomer to hell, an idea also found in *Slovo*.[103]
Christ shatters the iron bars, smites the devil with a hundred blows,
and then binds him. All the patriarchs are led out and Christ comes
again to the cross.

Although some passages echo *Slovo o zbureniu pekla*, there is little
evidence of a direct influence. But the *Questions'* popularity indicates
yet again the extent to which the harrowing theme captured the fertile
imagination of Eastern writers. Other Church Fathers who wrote on
this theme were Clement and his pupil Origen, both of Alexandria.

Saint Augustine

Of negligible importance to Eastern Christianity (unlike his centrality
to the West), St. Augustine nonetheless is a possible source of reference for an author interested in the harrowing theme, and writing
during a period of strong cross-cultural influences. Many of Augustine's sermons (219, 221, 233, 263, 265) allude to Christ's Descent and
His victory over death, and utilize the imagery of light and darkness,
which became a conventional method of dealing with this theme.

A lengthy treatment of the harrowing is found in Augustine's letter
to Evodius (164), in which he responds to questions concerning an
interpretation of I Peter 3:18, 19. Not certain whether all or only some
prisoners are freed from the bondage of hell, St. Augustine concludes
that at least Adam, the prophets, and the patriarchs would be granted
divine mercy and justice. Finally, Augustine asks, in a question that
reveals how deeply entrenched the doctrine of the Descent was already
in early Christian belief: "It is clearly shown that the Lord died in the
flesh and descended into hell. . . . Who, then, but an unbeliever will
deny that Christ was in hell?"[104]

Most influential, however, was the pseudo-Augustine homily Sermon 160, which consists of five parts: Christ's destruction of hell;
anonymous voices in Tartarus, which speak of the terror of the great
light; the Just calling for Christ's arrival (*Advenisti*); and then their
tearful thanks, and request that He establish the sign of the cross in

hell.[105] The homilist concludes the sermon by praying that Christ return
to earth a second time to lead mankind to heaven, and thus draws the
readers into the story by suggesting that the Descent applies to them,
also.
    A representative of the transition from the Patristic to the Mid-
dle Ages is St. Gregory the Great (d. 605). He was followed in the
mediaeval period by Peter Abelard, St. Bernard of Clairvaux, Peter
Lombard, Alain de Lille, St. Thomas Aquinas, Jacobus de Voragine,[106]
and, finally, Dante.[107] All of these writers affirmed that the purpose of
Christ's Descent into Hell (variously referred to as Limbo, Hell, and
the Bosom of Abraham) was to free the souls of the righteous who
deserved salvation, although a lively debate continued concerning the
numbers of souls saved: some believed only a few were led out into
paradise, others argued that all were freed.[108]

Ephraim Syrus

Yet another possible source of inspiration for the *Slovo* playwright
may have been the hymns of the fourth-century Ephraim of Syrus.
Ephraim's works were among the first to be translated into Old Bulgarian from the Greek in the tenth century; from there the text made
its way into Slavic lands.[109] As the English editor of his hymns, John
Gwynn, points out, it was the Syrian and not the Greek Church which
"took the initiative in the development of ritual."[110] The importance of
the hymns, and their great number in the Eastern Church is thus largely
due to the Syrian Church's influence.
    Ephraim's hymns, perhaps because of their dramatic character,
were widely popularized in the East.[111] For our purposes, the group
"Death and Satan" (Hymns 35 to 68), and "Death, Satan, and Man"
(Hymns 35 to 42) are especially noteworthy; all come from a larger
collection entitled *The Nisibene Hymns*. Frequently, Sin or Death has
the dominant speaking role in these hymns. In Hymn 35, for instance,
Sin, Hell, and Satan tremble and are terrified as the dead rebel. The
Hymn concludes with Sin counselling the devils to loose themselves
among Christ's disciples. Hymn 36 begins with a brief recapitulation of
Christ's Passion. In the rest of the Hymn, Death speaks in accents very
like those of Lucifer in the harrowing plays: "If thou be God show thy
power; and if Thou be man, feel our power" (*cf. Slovo*, ll. 371-376).[112]
In verses three to ten, Death boasts of conquering "all the wise men,"
Sampson, Goliath, Og, the prophets, priests, lords, and wise men. Only
Enoch and Elijah have escaped. The Hymn concludes with Death in

torment and confusion, as the Voice of the Lord sounds in hell, and the dead come forth. The image of Death weeping is continued in the next Hymn: "Death was weeping for her, ever for Sheol, when he saw her treasury that it was emptied."[113]

Although the main figures of these hymns are Sin and Death (and, less, frequently, Satan), they seem to closely resemble the pair of Satan and Hell from *The Gospel of Nicodemus*. It is noteworthy that Ephraim's hymns dwell on the harrowing of hell itself—that is, on its complete destruction, on the fear of Sin and Death, and later on Death's sorrows.

The Appeal of Adam to Lazarus in Hell

While Western writers were in the throes of the Reformation and had ceased to write about the harrowing, Eastern poets, playwrights, and prose writers were still drawing upon this theme.

A fragment, *The Appeal of Adam to Lazarus in Hell*, written no later than the sixteenth century,[114] deals with that scene in which the righteous await Christ's coming and ask Lazarus, who is about to depart for the land of the living, to take a message to Christ, reminding Him of their torment in hell, and hoping for His imminent Descent. Adam commands David to strike on his *gusli* (psaltery), and tells the prophets to rejoice because the day of salvation approaches. Adam has heard the shepherds' piping in the cave where Christ was born; their voices penetrated the gates of hell.

Many verbal parallels and echoes recall the *Gospel of Nicodemus*, the homilies of Eusebius and, in particular, Epiphanius, and hence, of course, *Slovo o zbureniu pekla*, although no actual harrowing is extant.

Conclusion

The seventeenth century, the time when *Slovo o zbureniu pekla* was being composed, brought together two very different cultures: Western European Baroque and mediaeval Byzantine Slavic. Because of the extraordinary cross-currents of the time, the multilingual scholars of Ukraine had available to them not only the usual works of the Orthodox tradition, but also many hitherto unfamiliar texts in Latin, Italian, Polish. Some scholars were being influenced by a revitalized Catholicism, others by the still-new Protestantism, and yet others undecidedly oscillated between Orthodoxy and the Uniate Church. With so many possible sources available to the writer of a seventeenth-century harrowing play, and so much shared material, it is impossible to determine with any certainty the exact sources of his material. We may, however, be assured that whatever the extensive influences possible, the writer's work, at base, had to be Orthodox, and this meant that the writer, of necessity, made himself most familiar with the writings of his own tradition.

The *Slovo* playwright, an author of considerable skill, appears to have been well versed in Biblical, liturgical, and apocryphal sources of the story of the harrowing of hell. Beginning with a firm knowledge of the Eastern Divine Liturgy (especially the Resurrection Odes), which may have suggested the light imagery at the conclusion of the play (1.476f), as well as the mingled images of hell as mouth, fortress, and chasm, the Liturgy also provided the concluding words of the play from the Great Doxology, Holy Saturday Office.

The *Gospel of Nicodemus* may have been a source for the play. But the material of the *Gospel* is also found in other sources. *Slovo*'s omission of the Seth story, and the brief procession of patriarchs (more hinted at than actual), as well as the inclusion of Solomon suggests that the Ukrainian writer may have used the pseudo-Eusebian homily instead of the *Gospel*. Likewise, the expanded dialogue between Satan and Hades may have been influenced by the pseudo-Eusebian homily. Curiously, no apocryphal, Biblical, or Patristic source uses the name Lucifer (clearly a Latin influence)—Satan is used instead, although a strong tradition of associating Lucifer with the harrowing is found in Cornish, Spanish, German, Bohemian, and Polish plays. The English and Italian use Satan or Beelzebub.

Possibly the Latin *Sermo de Confusione Diaboli* suggested the structure of only two speaking characters from among the righteous, St. John and Solomon. The sermon may also have suggested the list of Abraham, Isaac, Jacob and the patriarchs that the *Slovo* writer follows (ll. 77-79), and the attitude of St. John the Baptist, who almost smugly reminds the now-frightened Lucifer of his previous warnings and prophecies. Also from the *Sermo* may come the wording of Hades' explanation of Christ as the one who called Lazarus to himself "with one word only." Lucifer's odd fear of "another's fire" (*Slovo*, l. 448) is also clarified by the *Sermo*, in which the Prince of Darkness is flung into the fires of hell by the victorious Christ.

Hades' complaint of gastric disorders (*Slovo*, ll. 205-208) may have come from St. Barthlomew's *Questions*, in which Hades' stomach is also rent from fear; and Lucifer's newcomer position and comforting of Hades may also have its origin here. The boldness of Lucifer in his challenge to Christ and the sorrow of the defeated devilish forces is found in various sources, but perhaps most forcefully in the hymns of Ephraim Syrus. The apparently friendly relations between Lucifer and God (indicated in the first monologue of the Ukrainian play), and later between Lucifer and Christ (in Christ's sympathetic response to Lucifer's lamentations), also found in other Slavic plays, may stem from the Slavic legend of the dual creation of the world, probably based on the Bogomil's (a Bulgarian dualistic sect) main tenet of belief. (See note to 1. 23 of *Slovo*.) The treatment of Mary, in its emphasis on her maternal instincts and sorrows, and the importance of Solomon are distinctly Eastern.[115] The inclusion of Solomon may have been suggested by the Eusebian homily which replaced the *Gospel of Nicodemus* in the Slavic lands. His central role may also have been due to the popularity in the East of apocryphal works attributed to him (especially his connection with baptism), and to his familiarity as a clever, amusing hero of Ukrainian folk legends.

The apparent use of a variety of sources suggests a learned playwright, probably conscious of both Western and Eastern Christian traditional workings of the harrowing theme. Drawing upon these sources, and adding his own character-sketching and dramatic skills, the *Slovo* playwright enlivened an old, but popular theme.

NOTES

1 Karl Young, "The Harrowing of Hell," *Transactions of the Wisconsin Academy of Sciences, Arts and Letters*, 16, No. 2 (1910), 889-945 examines the texts of the *Elevatio*, from its simplest to its more elaborate form, in which the *(At)Tollite portas* becomes the dominant element. The earlier texts show that the *Elevatio* was celebrated just before Easter Matins. Also, the *Cum rex gloriae* antiphon in a form suggestive of dialogue includes the theme of the harrowing of hell. See Young's reprint of the *Elevatio* of *Agenda Ecclesiae [sic] Argentinensis . . . Coloniae, 1590*, pp. 912-913.

2 J.N.D. Kelly, *Early Christian Creeds* (London, N.Y., Toronto: Longmans, Green, and Company, 1950), p. 379.

3 Bo Reicke, *The Disobedient Spirits and Christian Baptism* (Copenhagen: E. Munksgaard, 1946), p. 8.

4 See Reicke for a detailed study of I Peter: 19, Christ's message to the dead.

5 See J.A. MacCulloch, *The Harrowing of Hell; A Comparative Study of an Early Christian Doctrine* (Edinburgh: T. and T. Clark, 1930) for a detailed examination and exegesis of these and related passages, as well as a full listing of all early Church references to the Descent.

6 All citations from the Eastern Divine Liturgy are taken from Most Rev. Joseph Raya and Baron José de Vinck, *Byzantine Daily Worship* (Combermere, Ont.: Alleluia Press, 1969), p. 848.

7 Robert Taft, *The Great Entrance* (Rome: Pont. Institutum Studium Orientalium, 1975), p. 100.

8 Allen Cabaniss, "The Harrowing of Hell, Psalm 24, and Pliny the Younger: A Note," in *Liturgy and Literature; Selected Essays* (University, Alabama: University of Alabama Press, 1970), pp. 68-69.

9 A. Rose, " 'Attolite Portas, Principes, Vestras . . .'; Aperçus sur la lecture chrétienne du Ps. 24 (23) B," in *Miscellanea Liturgicae in onore di Sua Eminenza il Cardinale Giacomo Lercaro, arcivescovo di Bologna. . . ,* I (Rome: Desclée, 1966), p. 467.

10 Taft, pp. 107-108.

11 Jean Daniélou, *The Bible and the Liturgy* (London: Darton, Longman and Todd, 1964), p. 304.

12 Daniélou, p. 315.

13 See M. Andrieu, *Les ordines romani du haut Moyen Age*, IV (Louvain: Spicilegium Sacrum Lovaniense, 1951), p. 317, and his introduction to *Ordo 41*, a Gallican ordo composed around 750.

14 Daniel Sheerin, " 'Signum uictoriae in Inferno'; An Allusion to the Harrowing of Hell in Late Medieval Dedication Rituals," The 21st International Congress on Medieval Studies, Kalamazoo, Michigan, 8 May, 1986, p. 4. I am indebted to Professor Sheerin for a copy of this paper.

15 Daniélou, p. 89.
16 Daniélou, p. 89.
17 Young, p. 894-895.
18 Paul Edward Kretzmann, *The Liturgical Element in the Earliest Form of Medieval Drama* (Minneapolis: Bulletin of the University of Minnesota, 1916), p. 130.
19 Kretzmann, p. 121.
20 D. N. Dumville, "Liturgical Drama and Panegyric Responsory from the Eighth Century? A Re-Examination of the Origin and Contents of the Ninth-Century Section of the Book of Cerne," *The Journal of Theological Studies*, 23 (1972), pp. 374-406.
21 Kretzmann, p. 133.
22 Raya, p. 825.
23 Raya, p. 835.
24 Raya, p. 836.
25 Raya, p. 835.
26 Raya, p. 851. O.B. Hardison, *Christian Rite and Christian Drama in the Middle Ages* (Baltimore: The Johns Hopkins University Press, 1965), p. 139, emphasizes the significance of the harrowing legend in Western liturgy, and in part attributes its prominence to the strong heroic imagery of the legend. Christian drama, notes Hardison, is a drama of renewal, which emphasizes elements of reversal, reconciliation, and rebirth. Much of what Hardison says may also be aptly applied to the Eastern Divine Liturgy.
27 A *troparion* is a short hymn which expresses the theme of the feast, or the intention for which the Liturgy is being celebrated.
28 Raya, p. 856.
29 Raya, p. 1007.
30 Raya, p. 882.
31 G. Mercati, "Antiche omelie e sacre rappresentazioni medievali," *Rassegna Gregoriana*, 4 (1905), pp. 12, 20.
32 V. Rezanov, *Drama ukrains'ka [Ukrainian Drama]*, I (Kiev: Ukrains'ka Akademiia Nauk, 1926), p. 19.
33 Karl Young, *The Drama of the Medieval Church*, I (Oxford: Clarendon Press, 1933), pp. 100-101, and Ivan Franko, "Apokryfy i lehendy z ukrains'kykh rukopysiv [Apocrypha and Legends from Ukrainian Manuscripts]" in *Pamiatnyky ukrains'ko-rus'koi movy i literatury [Monuments of the Ukrainian-Ruthemian Language and Literature]*, II, ed. Stepan Komarevs'kyi (Lviv: n.p., 1899), p. xxv.
34 Franko, p. xxxi.
35 According to H.C. Kim, ed., *The Gospel of Nicodemus* (Toronto: Centre for Medieval Studies, Pontifical Institute, 1973), pp. 2-3, Vincent de Beauvais and Jacobus de Voragine referred to the Late Latin recension

as the *Gospel of Nicodemus*. Since then, the title has been given to all forms of the *Gospel*.

36 But see G.C. O'Ceallaigh, "Dating the Commentaries of Nicodemus," *Harvard Theological Review*, 56 (1963), pp. 21-58, for the view that the *Gospel* was written in the seventh century.

37 M.R. James, *The Apocryphal New Testament* (Oxford: Clarendon Press, 1924), p. 95. Also, see the more recent edition and translation of E. Hennecke—W. Schneemelcher, ed., *New Testament Apocrypha*, I, trans. R. McL. Wilson (Philadelphia: The Westminster Press, 1963), pp. 444-484.

38 Jean Monnier, *La Descente aux enfers* (Paris: Librairie Fischbacher, 1905), p. 90.

39 Kim, p. 2. The question of orthodoxy and the use of apocryphal literature is a delicate one, not fully resolved by scholars.

40 James, p. 134, from the Latin form A. This famous phrase, taken from Psalm 24, is the centrepiece of most harrowing plays. F. Scheidweiler in E. Hennecke-W. Schneemelcher, *New Testament Apocrypha*, notes on p. 473 that this is a Septuagint reading which underlies the Old Church Slavonic translation.

41 I am indebted to H.C. Kim for the summary here.

42 See C. von Tischendorf, *Evangelia Apocrypha* (Leipzig: Avenarius and Mendelssohn, 1853), pp. 210-486; M. Speranskii, *Slavianskiia apokrifich-eskiia Evangeliia [Slavic Apocryphal Gospels]* (Moscow: Trudy vos'mogo arkheologicheskogo s'iezda v Moskvy 1890, 1895), II, p. 56; and Kim's more recent (1973) edition.

43 Francis J. Thomson, "The Nature of the Reception of Christian Byzantine Culture in Russia in the Tenth to Thirteenth Centuries and its Implications for Russian Culture," *Belgian Contributions to the 8th International Congress of Slavists. Zagreb: September, 1978*, Slavica Gandensia 5 (Ghent: Department of Slavonic Philology, Ghent State University, le Centre Belges d'Etudes Slaves, 1978), p. 108.

44 Thomson, p. 108.

45 Franko, p. 314. Mykola Chubatyi, *Istoriia khrystianstva na Rusy-Ukraini [The History of Christianity in Rus'-Ukraine]*, I (to 1353) (Rome, N.Y.: Logos, 1965), p. 744, remarks that the Church Fathers were among the first to be translated into Church Slavonic. Although apocryphal works were prohibited, they were avidly read and disseminated.

46 André Vaillant, ed., *L'Evangile de Nicodème* (Geneva, Paris: Librairie Droz, 1968), pp. ix, xiv.

47 Franko is contradictory on this point. On p. xx he suggests the eleventh or twelfth century, as does Speranskii (p. 62), but later (p. 314) ventures the twelfth or even thirteenth century.

48 Speranskii, pp. 144-151.

49 Franko, pp. 252-272, 293-304.

82 ABOUT THE HARROWING OF HELL

50 I. Porfir'ev, *Apokrificheskaia skazaniia o Novozavetnykh litsakh i soby- tiakh po rukopysakh Solovetskoi biblioteki* [*Apocryphal Legends About New Testament Characters and Events from Manuscripts of the Solovet- skaia Library*] (St. Petersburg: Tipografia Imp. Akademii Nauk, 1890), pp. 3-4.

51 For a list of the extant manuscripts see Aurelio de Santos Otero, *Die Handschriftliche Überlieferung der altslavischen Apokryphen*, Patristische Texte und Studien 23 (Berlin: W. de Gruyter, 1978-1981), pp. 61-98.

52 Thomson, p. 109.

53 Thomson, p. 109.

54 Thomson, p. 109.

55 Athanasius is notable for using the doctrine of the Descent in defense of the doctrine of the humanity of Christ. See Kretzmann, *Liturgical Elements*, p. 117.

56 See, for example, Saint Gregoire le Grand, *Homélies pour les dimanches du cycle de Paques*, trans. René Wasselynck, Ecrits des Saints 44 (Namur: Le Soleil Levant, 1962), Homily XXV, p. 94; Saint-Jean Damascène, *La foi orthodoxe suivie de Défense des icônes*, trans. E. Ponsoye (Paris: Saint-Denys, Institut orthodoxe français de théologie, 1966), pp. 153, 163; Saint Cyrille de Jérusalem, *Cathéchèses baptismales et mystagogiques*, trans. J. Bouvet, Ecrits des Saints 14 (Namur: Le Soleil Levant, 1961), pp. 314-315.

57 Kretzmann, *Liturgical Elements*, p. 120.

58 Jackson J. Campbell, "To Hell and Back: Latin Tradition and Literary Use of the 'Descensus ad Inferos' in Old English," *Viator*, 13 (1982), p. 130.

59 For the text of the pseudo-Eusebian homily see J.-P. Migne, ed., *Patrolo- giae cursus completus; Series Graeca* (Paris: Lutetia, 1857-1912), 86-1: 509-526.

60 See Santos Otero for a full description of the manuscripts, pp. 99-118.

61 Santos Otero, pp. 99-118.

62 Santos Otero, p. 100.

63 A. Vaillant, "L'homélie d'Epiphane sur l'ensevelissement du Christ," *Radovi Staroslavenskog Instituta*, 3 (1958), p. 7, lists six manuscripts of the homily; the two oldest—one in Old Macedonian, the other Cyrillic (Suprasaliensis MS)—appear to stem from the eleventh century.

64 Vaillant, *L'Evangile de Nicodème*, p. ix.

65 Franko publishes the Ukrainian homily in his *Pamiatnyky*, p. 317-326.

66 Franko, p. 321.

67 Franko, p. 325.

68 In the *Gospel of Nicodemus*, Satan addresses Hades as Beelzebub. In the homilies, it is always the other way around, that is, Hades calls Satan Beelzebub.

69 Franko, p. 317.

70 For the text of pseudo-Epiphanius, see Migne, *Patrologia cursus comple-tus; Series Graeca*, 43: 440-464. Kretzmann, *Liturgical Elements*, p. 12, argues forcefully on behalf of the independent origins of both the Euse-bian and Epiphanian homilies. The Epiphanian homily, he believes, is "one of the sources, if not the principal one, from which later writers and homiletes derived so much of their material" (pp. 118-119). Kretzmann cites the pseudo-Augustine "De Anima Christi" sermon (160) as one of those which bears a close resemblance to Eusebius' homily. During the mediaeval period, these homilies were used as "lectiones at the desig-nated time in the liturgical year" (p. 120). Most scholars, however, argue that the homilies are merely an elaboration of the *Gospel of Nicodemus* (MacCulloch, Rand, Vaillant, and others).

71 MacCulloch, p. 196.

72 A summary of Stavrovets'kyi's homilies is provided by Porfir'ev, pp. 39-41. V. Rezanov, *Iz istorii russkoi dramy; shkolnie deistva XVII-XVIII vv. i teatr ezuitov* [*From the History of Rus' Drama; School Drama of the 17th and 18th Centuries and the Jesuit Theatre*] (Moscow: n.p., 1910), pp. 384-385, notes the manuscript of a school play from Kalush entitled "Dialogus de S. Ioannis Baptistae in eremum discessu" found in Lviv in the library of Pavlykos'kyi. Unfortunately, I have not been able to trace this intriguing reference. The St. John play appears, by its title, to be based upon the Eusebian and Epiphanian homilies, rather than on the *Gospel of Nicodemus*. It is most curious that a *Slovo* manuscript comes from this same region and that one of its main characters is St. John the Baptist.

73 The homilies are ascribed to Eusebius of Emesa, as well as to Eusebius of Alexandria and to John Chrysostomus. For an examination of the homilies see MacCulloch, pp. 174-191.

74 MacCulloch, p. 184.

75 MacCulloch, p. 184.

76 Edward Kennard Rand, "*Sermo de Confusione Diaboli,*" *Modern Philol-ogy*, 2 (1904-1905), pp. 261-278.

77 See above, note 72.

78 J.H. Bernard, ed., *The Odes of Solomon*, in *Texts and Studies*, 8, ed. J. Ar-mitage Robinson (Cambridge: Cambridge University, 1912), pp. 129-130. There is some dispute about the date of the *Odes*. Rendel Harris and Alphonse Mingana, ed., *The Odes and Psalms of Solomon*, II (Manch-ester, N.Y., London: Longmans, Green and Quaritch, 1920), p. 197, sug-gest a much earlier date than the second century; they postulate that the *Odes* were written between 50 B.C. and A.D. 67, with some redaction by a Christian mystic in A.D. 100. In the most recent edition, James H. Charlesworth, "Odes of Solomon," in *The Old Testament Pseude-*

pigrapha, II (N.Y.: Doubleday, 1985), argues for a composition date of A.D. 100.

79 Bernard, pp. 17-25.
80 Harris and Mingana, pp. 197, 187.
81 Bernard, p. 24.
82 MacCulloch, p. 247.
83 Per Lundberg, *La typologie Baptismale dans l'ancienne Eglise* (Uppsala: A. B. Lundequist, 1942); Jean Daniélou, *The Bible and the Liturgy* (cited above); Bo Reicke, *The Disobedient Spirits and Christian Baptism* (cited above).
84 St. Cyrille de Jérusalem, 23 *Cathécèses*, p. 474.
85 I. Porfir'ev, *Istoriia russkoi slovesnosti* [*History of Russian Literature*] (Kazan: Tipografia Imperatorskogo Universiteta, 1891), p. 261; and M.N. Speranskii, *Russkaia ustnaia slovestnost'* [*Russian Oral Literature*] (Moscow, 1917; rpt. The Hague, Paris: Mouton, 1969), p. 435. O. Bilets'kyi, *Zibrannia prats' u piaty tomakh* [*Collected Works in Five Volumes*] (Kiev: Akademiia Nauk URSR, 1965), I, p. 140 notes the popularity of apocrypha associated with Solomon.
86 Bernard, p. 15, and also Chester Charlton McCown, ed., *The Testament of Solomon* (Leipzig: J.C. Hinrichs'sche Buchhandlung, 1922), p. 91.
87 F. L. Cross, ed., *St. Cyril of Jerusalem's Lectures on the Christian Sacraments* (London: S.P.C.K., 1951), p. 62.
88 Lundberg, p. 182.
89 Daniélou, p. 89.
90 Archdale King, *The Rites of Eastern Christendom* (Rome: Catholic Book Agency, 1948), p. 240.
91 Vladimir Lossky, *The Mystical Theology of the Eastern Church* (London: James Clarke and Co., 1957), p. 242.
92 Lossky, p. 243.
93 Lossky, p. 247.
94 Franko, pp. 293-294; he also notes that this legend has surfaced in oral accounts in many regions of Ukraine.
95 Franko, p. 293 (translation mine). This tale may be connected to the story of the "unhappy soul" in German harrowing plays. (See below.) It may also be useful to think of Solomon as a holy fool, one who simulates folly and is a type of sacred jester. See John Saward, *Perfect Fools: Folly for Christ's Sake in Catholic and Orthodox Spirituality* (Oxford: Oxford University Press, 1980) for the significance and wide-spread notion of folly, especially in Eastern Christendom.
96 Mykhailo Drahomanov, "Do spravy pro vertepnu komediu na Ukraini [About Puppet Theatre Comedy in Ukraine]," in *Rozvidky Mykhaila Drahomanova pro ukrains'ku slovesnist' i pys'menstvo* [*The Research of Mykhailo Drahomanov About Ukrainian Oral and Written Literature*], I (Lviv:

Naukove Tovarystvo imeni T.H. Shevchenka, 1899), p. 192. Drahomanov's laconic comment is not fully explained or proven.

97 W.J. Ferrar, ed., *The Proof of the Gospel Being the Demonstratio of Eusebius of Caesarea*, Translations of Christian Literature, Series I, Greek
Texts II (N.Y.: Macmillan, 1920), p. xxiv.

98 Ferrar, p. xxiv.

99 Ferrar, p. 111.

100 James, p. 166.

101 Santos Otero, pp. 56-59.

102 James, p. 167. For a more recent edition of the text also see F. Scheidweiler's translation in E. Hennecke-W. Schneemelcher, pp. 485-503.

103 F. Scheidweiler, p. 487, in his prefatory remarks to the translation, argues
that the Slavonic manuscripts are meaningless here, and that they have
omitted a brief passage which indicates that Christ, not Hades, says these
lines.

104 St. Augustine, *Letters*, 20, trans. Sister Wilfrid Parsons (N.Y.: Fathers of
the Church, 1953), p. 383.

105 For the text of this homily see Migne, *Patrologiae cursus completus;
Series Latina*, 39: 2059-2061.

106 While it is likely that these works were known to Slavic scholars, there
is no evidence of their great influence on the development of the Descent theme in East Slavic lands. Even that mediaeval bestseller, Jacobus de Voragine's *Legenda Aurea* is extant only in Polish, but not
in Ukrainian or Russian. See the list of extant manuscripts in Thomas
Kaeppeli, *Scriptores ordinis praedicatorum medii aevi* (Rome: S. Sabinae,
1970), pp. 350-359.

107 Dante, although not yet translated into Slavic languages, would probably
have been well-known in the period of the Counter-Reformation.

108 For a full discussion of the complexities of this issue and also the question
of hell or limbo, see Ralph V. Turner, *"Descendit ad Inferos*: Medieval
Views on Christ's Descent into Hell and the Salvation of the Ancient
Just," *Journal of the History of Ideas*, 27 (1966), pp. 173-194.

109 Démocratie Hemmerdinger-Iliadou (Montmorency), "L'Ephrem Slave et
sa tradition manuscrite," *Annales Instituti Slavici; Geschichte der Ost-
und Westkirche in Ihren Wechselseitigen Beziehungen* (Wiesbaden: Otto
Harrassowitz, 1967), p. 87.

110 John Gwynn, ed., "Selections Translated into English from the Hymns
and Homilies of Ephraim the Syrian, and from the Demonstrations of
Aphrahat the Persian Sage," in *Nicene and Post-Nicene Fathers*, 13, Series 2 (Oxford: James Parker and Col., 1898), p. 148.

111 They appear frequently in collections of hymns. See, for example, Dionisii Dorozhyns'kyi, *Prazdnychyi kartyny hreko-kadolytskoi Tserkvy* [sic]
[*Feast Day Images of the Greek Catholic Church*] (Lviv: Gustav Brake,

      1908).
112 Gwynn, pp. 196-198.
113 Gwynn, pp. 198-199.
114 Donald Raymond Hitchcock, ed., *The Appeal of Adam to Lazarus in Hell* (The Hague, Paris, N.Y.: Mouton, 1979).
115 Sandro Sticca, "The Literary Genesis of the Latin Passion Play and the *Planctus Mariae*: A New Christocentric and Marian Theology," in Sandro Sticca, ed., *The Medieval Drama* (Albany: State University of New York Press, 1972), p. 56.

Iconography and Symbolism

The *Slovo* writer may have been influenced by icons of the Descent in his depiction of the harrowing of hell, particularly because of the exalted place that icons hold in Eastern worship, but also because literature, art, and music shared a common language of images.[1] As Konrad Onasch points out, "The pictorial program of the Church initially emerged as dogmatic information at the same time as the first fully developed form of Byzantine hymnography. . . . In its structure and content the latter was based on the homiletics of the Church Fathers. These texts and their intellectual condensation in turn served as basic models for the imagery of the visual arts. . . ."[2] Basil, one of the most popular of the Greek Fathers in the East, considered the icon "equal in importance to the written word, the appeal to the eyes being just as authoritative as that to the ears."[3] John of Damascus, and Eastern Christians, believed that icons are "filled with the Holy Spirit."[4] The icon was not merely a representation of certain key events, but, as Michael Barida notes, it was intended to bring about "a transformation in the worshipper."[5]

The defense of icons, both before and after Iconoclasm, is based upon the doctrine of the Incarnation. As Barida explains it, "Through representations of Christ and the Christian Symbol of Faith (the Creed), the icon makes spiritual doctrine visible to us in imitation of the visibility of the Second Person of the Holy Trinity brought about through the Incarnation."[6] Unlike Western Christian art, Eastern icons are not meant to teach, "but to become a channel of divine light, a serviceable instrument of prayer and communion with God the Father, through the Son and in the Holy Spirit."[7]

After the end of Iconoclasm, the influence of the liturgy on Byzantine art became even more pronounced, and is perhaps seen most clearly in the *iconostasis* (wall of icons), which represents the twelve great feast days of the Eastern Church: the Annunciation, Nativity, Presentation in the Temple, Baptism, Transfiguration, Raising of Lazarus, Entry into Jerusalem, Crucifixion, Descent into Hell or *Anastasis*, Ascension,

Pentecost, and the Death of the Virgin.

In the teaching of the Church, the Descent is firmly connected with the Resurrection. This is particularly evident in the Eastern Church, where the icon of Christ's Descent into Hell is the icon of the Resurrection, and hence figures very prominently in church interiors.[8] The Greek term for the Descent is, paradoxically, *Anastasis*, or Resurrection—thus emphasizing the ascent, since the significance of Christ's descent is His ascent (along with the righteous) into heaven.[9] The icon, then, suggests a number of important themes: Christ's victory over the forces of evil, hence his qualities as warrior and victor; and, in leading out the saints, also as redeemer. These are also the main themes of the harrowing plays.[10] Beginning with the fresco in Kiev's St. Sophia (1037), which was inspired by the mosaic in the monastery of Daphne and Hosios Loukas (1000) in Greece, the theme of the harrowing of hell in the Byzantine world was depicted by a simple symmetrical arrangement.[11] Christ, in the centre, dominates the icon. He is presented as both conqueror and deliverer. Surrounded by a brilliant mandorla, usually of various shades of blue symbolizing his glory, Christ's divine rays fill the darkness of the hellish chasm. Under his feet lie two broken-down doors of hell, fallen to form the shape of a cross. Occasionally, a bound, trampled Satan is seen peering from out the fallen doors. Often, broken chains, keys and nails appear in the lower portion of the icon, representing the power of hell destroyed.

Very early icons show Christ raising Adam alone. Later, Eve was added and placed a little behind Adam.[12] Both these two figures are usually balanced by Kings David and Solomon. David's presence is justified by Psalm 106:10–16, which has been interpreted as a prophecy of Christ's Descent. Similarly, Solomon's apocryphal *Odes* (especially 17 and 42) apparently allude to the Descent into Hell. (See above, *Origins*.) St. John the Baptist generally stands behind the kings; his raised finger signifies that he has just announced the Second Coming.[13] Although they retain the same basic symmetrical arrangement, later icons are more complex and peopled. Old Testament prophets and patriarchs, Abel, the repentant thief, and angels fill the representation of Christ's Descent into Hell. Satan, or sometimes both Satan and Hades, are found trampled under Christ's feet, a reference to the *Gospel of Nicodemus*.

The *Slovo* writer follows the usual Byzantine configuration, including, as he does, Solomon, David, St. John the Baptist, and Christ in the central position. However, while Eastern art portrays Christ bearing a cross as a symbol of victory, and descending into a dark chasm, Western art usually depicts Him holding the banner of the Resurrection (a symbol of victory)[14]—a red cross on a white background—and entering through a door. Although *Slovo* generally seems to be an amalgam of both Western and Eastern traditions, it follows Western pictorial representations of the Descent, especially in the representation of the battle between good and evil. Christ and his army carry banners, not a cross; seeing these, Lucifer calls for his own banners to be brought to him. Rather than a simple, dark chasm, the setting of the *Slovo* play is a fortress and its environs, all evoking a mediaeval military siege, complete with two armies ranged against each other, great noise (see ll. 441–443), and violence. Lucifer and Hades speak about their dominion (l. 370), their palaces (l. 488), their hellish structures (l. 151), and their capital city (ll. 199, 484). They draw up the moat bridge, and secure the gates with strong chains and locks (ll. 214–216; 385–386). In addition to their obvious meaning, the chains could be an allusion to the action above the ground—the Flagellation—since chains are usually symbols of the Passion. The gate, always a central symbol of the Descent, may also refer to Christ's first liberation (the Nativity) from the Closed Gates, the Virgin. The righteous are kept in a prison (l. 228), and, continuing the metaphor, St. John the Baptist is referred to as a little bird—both a typical Ukrainian diminutive (used affectionately), and an appropriate reference to the imprisonment and apparently vain exclamations of the Baptist. The image of the bird escaping from a cage is a common symbol of death (see Psalms 67:19) found in catacombs, as well as a symbol of Christ being freed from the womb of the Virgin.[15]

Perhaps the *Slovo* author, if he was from Western Ukraine, drew inspiration from local scenery, as Antonovych suggests, when he notes the number of castle fortresses in Western Ukraine from the Commonwealth period.[16] The fortress or dominion of hell is constantly contrasted with heaven, the city of God. Lucifer insists on this separation before his impending violent encounter with Christ. He suggests that Christ should proceed to heaven, where he has both plenty of room to rule (ll. 371–373, 473–474), and where he may receive the praise of his apostles, saints, and angels. Like mediaeval and renaissance princes, Lucifer is loathe to give up his independence and his sphere of influence, a fact indicated by his unwillingness to pay tribute (l. 374) to Christ. The vanquishing of Lucifer and the harrowing of hell is a reminder of the devils' true relationship to God, and of His omnipotence in all matters.

At times, this fortress of hell is also called a hellmouth (ll. 88, 109, 332), again evoking Western images of hell. The hellmouth notion seems to have originated in early Christian times, during which the gaping jaws of Leviathan (Job:41) portrayed hell, and Jonas' exit from the whale's belly was used as the Old Testament prefiguration of the Descent.[17] The Renaissance, influenced by Dante, often portrayed hell as a cavern's mouth. Guarded by Cerberus (who appears in Polish Passion plays), hell was ruled by Pluto. By the mid-sixteenth century, this mouth is frequently depicted as a grotto or cave, rarely as a building; but in each of these versions, some resemblance to the original gaping mouth remains (in the works of Brueghel, and Bosch, for example). In Eastern art, the hellmouth seems to be a blend of chasm and building, with Christ standing on the broken-down doors or gates of hell, fallen to form a cross, suspended over a dark chasm.[18] Thus neither the image of mouth or building are clearly delineated, rather, merely suggested.

In addition to *Slovo*'s reference to hell as fortress and hellmouth, there are traditional allusions to hell as pit (ll. 93, 288). Associated with eternally burning flames (which, ironically, Lucifer himself fears, l. 443), and with horrifying tortures, the dark abyss of hell imagery is underplayed in *Slovo*, probably because of the difficulty of translating it into stage reality. Perhaps the most evocative description of the pit of hell in Orthodox Slavdom occurs in the apocryphal *Khozhdenie Bogoroditsi po mukam* [*The Journey of the Birth-Giver of God Through the Torments of Hell*].[19] In both *Khozhdenie* and *Slovo*, the spaciousness of hell is underscored, undoubtedly to increase the audience's sense of mystery and terror.

Finally, the last image associated with *Slovo*'s hell is far removed from icons: the tavern. Lucifer offers tar and infernal *kvass* [rye beer] to St. John the Baptist (l. 261), and similar beverages to anyone who does his deeds (l. 280). As hellish tavern-keeper, Lucifer is appropriately served by commander Venera (the Ukrainian name for Venus), whose name alludes to the general licentiousness associated with taverns—as well as with the devil. More particularly, the use of the name Venera may point to the Orthodoxy of the *Slovo* playwright, who was reacting to the "shameless" Catholic Renaissance art being introduced in Ukraine. In one sermon, Fabian Birkovs'kyi castigates the "heretics" who replace images of Christ and the Virgin with those of "fauns, . . . Veneras, Fortunas, summoning the shameless goddess from hell. . . ."[20] The second devil's name, Trubai ("one who blows a trumpet"), may be another subtle glance at imported Renaissance images; this one of fame.[21]

Continuing the metaphor of the tavern, Christ, having harrowed hell, promises to fill it with beer on the last day (ll. 507–508), that is, on Judgement Day, a reference to the filling up of hell with new souls. In contrast to the devilish group, the righteous and Christ seem to be represented with much less variety and with greater fidelity to traditional iconic representations. St. John the Baptist, the first of God's party to appear on stage, prepares hell for Christ's coming, as he prepared the world for the Saviour (Luke 3:4). David, usually portrayed as young and clean-shaven in Eastern icons,[22] is here found in his role as psalmist—he sings and praises the Creator as he plays on his harp (the recognized attribute of King David, I Chronicles 13:8). Adam and Eve have no speaking parts, and it is easy to visualize them in poses taken from icons: Adam stretches forth his hand, Eve lingers a little behind, her head bowed in prayer, conscious of her sin.[23]

Christ appears as a King in glory, surrounded and preceded by a multitude of angels (ll. 343, 405), a manifestation of His power and greatness. While most Eastern icons of the Descent show Christ alone or in the company of one or two angels, *Slovo*'s multitude seems to draw inspiration from other sources, possibly the icon of Christ as an Angel of Great Counsel, flanked by Michael and Gabriel,[24] or the icon of the Last Judgement itself—an icon teeming with figures.[25] Archangel Michael is also associated with a large heavenly host. The Kievan Rus' *Khozhdenie Bogoroditsi po mukam*, for example, begins with Michael and four hundred angels from all four corners of the earth appearing in response to the Virgin's request to see hell.

The liturgical roots of *Slovo* are revealed throughout the play and are visually prominent in Christ's actions: he makes the sign of the cross, blesses hell, and sprinkles it with holy water, an act symbolizing "purification from and the expulsion of evil."[26] With the exception of His promise of beer, His dialogue does not stray far from the formulaic *Attolite portas*. The bright rays of His halo, a symbol of His glory,[27] illuminate hell, and suggest, after such long darkness, an image of the sun.[28]

Probably old and bearded,[29] as in the icons of the Descent, Solomon brings the play to its conclusion: a song in praise of the Birth-Giver of God. The connection between Solomon and the Virgin is a typological one. Solomon's bowing to and enthronement of his mother, Bathsheba (I Kings 2:19), is said to foretell the Coronation of the Virgin.[30]

NOTES

1 Konrad Onasch, "Identity Models of Old Russian Sacred Art," in Henrik Birnbaum and Michael S. Flier, eds., *Medieval Russian Culture*, California Slavic Studies, 12 (Berkeley: University of California Press, 1984), pp. 176–177.

2 Onasch, p. 177.

3 Kurt Weitzmann, *The Icon: Holy Images Sixth to Fourteenth Century* (London: Chatto and Windus, 1978), p. 7.

4 St. John of Damascus, *Patrologiae Cursus Completus; Series Graeca*, ed. J.-P. Migne (Paris: Lutetia, 1857–1912), 19: 1252.

5 Michael Barida, "Iconography and Its Meaning," in *The Iconography of St. Nicholas' Church* (Toronto: St. Nicholas Ukrainian Catholic Parish, 1977), p. 17. A thorough overview of the Ukrainian icon may be found in Hryhorii Lohvyn, Lada Miliaeva and Vira Sventsitska, *Ukrains'kyi seredn'ovichnyi zhyvopys* [*Ukrainian Mediaeval Painting*] (Kiev: Mystets'tvo, 1976).

6 Barida, p. 17. For the most complete survey of this theme in the visual arts see Gertrud Schiller, *Ikonographie der christlichen Kunst*, III: Die Auferstehung und Erhöhung Christi (Gütersloh: Gütersholer Verlagshaus Gerd Mohm, 1971). Also very useful is Engelbert Kirschbaum *et al.*, *Lexikon der Christlichen Ikonographie* (Rome, Freiburg, Basel, Vienna: Herder, 1970).

7 B.T. Bilaniuk, "The Ultimate Reality and Meaning Expressed in Eastern Christian Icons," in *Studies in Eastern Christianity*, 3 (Munich, Toronto: The Ukrainian Free University, 1983), p. 3.

8 Leonid Ouspensky and Vladimir Lossky, *The Meaning of Icons*, trans. G.E.H. Palmer and E. Kadloubovsky (Olten, Switzerland: Urs Graf-Verlag, 1952), p. 189. The actual moment of Resurrection is never depicted in traditional Orthodox iconography since, it is argued, the Resurrection is "inaccessible to perception" (p. 189). Instead, two other icons serve this purpose: the icon of the Descent into Hell and, more rarely, that of the angel appearing before the women bearing spices to the sepulchre. These two icons are also examined by Hans-Joachim Schultz, "Die 'Höllenfahrt' als 'Anastasis': Eine Untersuchung über Eigenart und dogmen-geschichtliche Voraussetzungen byzantinischer Osterfrömmigkeit," *Zeitschrift für Katholische Theologie*, 81 (1959), 1–66, who studies the liturgy as the real source of Eastern piety.

9 Louis Réau, *Iconographie de l'art chrétien*, II (Paris: Presses Universitaires de France, 1957), pp. 531–532, examines the apparently contradictory nature of the term *Anastasis*. This Greek word points to the ultimate purpose of Christ's visit to hell: to redeem the souls and lead them into heaven. Some theological problems are associated with the chronology of the Descent, one of the central questions being whether

Christ descended into Limbo before or after the Resurrection. Most theologians (including the author of the *Gospel of Nicodemus*) adhere to the former opinion, although this poses a difficulty for the iconographer who must depict Christ's soul. To resolve this issue artists have reversed the chronology of events, and therefore portray Christ's body descending into Limbo. Others insist that it is Anima Christi descending into the hellish pit. Peter Meredith and John E. Tailby, eds., *The Staging of Religious Drama in Europe in the Later Middle Ages: Texts and Documents in English Translation*, trans. Raffaella Ferrari *et al.*, Early Drama, Art, and Music Monograph Series, 4 (Kalamazoo: Medieval Institute Publications, 1983), p. 113, cite a clever depiction of Anima Christi from a production in Mons: "Note that at this point there must be in the Limbo of the Patriarchs great brightness and melody, and the gates of Hell must fall down and the Godhead, which is like a soul in a tent of fine gauze (*une ame en eug pavillion de vollette*), must appear there with two angels censing before it."

The Descent in the body is rare, but references to it may be found in Ephraim of Syrus' *Sermo de Domino nostro*, and in "some Church Fathers." See Alois Grillmeier, *Mit ihm und in ihm. Christologische Forschungen und Perspectiven* (Freiburg: Herder, 1975), p. 157, note 167. The reversal of the usual Descent-Resurrection chronology is the subject of Antoinette Sally, "Le thème de la descente aux enfers dans le crédo épique," *Travaux de linguistique et de littérature*, 7, No. 2 (1969), 47–63. Sally discovers the ultimate source for such a non-canonical order in the Latin A text of the *Gospel of Nicodemus*, and in gnostic teachings.

Piotr Skubiszewski, "La place de la Descente aux Limbes dans les cycles christologiques préromans et romans," *Romanico padano, Romanico europeo* (Parma: Università degli Studi di Parma, Istituto di storia dell'arte, centro di Studi Medioevali, 1982), pp. 314–321, argues that two different concepts of the Descent existed side by side in the Middle Ages. One tradition, stemming from the Latin Church Fathers, regarded the Descent as a historical concept. Placed between the Crucifixion and the Resurrection, the Descent appeared as an "episode" in the Paschal history of Christ's life. The second tradition, stemming from the Greek Fathers, and found in the *Gospel of Nicodemus*, was also well known in the West. Here the Descent was regarded from an eschatological perspective. The Descent was placed after the Resurrection, since it was seen as a direct result of the power of the Resurrection and as Christ's final act in the battle against sin and death. Since the Resurrection had always been regarded theologically as the beginning of a humanity totally reformed and renewed in God, by consequence, the Descent became an eschatological symbol of the future of mankind. These two co-existing yet different concepts of the Descent explain the movable nature of the

Descent both in iconography and in the drama.

10 André Grabar, *Christian Iconography: A Study of Its Origins*, trans. Terry
Grabar (Princeton: Princeton University Press, 1968), p. 126, remarks
that the Descent into Hell, created as it was in late antiquity, was modelled after allegorical representations of the victorious Roman emperor.
Thus the triumphant warrior Christ with the trampled Satan (like the conquered city or province) was an already established image of victory,
and even of liberation from the "tyranny" of local leaders. The cross
may be interpreted as a type of trophy. Robert Hughes, *Heaven and
Hell in Western Art* (London: Weidenfeld and Nicholson, 1968), p. 194,
remarks upon the odd similarities between Christ as leader of souls and
Hermes Psychopompos—guide of souls—who led out the dead suitors
killed by Ulysses into the Underworld. J.A. MacCulloch, *The Harrowing
of Hell* (Edinburgh: T. and T. Clark, 1930) and Josef Kroll, *Gott und
Hölle* (Leipzig, Berlin: Teubner, 1932) examine descent myths in various
religions and cultures, arguing that the descent is a very old myth, not
created by Christians. Opposed to MacCulloch, Hughes and Grabar is the
thesis of F. Loofs, "Christ's Descent into Hell," *Transactions of the Third
International Congress for the History of Religions*, II (Oxford: Clarendon Press, 1908), pp. 290–301, who argues that Christ's Descent has
no relation to myth, rather it is a purely Christian idea stemming from
the apostolic age. Other significant texts concerned with the Descent
are Jean Monnier, *La Descente aux enfers* (Paris: Librairie Fischbacher,
1904), and J. Turmel, *La Descent du Christ aux enfers* (Paris: Bloud,
1908).

11 Konrad Onasch, *Ikonen* (Gütersloh: Gütersloher Verlagshaus Gerd Mohm,
1961), p. 364. Kurt Weitzmann, "Das Evangelion im Shevophylakion zu
Lawra," *Seminarium Kondakovianum*, 8 (1936), pp. 87–88, notes that
the very symmetrical grouping with Christ in the centre, a cross in His
hand and the broken doors under His feet are new aspects of the Descent
introduced into icons at the end of the tenth century. The older type
would merely include Christ and Adam (as, for example, the carvings of
the ciborium in St. Mark's, Venice, c. A.D. 6, the oldest extant version
of the scene). By the eleventh century the Descent icon reveals a new
interest: Christ is in the centre, Adam and Eve on the right, and David
and Solomon on the left (as, for example, in the beautifully symmetrical
Anastasis icon of Hosios Loukas).

12 According to Réau, p. 533, this is a late development of post-byzantine
painters from Athos.

13 Réau, p. 534.

14 George Ferguson, *Signs and Symbols in Christian Art* (N.Y.: Oxford University Press, 1961), p. 104. The banner is an allusion to the Emperor
Constantine's conversion. Having seen a cross in the clouds, Constantine

caused the symbol to be included in the design of his banner.

15 Carl van Treeck and Aloysius Croft, *Symbols in the Church* (Milwaukee: the Bruce Publishing Co., 1960), p. 104.

16 D. Antonovych, *Trysta rokiv ukrains'koho teatru 1619–1919* [*Three Hundred Years of Ukrainian Theatre 1619–1919*] (Prague: Ukrains'kyi vydavnychyi fond, 1925), p. 33. The image of hell as a castle or city is not, of course, unknown in the Christian tradition, and can be found in Augustine and Theodorus, as well as later writers. A drawing of the hell-castle with the hellmouth used for the Passion play at Valenciennes in 1547 has been frequently reproduced. See, for instance, A.M. Nagler, *The Medieval Religious Stage: Shapes and Phantoms* (New Haven and London: Yale University Press, 1976), p. 85. A very unusual Western depiction of the Descent may be found in the National Gallery of Art, Washington, D.C. There, a painting of the Descent from the German School c. 1570 depicts Christ hovering above a city filled with masses of people running in the streets.

17 Ouspensky and Lossky, p. 186.

18 Réau, pp. 534–35, remarks upon the artists' inability to distinguish limbo from hell. Thus it is possible to confound the icon of the Last Judgement with that of the Descent.

19 There are numerous translations of this masterpiece. See, for example, Serge A. Zenkovsky and Leo Weiner's version in *Medieval Russia's Epics, Chronicles, and Tales* (N.Y.: E.P. Dutton, 1963), pp. 122–129.

20 P.M. Zholtovs'kyi, *Ukrains'kyi zhyvopys XVII-XVIII st.* [*Ukrainian Painting, XVII–XVIII Centuries*] (Kiev: Naukova Dumka, 1978), pp. 16–17.

21 For Renaissance images of Fame see Samuel C. Chew, *The Pilgrimage of Life* (New Haven and London: Yale University Press, 1962), especially pp. 18, 22, 182, and 246.

22 Réau, p. 534. See, for example, the fresco of the Descent in the great Ukrainian cathedral, St. Sophia (Kiev), in Hryhorii H. Lohvyn, ed., *Sofiia Kyivs'ka* [*Kievan Sophia*] (Kiev: Mystetstvo, 1971), plate 111.

23 Réau, p. 534.

24 Bilaniuk, p. 11.

25 See, for example, the Apocalypse icon of the Kremlin Master, Moscow School, c. 1500, in the Cathedral of the Dormition, Kremlin, Moscow, reproduced in Kurt Weitzmann *et al.*, *The Icon* (London: Evans Brothers Ltd., 1982), p. 294. More obviously, the origins of the image of Christ surrounded by angels in His Descent are liturgical. (See above, *The Harrowing in the Eastern Liturgy.*)

26 Ferguson, p. 98. See Ps 51:7.

27 Ouspensky, p. 189.

28 F.J. Dölger, *Sol Salutis-Gebet und Gesang im Christlichen Altetum* (Münster: Aschendorffsche Verlagsbuchhandlung, 1952), pp. 336–364.

29 Réau, p. 534. Also, see plate 111 in *Sofiia Kyivs'ka*.
30 Ferguson, p. 44.

Slovo and the Harrowing Play
in Western and Central Europe

To gauge accurately the achievement of *Slovo o zbureniu pekla* and to locate it in a wider context, it is useful to survey the tradition of the harrowing play. Stemming from the thirteenth century, the first harrowing plays were born into a period of radical change in sensibility—a change which appears to be immediately responsible for an equally radical shift in the interests of literature, art, and philosophy.[1] This shift with its focus on the humanity of Christ revealed itself as a desire for a more personal religious experience, and is evident in a greater emotionalism found in art after that time.[2] Thus art and literature begin to consider the Passion, rather than the triumph of Christ. The harrowing of hell, although a victory, is equally (if not more importantly) a clear representation of Christ's humanity. As the Second Adam, Christ, through his human suffering, is debased and descends into the mouth of death, where He redeems mankind from the darkness into which Adam first had plunged all by his disobedience.

A survey of harrowing plays in Western Europe suggests the range of possibilities on this single theme: from the seriousness of the Spanish, Italian, and much of German drama, to the boisterousness of English and French plays.[3] Two basic models of harrowing plays emerge from such a study. The first is the single setting play, which encompasses five scenes: 1) the righteous in limbo rejoice in perceiving a bright light; 2) the devils fearfully prepare for Christ's coming; 3) Christ appears at the gates of hell; the *(At)tollite portas* ritual; 4) the harrowing proper, including the binding of Lucifer; 5) the righteous souls' praise of Christ. The second model, the double setting (a variation found in many German and Italian plays), usually substitutes scene one with an angel who awakens Christ from His slumber in the sepulchre, and then reveals the Resurrection as Christ sings *Resurrexi.* The last scene (scene five) may be developed into a procession of the prophets and, in both models, an additional scene, set in paradise, may follow the harrowing.

Both in chronology and in complexity, *Slovo o zbureniu pekla* stands at the end of this rich Western European tradition. Following neither of the above models, *Slovo* eschews traditional patterns (except for the *Attollite portas*) by beginning with Lucifer and the devils, instead of with the righteous. While some parallels may be drawn between the Ukrainian and Western types of the play, similarities may simply indicate a use of common sources (especially the *Gospel of Nicodemus*), rather than a possibility of literary influence or imitation.

By the time the *Slovo* playwright was composing, the Western European tradition was almost moribund. The later period of creation, aided by the particular concerns and interests of the Counter-Reformation in Ukraine, produced a play far different from its Western European counterparts. As Fichte accurately observes, "medieval drama is symbolic, ritualistic, and predominantly moral; it is never psychological. We do not question why a character acts the way he does; rather we look at how he acts."[4] By the time this mediaeval tradition is transferred into Eastern Europe, new influences allow for both the symbolic and the psychological. Hence, for example, the complex characterization of Lucifer in *Slovo*, in contrast to the much simpler devil of earlier Western drama.

In both Eastern and Western Europe the harrowing of hell story provided not only yet another opportunity to represent the grand theme of man's salvation, but also, from a psychological point of view, yielded the basic pleasures of literary art: delight and satisfaction at viewing the boastful forces of evil routed by the triumphant army of good. Christ, the hero of these plays, is not unlike a typical hero of romance, whose humanity is stressed at the same time as His actions are marvellous. But, at the same time, it is His divine nature that moves the harrowing tale into the realm of myth—the myth of the universal and unending conflict between good and evil, for even after this victory (as the Enoch-Elijah scene clearly points out), there is to be yet another, a final conflict. The audiences of the harrowing play thus joy in Christ's victory and in the folly of the devils, but are reminded of their own sober part in a similar scene of justice and destruction: the Last Judgement.

France

Scholars conjecture that in France the *Gospel of Nicodemus* was probably dramatized as early as the twelfth century, although extant evidence

survives only from later centuries.[5] *Le Jeu d'Adam*, composed about the
second half of the twelfth-century by an unknown author, may have
been one of the first French plays to include a harrowing sequence.
Possibly an Easter Play or a preparation for Lent,[6] *Le Jeu d'Adam*
includes in its *dramatis personae* the characters of God, Adam, Eve,
Satan, Devils and a choir—the essential characters of a harrowing play.
The first two scenes represent the temptation and Fall, and Cain and the
Abel story, while the dramatic fragment breaks off at the point at which
a formal procession of prophets takes place, thus suggesting that the
play may have been balanced and completed by its typological com-
plement: the exodus of the prophets and patriarchs from hell. Axton
and Stevens regard *Le Jeu d'Adam* as "a prototype of the Old Testament play-cycles in fourteenth century England and France. . . . events
dramatized are chosen for their traditional significance in worship and
iconography as prefigurations of the events of the New Testament."[7]
Evidence to support these speculations is found in the prophecy of
the character of Solomon who foretells the death and Resurrection of
Christ, as well as the deliverance of Adam from the bondage of hell:
"Del povre Adam avra pieté, / Delivrat lui de pecché" (ll. 815–816).[8]

Like the *Jeu d'Adam*, the twelfth-century Anglo-Norman fragment
La Seinte Resureccion may also have contained a harrowing sequence,
ending in the Ascension. The Prologue, for example, tells us that we
will see:

> Le crucifix primerement
> E puis le monument.
> Une jaiole i deit aver
> Pur les prisons emprisoner
> Enfer seit mis de cele part,
> E puis le ciel. . . .[9]

The description thus prepares us for a *mise en scène* which would
include an area described as a jail for the imprisoned righteous—an
area, it appears, that is distinct from hell and would, of necessity, be
limbo.

The first extant harrowing sequences stem from much later plays
than the *Adam* and *Resureccion*. The *Passion du Palatinus*, *Passion
d'Autun* and *Sion* fragment date from the fourteenth and fifteenth centuries, and their ultimate source may have been the popular, well-
circulated poem *Passion des Jongleurs*, written sometime at the end
of the twelfth or beginning of the thirteenth century. D.D.R. Owen
draws attention to the fact that the harrowing section of the *Passion du*

Palatinus has little in common with either the versions in *Autun, Sion* or the *Passion des Jongleurs*. He conjectures that "the episode in *P* [Palatinus] has been substituted for an original to which *S* [Sion] and *A* [Autun] both approximate, *A* being a slightly elaborated re-working of the source [the common source, a missing mystery play], but having the merit of completeness."[10]

The harrowing of the *Passion du Palatinus*, comprising 216 lines (ll. 1235–1450), follows the pattern of the *Gospel of Nicodemus* (and hence bears some resemblance to *Slovo*). Satan and Enfer quarrel about the consequences of the Crucifixion. The *miles gloriosus* Satan confidently boasts of his ability to withstand the power of Christ. Enfer follows the traditional mould: he is the cowardly, fearful type who flees at the approach of Christ. Satan, on the other hand, foolishly but boldly defies Christ, but is unable to withstand Him. The righteous greet Christ's coming with joy, and thank Him for their deliverance, which has come after more than a thousand years.[11]

The *Palatine* harrowing is amusing and vivacious with much name-calling and cursing among the devils, unlike the related but much fore-shortened (44 lines) version found in the *Autun* fragment. Unknown before 1903, the *Autun* is extant in two versions from the later half of the fifteenth century; a complete version (by Philippe Biart) contains a harrowing, the other a fragment (by Antoine Roman). Although a later text than the *Palatine*, the *Autun* may, in fact, represent an earlier dramatic tradition. Much controversy has surrounded the dramatic qualities of this text, although more recent scholarship argues that the narrative lines added to the text suggest the presence of a *lecteur*, and thus an acting version of the play, rather than a text meant for reading purposes only (as had been argued in the past).[12]

Epic in size, if not in quality, is the achievement of these fifteenth-century Passion plays which exceeded in length the *Passion du Palatinus* by ten or more times. The anonymous *La Passion de Sémur, Le Mystère de la Vengeance Jhesu Christ* and the *Mystère de la Passion* (the latter two by Eustache Marcadé) all belong to the first third of the fifteenth century. *Le Mystère de la Passion* by Arnoul Gréban, written about 1450, the *Autun* noted above (written in the later part of the century) and the *Mystère de la Passion* by Jean Michel (a revision of Gréban's work), appeared in 1486. This French golden age of Passion plays created works embracing the whole span of Christ's life, and employed as many as 400 people in various roles. Special companies of actors, formed of tradesmen and other citizens, were created to oversee the several days' production. The most famous of these, la Confrérie de la Passion, was licensed in 1402, and continued its activity until 1548, when the work was stopped by an edit of Parliament. An "outstanding feature" of French plays were their special effects, "sometimes so spectacular . . . that they were talked of for years afterwards."[13] A probable example of its repetoire may be found in a manuscript of the Bibliothèque Saint-Geneviève. Among the plays included in this book is *La Passion de Notre Seigneur*,[14] which includes a harrowing sequence, although it is not thus separately delineated. Satan, Beelzebub, the Lord, David, Isaiah, St. John the Baptist, Habakkuk, Adam and Eve make up the cast of characters.

Satan begins the sequence by admitting his guilt for causing Christ's crucifixion. Christ had always deceived the devil. Now His soul is troubled to death. Alluding to Lazarus, Beelzebub inquires about the person who gives life to the dead by a word only. Discovering the answer, Beelzebub begins to fear and begs Satan, ironically, "Par [ses] vertus" (p. 291) not to allow Christ to come to them. He is certain that He will take all their domains, riches, and seigneuries. The characterization of the fearful Beezlebub is thus in the tradition of Hades in the *Gospel of Nicodemus*, while Satan adheres to the portrait of a proud, overreaching devil.

Almost as soon as Beelzebub voices his fears, they are fulfilled. Christ, speaking in the vernacular, enters and commands the gates to open. David, Isaiah and St. John the Baptist speak of the light which has appeared in Limbo. The Lord calls out a second time, "Ouvrez, je suis roy glorieux," and the doors are broken down, while Habakkuk explains who the King of Glory is. Satan immediately begins to lament the spoiling of hell, but also tries to convince Christ to leave "nos liens." Christ, however, tells Satan he will suffer and will be bound in chains. Beelzebub, who is set to guard Satan, mournfully inquires why Satan had Christ crucified. While the devils lament, Christ calls all the prisoners to Him, and gives Adam his right hand. The harrowing concludes with praise by Adam and then Eve, who comments on Christ's justice: for evil He has given good in return.

A fifteenth-century unpublished text, called the Paris or the Michel Resurrection, includes a dramatic harrowing of hell which shows great attention to special effects, including various noises (thunder, cannon), flaming sulphur, a machine for pulling Christ up into heaven, and an elaborate tower to house the righteous. The description of the harrowing is as follows:

Here all the devils except Satan bring culverins and other weapons (*ferremens*) into Hell and close their gates with great bolts (*correilz*). And the Anima Christi with the above-mentioned four [angels] and the soul of the Penitent Thief go towards Hell, holding Satan bound. And the Anima Christi strikes the gates of Hell with his cross. [*The Attolite portas dialogue follows.*] Here the Anima Christi breaks the gates of Hell with the cross and goes inside with the four angels and the soul of the Penitent Thief. Then the souls in Limbo sing this hymn melodiously. *Conditor alma sidera*. Then the Anima Christi should remain near the room of Limbo (*chambre du Limbe*) until the devils have fled from there.[15]

The mid-fifteenth century *Passion de Sémur*, comprised of 9,582 lines, and requiring two days of performance, also includes a harrowing sequence, albeit a brief scene of souls in limbo awaiting Christ. But for the greatest and most representative of the French mystery plays one must go to the acknowledged masterpiece, Gréban's *Le Mystère de la Passion*.[16] Gréban's harrowing begins on the third day of the performance. In limbo Adam and Eve only (rather than the prophets), tenderly and reverently pray for an end to their suffering. Their prayers are seen to be directly and immediately answered by God, who sends Michael to comfort them with the news that Christ has humbled Himself for them by becoming a man. Isaiah, Ezekiel and Jeremiah add to the rejoicing of Adam and Eve, and the stage directions offer an optional "quelque motet" sung by David at this point. The whole scene is full of dignity and piety.

Meanwhile, a wise Lucifer appears to understand the true mission of Christ, and berates the naiveté of Satan and his devilish cohorts (Berich, Cerberus, Astaroth, Fergallus), who have been celebrating their "*chef-d'oeuvre*"—the death of Christ. Referring to Him as "ung homme sainte et venerable," Lucifer almost seems to be of the heavenly party. Upbraiding the foolishness of the devils, he refers to Satan as "faulx enemy" and to Berich as "faulx serpens"—phrases later ironically echoed in Christ's speech of victory which begins "Faulx dyable." Disabusing Satan of his illusions, Lucifer informs him of the fact that Christ will destroy their "manoir" and will release the prophets; this is the cause of the noisy rejoicing. Like Satan in the English Chester play, so here Satan becomes frightened and attempts vainly to stop the process he has already set in motion by going to Pilate's wife. The hell sequence is interrupted by the events of the Passion and the scene of Pilate's wife, but resumes on l. 26081 (and continues to l. 26283).

On the third day, the four archangels address Jerusalem as a cruel and desolate city. Gabriel urges the Virgin to take comfort, but she replies with confidence that her Son will arise on the third day, and therefore appears to need no solace. Satan and his devils shut the gates of hell, while Cerberus assures Lucifer that the doors will not be broken. But the spirit of Christ, armed with His cross and accompanied by four archangels, thrice commands "*Attolite portas.*" When the gates open, the Lord enters. In a long speech, during which time the devils lament, Christ rebukes the devils. Then taking Adam by the hand, He promises to lead all the prisoners to bliss. St. John the Baptist, Eve, David, Isaiah, Ezekiel and Jeremiah rejoice and bless the Lord as they exit. A great tempest is stirred up. An enraged Lucifer, complaining that he feels as if he were drowning in a red furnace, at last stoically accepts the depopulation of his realm: "Ce qui est perdu est perdu, / mais penssons tous au résidu, / de le saulver mieux qui pourra" (ll. 26268–26270).[17] The sequence ends with Lucifer, Cerberus and Astaroth making plans for the future.

Gréban's play thus neatly deals with the dramatic and theological problem of the complete defeat of the devilish forces. While Christ's victory is joyous and apparently absolute, the final moments of the scene prepare us for yet another future conflict between the forces of good and evil.

This overview of the French harrowing of hell play provides us with a microcosm of the larger picture of European drama. Beginning with small casts of characters, a simple structure and relatively un-adorned speech, the French harrowing evolves to an enormous length with a more complex psychology of character.[18] The early simplicity, which drew attention to the didacticism of the play, begins to fade or, at least, to be diffused.

An increase in the number and names of devils results in an in-creased dependence upon broad laughter and sensation. The poignant austerity of the English York play, for example, is absent in the late French plays with their large grotesque element. Perhaps as Owen remarks, "the staging of Christ's descent together with its attendant *di-ableries* was, theologically, something of a blunder." He goes to say, "From the doctrinal point of view, a simple and largely symbolical rep-resentation would have been safer."[19] Indeed, the message of Christ's sacrifice becomes dimmed; yet, from the audience's point of view, the *diablerie* constituted probably the most attractive and interesting parts of the *mystères*.

England

The subject of the earliest English religious drama known,[20] the harrowing of hell is represented in all four extant English cycle plays: N-Town (also known as Ludus Coventriae), Chester, York, and Towneley (Wakefield). Because the English harrowing of hell is one play in a cycle of plays, and because its structural position (immediately after Christ's most dreadful sufferings) marks the end of the Passion movement and the beginning of the joyful events of the Resurrection, the harrowing both reverberates with themes and ideas of plays which have already taken place, and looks forward to others. Primarily, the harrowing echoes the Fall of Lucifer, the Fall of Adam, and the Exodus of the Old Testament. Lucifer's pride, his attempt to overreach God in heaven is paralleled by his attempt to confine Christ's soul to hell. In this effort, Lucifer not only loses Christ and the righteous of the Old Testament who longingly awaited the coming of Christ, but also loses his right to the soul of man because of his presumption.[21] Bound tightly in chains, Lucifer can no longer wander the earth.

As the Second Adam, Christ through his suffering redeems mankind from the darkness into which Adam had plunged it by his disobedience. The tree of knowledge becomes, in the Passion sequence, (the tree of) the Cross, and it in turn becomes the tree of life. Finally, the joyous exodus of the righteous from hell into blissful paradise echoes the Exodus of the Israelites from the bondage of Egypt. The English versions, perhaps more than any other harrowing drama, play with these typologies and parallels with the result that past and present as well as future appear to exist simultaneously.[22] Prefiguring the Last Judgement, the harrowing of hell intimates many of its concerns: the final conquest over death and evil, and the separation of the righteous from the evildoers.

Undoubtedly because the role of the harrowing play is the same in all four English cycles, minimal (as compared to the harrowings of other countries) variation occurs among the pageants. In all four plays, the harrowing serves "as the dramatic climax of Christ's career," and if, as Travis argues, Christ is understood to be the hero of these plays, then "the Harrowing is not only the climax of his career but [also] the climax of his cycle."[23] The harrowing thus serves as the "glorious peripeteia" of classical drama, and leads both to the joy of the liberation of the souls and, later, to the Resurrection of Christ himself.[24]

Despite the similarity of content, the plays vary in the positions they occupy in the larger scheme of the cycles, and also in the choice of episodes they dramatize. The most obvious example of variation occurs in the N-Town play,[25] in which the harrowing, divided into two parts, is placed between Christ's death and His deposition. Never "performed as a whole in the form in which it has been preserved," the N-Town cycle is an amalgam of three play traditions: the Old Testament, Marian and Passion plays.[26] Probably produced on a stationary "polyscenic" stage, with mansions not unlike those of Valenciennes, the N-Town play would have clearly displayed in two mansions the mystery surrounding the Descent: while Christ's body was being taken from the cross, another actor playing Christ would show that only His soul was approaching hell.[27]

Despite the clarity of the theological issue, the play's construction is awkward and loses any real sense of drama, suspense and awe because it falls into two parts. In play 33, Christ's soul urges mankind to rejoice, for He will rise again on the third day. Now, He will descend to hell, "and feche from the fendys fell / all my frendys that ther-in dwell/ to blysse that lestyth Ay" (ll. 991–993). Commanding the gates of hell to open, Christ then cries out that He will break the gates and deliver mankind. Belial, whose role is restricted to a single stanza, admits that he doubted, but now knows that this is God; "Alas alas out and harrow" (l. 1002) is his mournful cry. Christ throws down the door. An intervening scene then takes place: the burial and the guarding of the sepulchre. Then, the second part of the harrowing (play 35), nine stanzas long (three more than part I), emphasizes the bliss which awaits the liberated souls. Anima Christi calls forth Adam and Eve and all the Saints to paradise and bliss, while the fiend is to be "wrappyd" (l. 1349). Adam thanks Christ for forgiving his trespass and Eve, identifying herself, blesses the Lord. St. John the Baptist and Abraham introduce themselves. Christ binds the devil for his "envyous cruelte" (l. 1397). The play concludes with Belial's sorrow, and Christ's declaration that He will now arise.

The N-Town play's construction (six stanzas in part I, nine in part II), suggests that the primary emphasis is not on the harrowing in its strict sense; that is, the anticipation of Christ's coming, the Devil's joyful preparations to receive Him, and the peripety which occurs (the Devil's fear, his sudden comprehension of the Lord's power and majesty, as well as his Godhead) is not as important to N-Town as it is to the other English cycles.[28] The actual harrowing takes up only three stanzas. What appears to be more important is the theological implication of this play: Christ, the King of virtue, descends in spirit

to free mankind. Thus, the second part is longer and centres on praise
of the Lord for the deliverance of all the souls.

The device of the characters of Adam, Eve, John the Baptist, and
Abraham introducing themselves to an omniscient God may appear
to be awkward, even ludicrous. Certainly, it seems to be a primitive
device, but one frequently used in mediaeval drama.[29] The slight number of righteous characters on stage, and their formal blessings seem to
suggest the historical rather than transcendent quality of the scene. Evidently, the N-Town artist wanted to downplay the dramatic possibilities
of the harrowing.

Very different from this simple and awkward version is the Chester
harrowing. Originally thought to be the oldest of the four extant cycles,
the Chester now seems to have first appeared around 1375, roughly the
time of the York plays.[30] The Chester harrowing, play 17 of the cycle,
consists of three scenes. The first is the traditional one associated with
the harrowing: the patriarchs and prophets await the coming of Christ.
Adam first discovers a great light shining in the darkness of hell, a
light which he feels sure is a sign from the Saviour, indicating His
imminent coming. Isaiah, Simeon, David and John the Baptist each
in turn comment upon the appearance of the light, and recall specific
instances from past episodes in the cycle. St. John reminds us of his
role as Christ's messenger, Simeon recalls his part in the presentation
at the temple. Adam's son Seth relates the refusal of the archangel
Michael to provide him with the oil of mercy for a period of 5,500
years. That time has now come to an end. All of the prisoners of hell
kneel down while David prays to the Lord for their deliverance.

This type of detailed dramatization of the harrowing theme, so
close to the *Gospel of Nicodemus*, continues in the next episode.[31] Satan
blusters and commands his devils to revenge themselves upon God's
Son, who must be a man because He dreaded death. Three Devils ask
Satan who this man may be who wishes to deprive Satan of his power.
Admitting his part in rousing the people against Christ, Satan also
recalls that He snatched Lazarus from their teeth. Quaking with fear,
the devils now beg Satan not to allow Jesus to enter hell. The Lazarus
story, although taken from the *Gospel of Nicodemus*, traditionally was
regarded as a prefigurement of Christ's Resurrection. The devils thus
fear the might of a man who has already conquered death.

In the third scene, Christ approaches the gates of hell. The devils
raise a clamour. Jesus cries out, first in Latin, then in English, the words
from the twenty-fourth Psalm. Meanwhile Satan is being taunted by

his underlings who urge him to fight for his position, for otherwise he cannot be their king. Christ calls out a second time, and even before the gates open and the combat is complete, Satan is hurled from his throne. Taking Adam by the hand, Christ offers peace to all, and employs Michael in leading the just out of hell into paradise. Satan sorrows and is strictly confined.

The Chester harrowing includes two additional scenes not found in the other English cycles: a scene in paradise, and another scene in hell. Upon his arrival in paradise, Adam, seeing three unknown men already there, inquires with surprise who they may be. He discovers that they are Enoch, Elijah and the repentant thief. Enoch and Elijah tell Adam about yet another battle, one which will occur in the future: the final struggle against Antichrist at the end of time. All the characters exit praising the Lord and singing the *Te Deum*.

The last scene, the comic alewife episode, is quite probably a later addition, as Peter W. Travis forcefully argues.[32] Possibly a Protestant version, the alewife scene would have been intended to leaven the seriousness and importance of the entire original Catholic pageant. The last scene concerns an alewife who has deceived many by brewing ale with ashes and herbs. Her sorrow at being left behind in hell is turned to humour as Satan and his devils attempt to cheer her; one even promises to marry her. Full of farce, the last scene leaves us with the image of Satan as an ineffectual villain; deserted by his hellhounds and surrounded by their unruly behaviour, he can only vent his anger by calling Christ a hypocrite. A popular episode in German plays (see below), which possibly bears the mark of later Protestant revisions or additions, the alewife scene is extant in four out of five Chester manuscripts, although there is some debate about whether the scene should indeed be regarded as part of the original play proper.[33]

With or without the alewife scene, the Chester harrowing still raises some problems of staging, since the central part of the action occurs in hell, but the concluding scene occurs in paradise. Perhaps the traditional hellmouth would need to be abandoned in favour of a hell-like atmosphere created by the costumes of the fiends. Alternately, the saints could make use of the area directly in front of the pageant wagon, the unspecified locus, which, for the purposes of this brief scene, could be made to represent heaven. Or, perhaps the roof of the covered wagon could serve as heaven. The righteous, then, after abandoning hell, could exit through a set of rear curtains, climb up a ladder and greet Enoch and Elijah at the top, in heaven.

In all events, the Chester harrowing is more complex than the N-Town play. Both the staging and the characterization are handled in a more sophisticated manner, although much simplicity remains. The speeches are plain and unadorned. St. John the Baptist, for instance, begins by revealing "Yea, Lord, I am that prophett Johan" (l. 57). Simeon, too, identifies himself in the manner of the N-Town characters: "And I, Symeon." (l. 41) Adam's role, the longest in the play, suggests that a typological approach (like that of Meyers)[34] is indeed fruitful to pursue. In his opening monologue, Adam reminds the audience of his Fall, the reason that his kin now inhabit hell. Satan, the second most important figure, is more fully developed than Belial in the N-Town play, yet he is still not very complex. A ludicrous character, Satan is taunted and ridiculed by his devils once Christ appears. Lacking authority, the fiend is easily overthrown. The outcome of the contest is never in question.

Christ, the central figure of the play, enters almost exactly halfway in the text (l. 153). Dignified, solemn in all three of his speeches, he is the complete opposite of the ridiculous Devil. Only the affectionate "Peace to thee, Adam, my dearlynge" (l. 205) humanizes the divinity. The formal eight-line stanzaic pattern and the *Te Deum* reinforce the orderly, dignified presentation of the harrowing; the orderliness is disturbed only by the clamour of the devils' pots and pans during Christ's entry.

Perhaps the finest of the English harrowing plays, the York play 37 is also the longest: 408 lines, 34 stanzas.[35] Like the Chester, the York is close to chapters two and eight of the *Gospel of Nicodemus*. But unlike the Chester, the York begins with Christ, not with Adam. As in the N-Town play, so here Christ reminds the spectators that He suffered and died for them, and will arise on the third day. He promises to show man a light as a sign of his imminent deliverance.

The scene shifts to hell where Adam and Eve, standing inside the gates, rejoice at the appearance of this promised light which brings them hope and solace after 4,600 years. Isaiah and Simeon similarly regard the light as a symbol of Christ's coming. St. John the Baptist, after recalling the baptism of the Lord, confidently exclaims that Christ's light will kill their cares. Moses also has had knowledge of the light; it is like the light of the Lord's transfiguration.

The York harrowing thus replaces David of the Chester with Moses, but uses the same technique of allowing the characters to recall a variety of events from past episodes in the cycle, events which reinforce in the audience's mind the preordained nature of Christ's coming.

This choric recitation by Old and New Testament prophets of their knowledge of Christ is disturbed by the entrance of two rowdy devils. The first orders his cohort to "bynde ther boyes" (l. 97) because they are too merry and call on Christ. Beelzebub (Belsabub) wants to "save" those in limbo by never allowing them to leave hell. He calls Astrotte, Anaball, Bele-Berit, Belial, and Lucifer to counsel.

Hardly has the command gone out, when Jesus from outside the gate orders: *"Attolite portas, principes."* While Satan wants to know who it is who calls himself King, David responds by praising Christ as a virtuous, fierce, strong, ruler. Disputing with David, Satan argues that all men are his thralls. But his assured replies are interrupted by a devil who fears the hideous (l. 138) cry of Christ. Belial orders the gates of hell shut and manned. The devils are ordered to attack Christ should he call or cry out.

Another disturbance breaks out; a devil reminds Satan that Jesus was the one whom Judas betrayed. But Satan believes that he knows all of Christ's tricks and guiles, including the raising of Lazarus. He had, therefore, counselled the Jews to do away with Christ; and then he entered Judas. While Beelzebub fearfully inquires whether Christ can be prevented from using his powers, Satan attempts to calm him, and urges the old devil to take heart.

As Satan speaks, Christ's voice is heard outside the gates: *"Princeps, portas tollite."* Satan fearfully cries out and asks who this man is. David reminds Satan of his prophecy: Christ will break down the bars and will destroy the works of hell. Christ shouts another time, "Opynne vppe, and latte my pepul passe" (l. 194). Confusion ensues as a devil and Beelzebub cry out that the bands of brass are broken. Satan orders Beelzebub to "sette" Christ "sadde and sore" (l. 204), but he rebelliously replies, "come thiselffe and serue hym soo" (l. 206). While Satan taunts the devils for their cowardice, he calls for his armour. Jesus tells Satan that the prisoners of hell were always His; now is the time set by the Father to deliver them.

Satan disputes with Christ, emphasizing His human nature, but Christ replies that He had hidden his Godhead, and reminds Satan of the prophecies which He has come to fulfill. A theological argument ensues with Satan quoting Job and Solomon, who wrote that those who enter cannot leave hell. Jesus replies that all those in hell were there because of His will. He will lead them out into peace and bliss, although some will remain: the suicides, Judas, and all those "that liste noght to lere my lawe" (l. 313).

Satan gives Christ his hand; if Jesus speaks true, then the Prince of Darkness will have even more inhabitants in hell than he does now. But Christ wants to prevent Satan's wandering and orders Michael to bind the fiend and throw him into hell's pit.[36]

Adam and Eve praise Christ's might; St. John the Baptist expresses his love of Christ; David prays his soul will not be left in hell. All praise God together. Christ orders Michael to lead the righteous out of hell. Christ's soul returns to the tomb, where His body lies during the harrowing. Michael asks Christ to bless all, and Adam concludes the play, urging all to love the Lord, and to sing for solace "*Laus tibi cum gloria.*"

A more elaborate treatment than the Chester, the York play presents more fully developed characters. Jesus in particular has a long role in the play and twice conquers Satan, once in the usual physical conflict—the breaking down of the gates of hell—and a second time in a verbal dispute.[37] Satan, too, is more fully characterized. Unaware of Christ's divine lineage, Satan boldly lays plans to have Jesus killed. But once in full possession of the facts, face to face with God's Son, Satan maintains a strong stand using arguments from Scripture and claiming knowledge of Christ's "parents"—Joseph and Mary. The central dramatic conflict lies here, the two forces, good and evil, clearly opposed.

Also more developed is the devilish entourage of Satan, consisting of numerous fiends, with Beelzebub at their head. Beelzebub's "Sir Sattane" and his anxiousness at Christ's arrival recall his ancestor in the *Gospel of Nicodemus*. But his fear that Christ will deprive them of their prey (l. 175) is a pale version of Hades' strong proprietorial feelings about hell in *Slovo*.

While these central scenes are well-developed, they are also more powerful than the Chester because of the paring down of events: the alewife and the meeting with Elijah and Enoch are absent from the York version, the dramatic emphasis of which rests with two scenes—the awaiting of Christ, and the debate between Christ and Satan. The influence of the traditional vernacular debate and of *flyting* may be present here. Suspense and drama are well-worked out in this play, with its emphasis on a strong, virile Christ who is matched with an intelligent, not ludicrous, Satan.

Another copy of the York harrowing exists in the Towneley (Wakefield) manuscript. The two copies are "substantially the same,"[38] although there is some confusion about the name of the devils. In addition, the Towneley[39] includes another harrowing, also written down in fifteenth-century Yorkshire dialect. *Extraccio animarum*, along with five other plays, is very close to the York model. Both rely heavily upon the vernacular *Gospel of Nicodemus*.[40] The chief differences between the Towneley and the York lie in the expansion of the scenes involving devils. The terrified devil of the York play (known as Diabolus I or Rybald) is more developed than his York counterpart. His cowardice sets off the confidence of Satan, who, as Gardner points out, is in the tradition of Towneley tyrants: Herod and Pilate.[41] Beelzebub is closer to Hades of the *Gospel of Nicodemus*. Seemingly older and more experienced than Satan, Beelzebub does not underestimate the might of Christ. Christ, while essentially the same as in the York version, is perhaps even more dignified and mysterious. Speaking in Latin, rather than in English, Christ approaches the gates of hell. His mysterious powers not only cause the gates to open, but also cause Satan to descend into his pit—without the help of St. Michael (suggesting the use of a trap door).[42]

Structurally, the harrowing play in the English cycles unites and summarizes the various threads and themes. The Old Testament figures who appear in the plays are types who testify to the truth of Christ. The battle and victory over the devilish forces prefigure Christ's triumph on earth, and over all the devil's followers. Finally, the leading out of the saints both looks forward to the Last Judgement and the separation of good from bad souls, and looks back to the Exodus (*Processus prophetarum*).[43] Parallelism of plot and structure is thus central to an understanding of these plays.[44]

In the Cornish drama, only one complete, brief harrowing survives in the play *Resurrexio Domini Nostri*,[45] the last play of a fourteenth-century Middle Cornish trilogy. Unlike the English Corpus Christi cycle plays, the Cornish *Ordinalia* is a Passion cycle, containing many similarities to the great French Passion plays (and thus has no Nativity, ministry, or Last Judgement scenes).[46] Although, as Bakere notes, the *Ordinalia* at first seems "loose-knit and episodic," it is actually "a powerful and closely knit celebration of the Passion, and thus, of Christ as Redeemer."[47] The Cornish harrowing of hell centres on Adam and Eve, since the harrowing "is the fulfillment of the promise that Christ will redeem them from their fallen state."[48] The play begins as the Spirit of Christ approaches the gates of hell and threateningly calls out: "Ye princes of the devils, / Immediately open the gates, / If you do not, there shall be wars, / Certainly before passing" (ll. 97–100). Again, echoes from Psalm 24 form the central passage of this text. Christ twice calls out before the gates are finally broken down. As in the *Passion d'Arras*, so in the *Resurrexio* Lucifer responds to Christ's *Attolite portas*.[49] Lucifer's vain cries, "Oh! out! help! thieves" (l. 125) emphasize the devils' view of Christ as an intruder, a thief, and a despoiler. The characterization of the ineffectual, naive Lucifer who scurries about urging Beelzebub to send forth lightning and thunder to burn Christ suggests a comic, powerless devil who would be a god, but cannot.

Beezelbub, both here and in the *Gospel of Nicodemus* (as well as in Eastern versions), is the wiser of the two devils, or, in comic terms, the straight man. Intuiting that no action will avail them now, this practical devil counsels Lucifer to flee into a hole until Christ returns to heaven. But the Spirit approaches and, as in the traditional sources, stretches out a hand to Adam, who, with Eve, prays for mercy. Extending peace and laughter to all, the Spirit sends a thankful Adam and Eve to heaven with the Archangel Michael, while He himself returns to the sepulchre. The idea of Christ wishing the emerging inhabitants of hell laughter seems at first inappropriate, yet, upon second consideration, it is fitting, since clearly the joy of laughter and delight of heaven, absent in hell, is what He bestows upon them.

Scene two occurs in heaven, where Adam encounters the thief Dymas, together with Enoch and Elijah, who explain their presence there and foretell their battle with the Antichrist. The scene then shifts back to hell where the devil Tulfric, angered by the harrowing, would cast Christ into the hellish fire. Beelzebub once again is the moderating force, wisely remarking that all action is useless. The play concludes with the sorrow of Satan over the loss of so many souls and the horror of his near-blinding by the light of Christ's presence.

The Cornish play is as complex as the Chester in its shifting of scenes from hell to heaven and back to hell again. Considering the usual staging of such plays in large amphitheatres, the Cornish play must have suggested the shift in scene in the easiest and fastest manner—perhaps merely by a "passage" of a few feet to another area where the prophets would reveal, by their costumes as well as by their speech, the new location.[50]

Conspicuously absent in the Cornish play are the Old and New Testament prophets who traditionally form, if not the first scene of the play, then certainly a part of the exiting procession. With fewer characters than any of the English texts, the Cornish play is almost evenly divided in its *dramatis personae* between the forces of good and evil. This simplified structure clearly suggests the outcome of the action, particularly since the divided forces of the devil hold no threat, no terror. The infernal forces are objects of contempt and ridicule, with the exception of Beelzebub who, in his stoic acceptance of the harrowing, bears a curious albeit comic resemblance to Job. Unlike the Beelzebub of the *Gospel of Nicodemus* who quakes and fears at the same time as he wishes to entrap Christ, the Cornish Beelzebub almost appears not to be of the devil's party. Thus Tulfric and Lucifer are merely outwitted rogues at the end of the play, whereas Beelzebub maintains an aura of dignity.

The pious, repentant Adam and Eve, the Spirit's physical contact with them—as if He were creating them afresh—and His blessings form the moving climax of the piece. The meeting in heaven confirms the achievement of eternal bliss for Adam and Eve, while the conversation with the prophets reminds the audience that God's battle with evil is not yet done. The concluding comic scene of the devil's mourning also takes its clue from the apocryphal *Gospel*, but serves to end the play in a different key from most harrowing plays. Like the later Chester alewife scene, the Rhine and Redentin Easter plays, and the *Slovo* Solomon scene, so the Cornish devils' scene serves to divert the audience's attention from ultimate things, from the Last Judgement, to a comic appreciation of the devils' predicament—in fact, to a human response, that of pity or even sympathy for poor Lucifer who is nearly blinded by Christ's glorious Descent.

Spain

While English and French mediaeval drama was flourishing, the drama of Spain slumbered on. As J.P.W. Crawford notes, "Not a single Castilian play is known to have been composed" during the time of the "unfolding and culmination" of both mediaeval French and mediaeval English religious drama.[51] Perhaps, as Ronald Surtz suggests, the Spanish people were content to display their faith in the drama of the Mass—and in the drama of war—rather than in the theatre.[52] For whatever reasons, Spanish religious drama did not begin to unfold until the sixteenth century; yet once born, it flourished in a profusion unknown in any other country. Calderón de la Barca alone wrote over seventy *autos*.

The independent path which Spanish drama followed is revealed especially in its form. Unlike English and French plays, the Spanish had little interest in cycles. Only the *Autos Cuadragesimales* by Vasco Diaz Tanco came close to the cycle format. Composed of seventeen plays, including a Passion sequence, the *Autos* (unfortunately not extant) were intended for performances on Sundays in Lent, Thursday and Friday of Holy Week, and Easter.[53]

Although it is impossible to know for certain, it appears by the number and subject of extant Spanish religious plays that the Easter season was much less significant than that of Christmas. Of the Easter plays extant, very few include a harrowing sequence. Among the plays from Burgos (1520), there is an *Égloga de la Resurrección* by an anonymous author that includes one of the earliest harrowing sequences. (See Joseph E. Gillet's edition, "Tres Pasos de la Pasión y Una Égloga de la Resurrección," *PMLA*, 47 (1932), pp. 949–980.) In limbo, the prophets (David, Solomon, Isaiah, Zacharias, Hosea) and the Erythraean Sibyl sing prophecies of deliverance (ll. 1–140). On the third day, Mary at the sepulchre appeals to God the Father to permit the Resurrection of His Son (ll. 141–170). Christ appears with His angels and sends Gabriel to announce His Resurrection to Mary (ll. 171–190). The brief harrowing (ll. 191–230) follows the traditional sources. A great light appears in hell. Christ descends and a short dialogue ensues between Christ and Lucifer, who is seated on his infernal throne. Lucifer inquires about the identity of Christ, who approaches the captives. When Christ replies that He is God come to release the souls, Lucifer responds in the same possessive and uncomprehending tone: these have been his captives for 4,000 years. Christ explains that it is now the time of the new order, the time of mercy, when the souls of the dead must be freed. Commanding the gates of hell to open, Christ leads out the patriarchs and prophets and presents them to the Virgin Mary (ll. 231–270). Adam and Eve ask Mary's forgiveness (ll. 271–300), and David concludes the play by receiving in the name of all the prophets the Virgin's blessing (ll. 301–340).

This anonymous play includes the germ of all traditional harrowing plays: the dialogue between Christ and Lucifer, the *Attolite portas*, and the release of the captives. Lucifer's character is very roughly sketched; he is perhaps created in the tradition of the Spanish comic *bobo* or *simple*, the fool who does not quite understand what is transpiring, and thus conveniently evokes the necessity of some theological explanation.[54] Christ, not surprisingly, holds a central role in the *Égloga*, not only as redeemer but also as Son of Mary. This typically

Spanish touch, the introduction of the Virgin into the harrowing, reflects the tremendous significance that the cult of the Virgin has always had in Spain. In contrast to other harrowing plays is the marked absence from this early harrowing play of the presence of Lucifer's devilish entourage, a usual source of comedy.

The most elaborate Easter play extant is the *Auto que trata primeramente cómo el ánima de Christo decendió al infierno* (1549) by Juan de Pedraza, a weaver of Segovia. Joseph E. Gillet has edited this play for the *Revue Hispanique*.[55] Both Gillet and Crawford concur that the play was performed in church, probably on Easter morning.[56] Although a complex play, consisting of 1173 lines, and much varied action, this *auto* has no act or scene division.

After the comic prologue (a dialogue between a shepherd and a priest), the harrowing begins the action (ll. 161–287), and is followed by the Resurrection, as well as various other scenes, including the unusual race between the apostles John and Peter (ll. 288–1173). The harrowing itself is introduced by angels who sing of Adam and his lost liberty. After Christ commands the gates of hell to open, Lucifer asks the familiar question: who is the King of glory? Having posed this question twice and received the same response from the angels, Lucifer humbly seems to concur; Christ is certainly the long-awaited one, who will free the captives.[57]

Christ commands the captives to leave hell. Addressing Christ as Lord and Redeemer, Adam speaks of his sin, Christ's sacrifice, of his own new-found liberty and his adoration of the Lord. The harrowing ends with the exit of the patriarchs who sing Zacharias' song *"Benedictus Dominus deus ysrrael"* [sic].

It has recently been suggested that rather than a play acted in church, the *Auto* may instead have been intended for miniature figures, not live actors.[58] Shergold cites the "very unecclesiastical" tone of the prologue and epilogue as slim evidence to support his case. As he points out, however, the *retablo* was already referred to in 1539, and had apparently been brought to Spain by "foreigners" in the previous year.[59] Like the Ukrainian *vertep*, the Spanish *retablo* was divided into compartments, the Nativity being played in one section, the Passion in another. Wooden figures replacing actors were moved by clockwork.

Three Resurrection plays (only one of which has a full-fledged harrowing) are found in the most important monument of Spanish religious drama, a codex of ninety-six plays, edited in four volumes by Léo Rouanet under the title *Colección de autos, farsas y coloquios del siglo XVI,* and dated 1550–1575.[60] Play LIV, *Auto del Despedimiento de Christo de Su Madre* once more focuses on the Virgin and her response as a mother to the Passion. The harrowing of hell is not presented on stage. Instead, we see only the consequences of it: a liberated Adam who appears on stage with a cross, talking of his redemption.

In play LX, *Auto de la Resurreción de Christo* (1578, Madrid), again the harrowing is narrated rather than represented. The allegorical figure of Libertad (Liberty) comments on the triumph of liberty and on the release of Adam and the righteous from captivity (ll. 233–237). The key events of the Descent, harrowing, and liberation are all related by the figure of Time.

Play XCIV, *Aucto de la Redención del Género Humano* is, with a few exceptions, identical with the last *auto* of Bartolomé Palau's *Victoria de Christo.*[61] Unique in Spanish drama, the play is divided into six parts, and presents a chronological view of the subject of the spiritual captivity of mankind from the Fall to the Last Judgement. A very popular text, it underwent nine editions. The characters of the sixth part include allegorical figures such as Redención (Redemption) and Culpa (Sin), as well as Lucifer, Satan, Christ, Adam, Eve, and "other holy fathers."

The play begins with an "Argumento" which tells of Christ's Descent. Then Paz (Peace) sings that this is the day of enlightenment as prophesied by David. Lucifer angrily enters, demanding to know who is making so much noise. He begins to boast of having in his possession Joshua, Moses, Sampson, David, Goliath and the head of Holofernes! Redemption, speaking to Sin, explains in Latin, *"O Mors, ego mors tua,"* and, turning to Lucifer, remarks that Christ's blood will pay for the captives' release. Berzebu (Beelzebub) takes on the usual role of Lucifer and naively refuses entry to the Redeemer, arguing that the devils do not know this "señor" (ll. 291–295). Redemption responds with an unusually full explanation of Christ's power. She tells of the miracles of Cana and of the miraculous feeding of the multitude.

Lucifer's role in this harrowing play is surprisingly slight. He confesses to speaking with Pilate's wife and urges his demons to defend the captives. Redemption, on her part, calls upon David and the prophets. Christ enters at line 461, and touching the doors of hell (*tocando en las puertas*), he sings *Attolitas portas.* Then ensues the usual question "Quis est iste rrex glorie?" [*sic*] which Lucifer repeats in Spanish, perhaps for those in the audience who did not understand the ecclesiastical language. Christ, however, responds in Latin, and then calls Eve, Adam, and Abraham to himself. Adam thanks Christ. Eve, more effusive and talkative than her spouse, explains that during their 5,000 years of captivity she had always lived in hope of this day. Thanking Christ, she urges all to sing a song to welcome Him, the *Benedictus*.

In comparison to English and French drama, Spanish drama places only a very slight emphasis on the harrowing of hell as part of the Passion and Resurrection plays. Tending more toward the serious, Spanish drama lacks the usual sources of comedy, the numerous devils. Lucifer himself is a secondary, almost pathetic figure, while Christ and the Virgin figure prominently.

Italy

Like Spain, mediaeval Italy (except for the north) offers scant evidence of dramatic activity, although the drama seems to have arisen already in the thirteenth century. In the Friuli Chronicle, Giulano, the Canon of Cividale, noted that in 1298 on three succeeding days a *Ludus Christi*, including the life and Resurrection of Christ, was played.[62] Little else is known about this production, and we can only guess that perhaps a harrowing of hell was contained within the play. If so, it would have been the earliest harrowing to have appeared in Italy.

By the fourteenth and fifteenth centuries dramatic activity begins to increase in the north. Perugia in Umbria is the cradle of the vernacular drama. Here in 1258 the hermit Ranieri Fasani began the religious revival of the *Disciplinati*, or Flagellants, a movement which later spread throughout the Italian peninsula. Part of the religious fervour of the *Disciplinati* revealed itself in songs of praise—to God, the Virgin, and the Saints—called *laudi*. From these vernacular songs developed sung or chanted dialogues, the germ of Italian mediaeval religious drama. From fourteenth-century Perugia an anonymous harrowing play has survived which was performed during Holy Week.[63] According to Mario Apollonio, the Perugia *laud* served as a model for the *Disciplinati* of Umbria.[64] The Perugia play, *La Discesa di Gesù all' Inferno*, begins with the traditional scene of the Patriarchs in limbo. As a light begins to shine, the righteous (Isaiah, Simeon, St. John the Baptist) recognize it as coming from the Son of God. The souls identify themselves (e.g. "Io, l'antico Simeone" l. 13), and proceed to tell of their past.

In the next brief scene Satan, in conference with Infernus, gloats that today is the day when the Son will meet death. To Infernus' inquiries of this man's identity, Satan replies that it is the one he tempted in the desert. When Satan affirmatively answers Infernus' question whether this is the same man who resurrected Lazarus, Infernus begins to fear His approach. While Satan urges his devils to be vigilant and prepare for His coming, all the souls in limbo call upon Infernus to open the doors of hell. Perhaps still doubtful of the nature of this expected guest, Infernus once again inquires about this King of glory, and is answered by King David. An angel commands the doors to open. Instead, the unrepentant and now despairing thief, Gestas, is presented to Satan, who welcomes him. Apparently to be understood as an action occuring at the same time as this scene is Christ's welcoming of Dymas, the good thief. Christ commands him to proceed to paradise. Dymas is given Christ's cross as a sign of his readiness for heaven, to which he is led by Gabriel.

In the next scene Christ approaches hell to present Satan with "tribute" (ll. 203–204), namely His Blood, which will redeem mankind. While Infernus inquires yet again, "Who are you who spoils Limbo and who battles so furiously?" Christ ties up Satan. The demons reprove their King for allowing the harrowing of hell. Christ calls all the souls to Him, and promises them paradise. Each briefly addresses Christ: Adam, Abraham, Jacob and Simeon. Others are named (Daniel, Jeremiah, Zacharias, St. John the Baptist), but have no speaking role. All are blessed and then sing *Alleluia* as they are led out by Gabriel. The last scene takes place in paradise with Enoch, Elijah and Dymas. Christ concludes the play, indicating his intention to visit the Virgin.

As may be seen by this brief summary, the Perugia play is very simple in its structure and characterization. It conforms in most aspects to traditional harrowing plays, with two notable exceptions. Eve does not appear in this play. The usual *Attolite portas* and the ritual of questioning is not as formalized as in other plays. As a whole, the play is interested in the basic contrasts between good and evil (good-unrepentant thief, angel-devil, Christ-Satan), rather than in individualized types.

Mario Bonfantini, however, refers to *La Discesa all' Inferno* as "without doubt the most important theatrical monument of all the 'Sacre Rappresentazione' in Umbria."[65] Poetically, even rhapsodically, discussing the play, Bonfantini finds that the work has been constructed like a piece of music. The opening scene he calls "Un largo movimento," "un grandioso inizio sinfonico."[66] Despite Bonfantini's praise, *La Discesa di Gesù all' Inferno* is not one of the more interesting of the harrowing plays; and, in fact, it shows little original (if any) deviation from the *Gospel of Nicodemus* and from other possible models. Joseph Spencer Kennard, for one, confidently asserts that "the French mystery-plays undoubtedly influenced the Italian drama."[67] Certainly this Perugian play bears some resemblance to its French counterparts. Two related *laudi* from Umbria appear in Guiseppe Galli's *Laudi inediti dei Disciplinati Umbri*.[68] Lauda XVI takes place in limbo, where David, Isaiah, Jeremiah, Abel, Adam and Eve discuss prophecies of salvation. This is a very brief *lauda* (pp. 103–105), possibly a fragment from which no harrowing survives.

Lauda XVII is also brief, but unusual. Christ first appears in dialogue with sinners who are then returned to hell. The Son of God then calls upon the just and prepares them to go to His Father.

The *sacre rappresentazioni* (religious drama of popular origin) have their origins in mid-fifteenth century Florence. At first like *laudi*, *rappresentazioni* were always sung; "It is probable, however, that, at a later date, parts of the *rappresentazioni* were declaimed and other parts sung."[69] Because of the musical nature of these plays, it is not surprising that they are generally brief, with few actors—certainly much fewer than appear in the French drama. While dialogue is of secondary importance (hence also characterization and even structure), spectacle is crucial, as is most clearly indicated by the eyewitness account of Bishop Abraham of Souzdal.[70] Bishop Abraham had accompanied Archbishop Isidore of Kiev and John Palaeogus VII, Patriarch of Constantinople on a mission intended to unite the Western and Eastern churches. In Florence the Bishop witnessed a St. John's Festival in June of 1439, and saw an Annunciation and Ascension play. His recollections draw attention to the Florentine fascination with theatrical machinery, lighting and other visual effects.

An anonymous fifteenth-century Florentine Resurrection play has survived, which gives us some indication of the nature of these productions. *Rappresentazione della Resurrezione di Gesù Cristo*[71] a play of 892 lines, begins with an angel who announces that Christ will return in glory and will spoil hell. A scene between a priest (Sacerdote) and Pilate, and the dicing scene precede the Descensus proper in which Christ, flanked by angels, enters with a banner and announces his Descent into Hell and his intention to release the souls from darkness. An angel orders the doors to open, but instead is greeted with Satan's question, "Who is this King of glory?" When the angel replies, Satan attempts to resist, but is tied by Christ with chains. As Satan laments,

"Oimé, oimé," Christ warns him that his cunning will be of no avail. Finally, the Prince of Darkness is forced to acknowledge Christ as the Lord.

The Son of God then calls the souls to Him. Adam, speaking on their behalf, tells Christ that he knows all are liberated by His blood. Then each of the righteous speaks in turn: Abraham, Joshua, Noah, Gideon, David. When David urges a song, all begin singing *Misericordias domini in eternum cantabo*. Christ responds that this is the tropary of victory. The saints proceed to heaven, where they encounter the repentant thief, then Enoch and Elijah, who welcome Christ. David again breaks into a song of joy and cannot refrain from one of his psalms. Christ tells the souls that they will rest in this place until He ascends to the Father. Now He will visit and console Mary. A number of brief scenes follow: Christ's dialogue with Mary; the Priest's discovery of the empty tomb; the three Marys; Christ's appearance before the Magdalene and the other Marys; on the road to Emmaus; and doubting Thomas.

This Florentine play is grander in scope than the Perugian play with its many brief scenes which encompass a much larger time frame. The episodic structure emphasizes action and display. It is fitting therefore that it ends with doubting Thomas' desire to see and feel Christ's wounds. The harrowing itself, however, is brief (only three pages). Unlike the Umbrian play, the Tuscan does not follow the *Gospel of Nicodemus'* structure. Clearly the emphasis here is on Christ, who figures prominently in each scene. There is never any doubt about His victory, and Satan, his opponent, seems merely weak and ineffectual, rather than cunning and Promethean. Again, as in the Umbrian play, Eve is absent from this account of the harrowing.

To the north and east of Florence lies Pordenone, which has also preserved a fifteenth-century Resurrection play entitled *Festum Resurrectionis*.[72] The Pordenone play reveals by comparison just how spectacular the Florentine drama is, for the Pordenone harrowing takes place in the first thirteen lines! While the opening sequence follows the *Gospel of Nicodemus* and the Umbrian example with the souls perceiving a light in limbo, only Adam and Isaiah speak. Then Christ immediately orders, *"Attolite portas."* The central episode occurs in Latin, unlike the example of the Florentine and Perugian play which are in Italian. After Christ replies, *"Dominus virtutem. . . ,"* the stage direction tells us that Christ spoils hell (1. 13). The Descensus is then followed by two brief scenes: the first with the three Marys, the second with Peter and Thomas. An angel concludes the play.

Only one Italian Resurrection appears to be extant from the six- ↳ ⅙ ↩
teenth century.[73] From Rome we have an anonymous play which begins
in an unusual fashion with Dionysus the Areopagite, who announces
the Resurrection. Pilate is troubled by recent events, and the Pharisees
ensure that Christ's sepulchre is well guarded. Only then does the action move to limbo where the righteous call upon the Lord in song.
The soul of Christ appears in limbo and beats upon the doors. Satan,
more assured than his other Italian counterparts, answers with arro-
gance and asks why Christ has come to disturb him. To these remarks
Christ responds, "Why don't you open the door," and then commands
in Latin, "*Attolite portas. . . .*" Satan follows the formula, "*Quis est rex
gloria*," and Christ replies with the traditional Latin response. Finally,
breaking down the door, Christ ties Satan and calls the souls to Him.
They reply by singing *Adoramus te.*

Although the harrowing ends here, the play continues by following
the Descensus with a scene between Christ and the Virgin; then the
discovered empty sepulchre; the three Marys; Christ's appearance to
Peter and to the Magdalene; and finally Luca and Cleofas, after which
the play breaks off.

Like the Spanish drama, the Italian is sober in its devout tone,
simplicity of structure and characterization, close adherence to Biblical
and apocryphal sources, and eschewing of comical scenes. The latter
were left to *intermezzi* or interludes, which gradually moved away in
subject matter from the serious play with which they alternated and
which they originally explained.

Germany and Austria

The harrowing of hell theme was extremely popular in Germanic lands,
as numerous extant plays attest. The oldest of these, the Easter play
of Muri (c. 1250), contains the earliest known fragments of a German
vernacular harrowing of hell, a dialogue between Christ and the Devil
(as Christ stands before the gates of hell), and a brief scene of the
righteous welcoming their Saviour.[74]

Most Passion and Easter plays of the twelfth and thirteenth centuries were, however, written in Latin. Not until the fourteenth century does German begin to predominate, and by the fifteenth and sixteenth centuries, German is used almost exclusively.[75] The Frankfurt
Dirigierrolle,[76] an early fourteenth-century director's copy of a two-
day Easter play, contains stage directions, the order of appearance of

the actors, and the first lines of their speeches. The second day of performance sketches out a brief harrowing, but no text survives.

The Monastery of St. Gall has preserved a fourteenth-century text probably written in central Western Germany.[77] West comments that this play, like the Frankfurt *Dirigierrolle*, "represents a transitional form between the early, liturgical presentations and the longer, secularized performances of the fifteenth and sixteenth centuries." He goes on to remark that, indeed, the St. Gall play may have been the source for longer plays of the Frankfurt groups, and of the Tyrol Passion Play.[78]

A very brief play of only forty-five lines, the St. Gall begins with Christ rising and singing, "I am risen and still I am with thee."[79] He then goes down to hell carrying the cross and singing "Lift up your gates." The Prince of hell is commanded to open the door and bring forth his servants. But Lucifer instead inquires about the identity of the King of glory. Never in 5,000 years has he heard such loud knocking. After an angel responds, Christ once more orders Lucifer to open the gates or He will take away his power. Weakly replying, Lucifer acknowledges the grim tidings. Christ pushes the door with his foot and enters as Adam and various nameless souls sing the *Canticum triumphale*. After Adam tells of the souls' great longing, Christ seizes his hand, promises that all shall live forever without sorrow, and leads them to paradise, where the souls sing "Holy! holy! holy!"

Although stemming from approximately the same period as the St. Gall text, the Innsbruck Easter play is much more sophisticated. Likened to the famous Redentin play, the Innsbruck nonetheless contains many of "the usual weaknesses of the medieval drama"—lack of unity, long drawn-out mirror scenes, disregard of probability, and a lack of character development.[80]

The Innsbruck harrowing is preceded by a number of brief scenes which take place on earth, including a farcical scene of the watchmen who have come to fisticuffs because Pilate has scolded them for falling asleep at Christ's sepulchre. It is this comic scene that precedes the harrowing.[81]

As in the later Vienna play (and in the Bohemian Resurrection play), so in the Innsbruck an angel begins by singing *"Exsurge, quare obdormis, domine?"* and then urges Christ to rise and redeem the poor souls in hell. Christ responds by arising and singing *Resurrexi*.

This short scene is interrupted by another, equally as brief, of Pilate and the watchmen. We are then awkwardly taken back to Christ who now stands before the gates of hell. Evidently, the dramatist felt the need to suggest some passage of time, and thus interrupted the harrowing sequence with this cumbersome device. At the gates of hell an angel sings *"Cum rex gloriae Christus,"* and is followed by Adam who sings *"Advenisti"* from the other side of the gate. Angered by the noise, Christ commands the gates to open and replies to the Prince of Darkness with the traditional formula. Lucifer refuses to open his gates, and saucily answers Christ, who thereupon spoils hell. He is greeted by Adam and Eve who remind the audience of the Fall by explaining to Christ who gave them "the bad advice" (l. 321) of eating the forbidden fruit. Calling the souls to His Father, Christ sings *"Venite, benedicti patris mei."* As the righteous depart, an unlucky soul is apprehended by the Devil, who gloats at his catch.[82] The scene becomes comic as Lucifer rushes about, crying out in a loud voice that hell be filled once more with all manner of men and women. These are quickly brought before him and each soul identifies itself. The segment ends with Satan throwing them all into hell. This comic scene of the Prince of Darkness replenishing his kingdom by ushering in various tradesmen is a comic inversion of the serious action of the King of glory leading the righteous into the kingdom of heaven. As in the French drama, so in this German play the comic action seems to divert attention away from the serious salvation theme, as it turns into satire and farce.

Dramatic activity increases in the fifteenth century, during which the Tyrol, Lucerne, Rhine, Vienna, Donaueschding and Redentin plays are produced. Stemming from the late fourteenth, early fifteenth centuries is the Tyrol Passion play cycle, which took three days to perform. The Tyrol harrowing appears to be closely influenced by the Innsbruck play. The Lucerne play (1453), extant only in fragments, also contained a harrowing which formed the basis of the Donauesching play, a long play of 4,106 lines of which but 126 form a harrowing sequence.[83] Like the Innsbruck, the Donauesching begins with an angel who urges Christ to arise, and who offers Him the golden crown of glory (to replace the crown of thorns), and a banner displaying the red cross. Salvator arises from the sepulchre where He has slept, and the two then descend into hell, whereupon the angel begins the *Tollite portas* formula. As in the St. Gall play, so in the Donauesching, Christ, with a foot in the door of hell, orders the gates opened. To the accompaniment of strange noises made by the devils, Lucifer inquires about the identity of Christ. Christ himself responds three times until a wild cry is raised by the devils and Christ harrows hell, binding Lucifer. The angel sings *"Venite benedicti patris mei,"* and the righteous reply in song *"Advenisti, desiderabilis"*

(l. 3889). Taking Adam by the hand, Christ hears his thanks, followed by those of Eve, St. John the Baptist, Daniel, Noah, Abraham, David, Isaiah, Moses and Jeremiah. The play concludes with the angel leading them out of hell into paradise.

The Rhine Easter play, stemming from western central Germany and written down in 1460 (according to the concluding remarks of the scribe), is the first of the German plays to present a more elaborate harrowing sequence, the most complex after the Redentin play.[84] Comprising 288 lines, the Rhine harrowing still includes a good deal of Latin, both in its songs, and in what might be called the ritual parts of the play. This long Easter play of 2285 lines begins with an Angel who sings "*Silete!*"—a device to encourage the audience to pay attention—which is used periodically in the play, particularly preceding more solemn portions of the action. The Descent begins immediately after the Angel's introduction, when, in a stage direction, we are told that Salvator's journey to limbo is preceded by angels who sing "*Te Sanctum Dominum.*" A brief, comic scene intervenes involving Jews who rejoice at the spilling of blood. The angel's command of "*Silete*" marks the end of the scene and the beginning of the harrowing. Salvator, who had (according to the stage directions) been proceeding slowly to limbo, now enters singing "*Tollite portas*," the ritual formula which begins the true action of the harrowing. David twice replies to Lucifer's question, "*Quis est iste rex gloriae?*" Introducing himself to the audience, Adam reminds us of his Fall and of the loss of paradise—useful reminders topologically, since we will be witnesses of the regaining of paradise. A frightened Lucifer calls Wedderwosch for advice, but before Wedderwosch's words are out of his mouth, Salvator sings the "*Tollite portas*" formula a third time. The devils scurry about in confusion while hell is harrowed. Christ calls the righteous to Him in Latin, then in German, and the souls joyously respond, singing "*Advenisti.*" A type of procession then occurs, when the righteous welcome Christ, each in turn declaiming lengthy speeches, beginning with Abraham, and followed by Noah, Isaiah, Zacharias, Eve, Moses, and Jacob. The souls genuflect, sing, and follow Christ to paradise. A comic scene of *diablerie* succeeds the serious action, in which Lucifer calls for new souls to fill hell and is presented with a variety of characters from all walks of life, including a priest, a merchant, a knight, and a doctor.

The Vienna harrowing survives in a single manuscript, dated 1472; it is longer than many of the German plays, but remains, nonetheless, rather perfunctory, comprising only 140 lines.[85] Michael begins the

play, urging Christ to rise and aid the poor souls in hell. Jesus responds
with *Resurrexi*. Gabriel reminds Christ that since He is the light, He
should take light into the darkness where the souls await Him. The
scene changes to hell, where Adam and Eve, repentant yet hopeful,
await the end of their pain. Jesus approaches and sings, commanding
Lucifer to open the gates. Then the usual questions ensue, which
Gabriel answers. Beginning to fear, Lucifer requests assistance from
Satan and orders the doors barred and closed. However, his actions are
in vain; Christ harrows hell. He is bid welcome by Eve. While Lucifer
laments the loss of his subjects, Jesus calls all to His Father's kingdom.
Comforting his master, Beelzebub promises to help fill hell once more,
but Lucifer is not consoled and irritably asks, cannot anything be kept
from Christ? Satan then tells of a devil who seized one soul, but it
cried out to Michael, who ordered the devil to flee. Lucifer's despair
deepens. Satan concludes the scene.

Although earlier than the Vienna and Donaueschling play, the Redentin play of 1464 is probably one of the best known and best constructed of the German Easter plays. A.E. Zucker argues that not only
does it excel "all others of its kind in German," but that it also is
"superior to the English plays in unity, motivation, satire, humour, re-
alism, and the characterization of saints, sinners and devils."[86] These
are large claims indeed. An examination of the Redentin harrowing
will, however, bear out many of them.

The Redentin harrowing is, first of all, a much fuller treatment of
the subject than we have hitherto seen in German drama. Beginning in
scene eight, the ante-chamber of hell, the souls exult.[87] Abel, the first
man to die, is the first to speak in the play. He asks what the light is that
has suddenly appeared in heaven. Adam explains that this is the light
of the Lord. Isaiah and Simeon identify themselves in the same simple
way we have seen in other plays ("I bun Symeon de alde"—l. 295).
After discussing the Lord's imminent arrival, they sing "*Luminem ad
revelationem gentium.*" The first scene of the Redentin thus follows
the traditional format found in other Western European plays.

The second part of this scene introduces St. John, who is apparently unknown to the others. His role in hell is that of the Precursor.
Telling the story of baptism, John explains that Christ is nigh. Seth
narrates the oil of mercy story, and recalls that since 5,600 years are
past, the redemption must be at hand. Further, he explains the origin
of the Cross and the tree from which it was carved. Isaiah urges all to
rejoice.

Sc. 9

Scene nine contains a dialogue between Lucifer and Satan. The suspicious Lucifer wishes to know where Satan has hidden for the past three days, and what news he brings. Unlike Lucifer in *Slovo*, the Redentin Lucifer appears to be uncertain of the loyalty of his troops, and does not seem to have the same powers of intuition. Taking on the boastful role usually assigned Lucifer, the Redentin Satan proudly explains that he has been garnering "a great treasure" (1. 383). He has been among the Jews and has set a trap for Christ who fears death. The wiser Lucifer, clearly knowing who Christ is, contradicts his underling: God cannot die. He will harrow hell and deceive Satan. Satan persists in believing that Christ is a mortal and claims to have seen Him reading His last will, drinking vinegar and gall. Satan admits that he directed the spear into His heart. Crumnase (Crooked Nose) supports Satan's claims and brings forth Judas, a recent arrival in hell.

Continuing the interrogation, Lucifer demands to know where Christ's soul is. It is lost, says Satan, because at the very moment that His soul was freed, Satan was called by Lucifer and so failed to catch it. Bethinking himself of another possibility, Lucifer inquires whether this is the same man who raised Lazarus. When Satan replies in the affirmative, a terrible fear strikes the devils. In a vain about-face Satan now urges that the gates of hell be well-defended. All is confusion as the noise of the merrymaking of the souls strikes further terror into the heart of Lucifer.

Sc. 10

The stage directions of scene ten indicate that Christ approaches the hellmouth. Espying Christ, David urges Him to redeem the souls that are all in pain. David sings and is followed by Adam, who rejoices and urges all to join in song. Eve welcomes Christ. Jesus enters on 1. 510 with angels preceding Him. Gabriel exchanges words with the devils who ask who this King of glory is. Lucifer then asks who storms his castle; the phrasing clearly suggests the mediaeval influence of the unknown challenger-knight. Christ is the warrior. Raphael responds to Lucifer's question. Then the devils pose the question once again, as the angels sing *Tollite portas.* Lucifer vainly attempts to command the angelic forces. He orders them to stop "storming," and reiterates his claim to the souls in hell. Not heeding Gabriel's warning that he will be bound for all eternity if he fails to open the gates, Lucifer persists in demanding that his "nest" (1. 517) be left in peace.

The Redentin Lucifer thus comes closest to the *Slovo* Lucifer in characterization. Both face invasions; their castles are under siege. They are sympathetic in their desire for peace on the one hand and, on the other, in the clearly hopeless but courageous effort to maintain morale and face in front of an invincible force.

Told yet again who Christ is by David, Lucifer finally admits that all weapons, all struggles are useless. The pitiful Satan, now completely terrified, can only ask uncomprehendingly why Christ is so "discourteous," and why He causes so much suffering (ll. 563–566). Calling him "dragon" and "damned snake" (ll. 567–568), Christ then "with great violence" harrows hell. Seizing Lucifer, He binds him and orders the rabble of hell away.

Perhaps not as dignified as in other plays, Christ in the Redentin play is clearly presented as the triumphant warrior, pitiless toward his enemies, awesome in his strength. Singing *"Venite benedicti,"* He urges the righteous to come to Him so that He may lead them to heaven. He grasps Adam by the right hand and then calls Eve, who asks Christ's forgiveness.

The dramatic scene of invasion and the joy of the righteous is then modulated into a comic tone, when scene ten ends with *diablerie.* Tutevillus seizes St. John because, he says, the Baptist's pelt will be useful to the devils when it rains. John, however, warns of a catastrophe if he is not freed, and so manages to escape. Here again we see the *"anima infelix"* in a different guise. In this more complex play, the devils, angels, and the souls are individualized and the episodes of earlier German plays expanded.

Scene ten concludes with Lucifer's lament that Christ's victory was an unfair trick. "What a violent fellow this is!" (l. 656) Lucifer exclaims, leaving the audience with a sober view of judgement after the comic intrusion of Tutevillus.

Scene eleven of the Redentin play takes place in heaven as Michael leads the singing procession to Enoch, Elijah and the thief. Before crossing the threshold, the souls remind Adam and, of course, the audience of past events. A capsule history of the Fall is narrated: the final triumph is about to be achieved—they will meet with God himself.

Indeed superior to all other German harrowings, the Redentin play is evidently more than just a mere reciting of the details of the story. The anonymous author may very well have participated in military campaigns. Certainly this harrowing gives some idea of the terrors of invasion and the destructiveness of the victor. The characters are unusually fleshed out. Lucifer is cautious and wise at first, then admirably reveals bravado in a hopeless battle. By the last scene he comes full circle, appearing to diminish in status when he claims unfair victory.

He is no longer a formidable opponent, but a babbling idiot. Part II of the Redentin play takes up this treatment of Lucifer in scene nineteen, where the chained, lamenting Lucifer reiterates the details of the harrowing and questions its justice. All the souls, he claims, "Whether they were sinful or not" (l. 1064), were led out. The task of rebuilding hell then begins as people from all classes, all professions are carried in.

The Redentin Christ is one of the most awesome Saviours of any harrowing play. Rewarding the good, severely punishing the wicked, the Redentin Christ is majestic and severe.

After the masterful achievement of Redentin, the sixteenth-century Aldsfeld Passion Play, also a three-day event, appears simple and unsophisticated. The harrowing begins with Christ rising from the sepulchre (l. 7043)[88] and the angels preceding Him in a procession, singing *"Cum rex gloriae."* As the souls in hell rejoice and sing, Lucifer inquires of Satan the meaning of their happiness. Satan explains that there is a report that Jesus has risen and will come here. Lucifer cries horribly but is calmed by Satan who assures him that it is only a rumour. Theologically, the ignorance of both Lucifer and Satan is an odd notion, for the devils are traditionally responsible for Christ's death. Instead, in the Aldsfeld play, the devils are almost "innocent" victims because they have not brought about their own downfall. The *"Tollite portas"* and *"Quis est iste"* ritual thus makes little sense dramatically, since both Satan and Lucifer indicated that they already knew Christ's identity. The spoiling of hell, which occurs after Christ explains that He is both man and God, is perfunctory compared to the earlier Redentin play. As Christ calls the souls to Him, Adam and Eve bid Him welcome, bless Him and sing *"Gloria tibi, trinitas"* (l. 7181). Only then do the nameless souls identify themselves as Simeon, John the Baptist, Daniel and Moses. Lucifer is bound and the *maledicti* beg to go with Christ, but they are ignored (another deviation from the Redentin play). Christ proceeds to lead out the righteous, and Eve concludes the scene praising Him as she stands at the gates of heaven.

Like the Spanish and Italian harrowing plays, the German are serious, straightforward dramatizations of this apocryphal theme. With the exception of the Redentin and the Rhine plays, German plays treat this subject in a generally perfunctory manner. Only the Redentin and the Rhine plays go beyond the usual formulaic patterns to present a well-unified play with detailed characterization, lively devils, and an imposing Christ figure.

Bohemia

As early as the thirteenth to the fourteenth centuries, the Bohemians came under the influence of European literature. But the Bohemians' golden age of mediaeval drama (as far as we are able to ascertain) included few passion plays.[89] One, a fourteenth century Resurrection play, *Ludus de resurrectione domini . . . Hra o Kristovu Zmrtvýchvstání o Jeho Oslavení* [*The Play About Christ's Resurrection and His Glorification*], recorded in the sixteenth century, probably between 1516 and 1526, includes a harrowing sequence.[90] The text begins with a prologue by "Praecursor" who, in rhyming couplets, informs the audience of the action they are about to see. The opening sequence begins, as in *Slovo*, with Lucifer. Speaking to his devilish cohorts, which include Beelzebub, Astaroth and Urbata, Lucifer regrets the fact that there is no place in heaven for him. He proudly recalls that he was the most beautiful angel in heaven. But since he can no longer be in heaven, Lucifer vows to be the most terrible of devils in hell, and urges his cohorts to assist him in his revenge by filling up hell.

Like *Slovo*, then, the Bohemian play begins with Lucifer's recollections of the past. But unlike *Slovo*, the introduction is brief and Lucifer's character is but vaguely sketched. Rather than revealing character or structurally preparing for Christ's arrival, the monologue is actually a prelude to a dramatic, satiric action of *diablerie* with little connection to Christ's imminent harrowing of hell. In a scene reminiscent of the Rhine Easter Play, Lucifer's command to fill his kingdom is answered by his devils who promptly respond by carrying in various tradesmen—a miller, a tavern keeper, a tapster, a shoemaker and a baker. Each is judged in turn by Lucifer, who metes out appropriate punishment.

After a scene on earth between Pilate and Caiphas, the harrowing proper begins with an angel singing *"Exurge, quare obdormis,"* and then asking in Czech, "How long will you sleep O Lord? It's time to rise from the dead."[91] The Bohemian harrowing thus begins at the sepulchre, as do most German plays. Christ, rising, sings *"Resurrexi"* after the angel once more urges him to rise; and then He explains that He has left His grave in order to spoil hell. These events are followed by a brief scene on earth with Caiphas, who urges his friends to keep Christ's apparent Resurrection a secret.

In the next scene Christ appears at the gates of hell with an angel who sings *"Tollite portas,"* after which Christ commands the gates of hell to open. The traditional formula then begins with Satan, who inquires in a horrible voice, *"Quis est iste rex gloriae?"* The angel replies to his question, posed three times, and then the gates finally open on the souls who sing *"Advenisti desirabilis."* Christ addresses all, then gives Adam His hand. Adam, accepting his guilt and suffering, welcomes Christ. Another soul tells of the Fall, blaming all on Eve, who then introduces herself as Eva, the one who ate the apple. The good thief speaks briefly. The play comes to a close with Christ's promise to remain in hell until the third day, and with His command to Michael to lead the souls to heaven. They exit singing *"Salve festa dies."*

Most likely influenced by German plays, this Bohemian harrowing does not possess the unity of structure or development of characters that, say, the Redentin play reveals; but it does contain a fascination with both the solemn and the comic evident in the most masterful of Western plays.

Poland

The history of Polish theatre before 1580 is, for the most part, speculative. Although there was a flourishing liturgical drama (in Latin) there is no extant evidence of any plays written in the Polish language before Mikołaj from Wilkowiecko's sixteenth-century Resurrection play, *Historyja o Chwalebnym Zmartwychwstaniu Pańskim* [*History of the Glorious Resurrection of Our Lord*]. Probably published in Cracow,[92] the cradle of Polish liturgical theatre,[93] *Historyja* is both of intrinsic and of comparative interest as a possible source for the Ukrainian *Slovo o zbureniu pekla*. Stanislaw Windakiewicz, the play's first editor, calls it the best (and the only) printed text of a Passion play in Poland.[94] Windakiewicz also firmly believes that this Polish play is a close cousin of both the French Passion play of Gréban, and the German plays of the fifteenth century.[95] In a more recent book, Julian Lewański has examined the possibility that Mikołaj was not only the author of the text, but perhaps also its censor, editor, and revisor.[96] Jerzy Ziomek, on the other hand, questions both the authorship and the date of the work.[97] Possibly a much earlier work, it may have been (like the English mystery plays) written down at a much later date. Ziomek suggests that an earlier version of *Historyja* may have been in circulation already in 1551, when a reference appears to "Historyj częstochowskich"—an allusion to the icon of Częstochowa and, presumably, to that part of the scene in the play which appears immediately after the harrowing: when Mary is informed of her Son's Resurrection.[98] Probably the earliest date possible for *Historyja* would be 1544, when Wawrzyniec from Łasko copied an anonymous version of the *Gospel of Nicodemus*.[99] The circulation and popularity of such a text would have encouraged the writing—and staging—of Passion plays.

A play of 1470 lines, *Historyja* most likely used "simultaneous" staging in mansions.[100] The written text is preceded by brief instructions about the time and place of the play's staging: *"inter festa Paschae et Ascensionis Domini,"* either in church or in the cemetery; and its author suggests that if doubling is used, twenty-one people may suffice to play all the parts.[101] For the purposes of quieting the audience, the author advises singing "Przez Twe święte zmartwychwstanie" [By Your Holy Resurrection]. Then a 120 line Prologue follows, addressed to all believers.

Scene four (ll. 470–913) presents the harrowing sequence. Like the rest of the play, it offers clear indication of a link with liturgical services: hymns and readings from the Bible occur frequently in the text and remind the audience that they will see a dramatized event taken from Scripture. Scene four begins with the Evangelist reading Psalm 23 (24), and then Christ immediately appears, clothed in priestly robes (alb, stole and cope). However, the appearance of Christ and the solemn opening suddenly seem undercut by the colloquial address of the Lord, who calls out "Hey, devilish princes/ Open up your gates" (ll. 481–482). Lucifer answers in a similar style and questions the visitor about His identity. After Christ's reply, which paraphrases the Psalm and underscores the Lord's might, Lucifer still seems comically oblivious to the seriousness of the event. He sends Cerberus to the door to find out who is banging on it. Cerberus opens the door slightly and, smelling the horrible stench which has escaped, quickly closes it. Cerberus then explains to Lucifer that their visitor is heavenly, Jesus of Nazareth, and He carries a banner with a red cross. Although Cerberus seems alarmed, and the righteous begin to make a great noise, Lucifer shrugs off Cerberus' words with a "Bah" and asks for tar, which he will offer his prisoners. Adam warns Lucifer that he will have to drink tar himself, and Isaiah reminds the devil of words he used frequently in the past: "O death, where is thy sting?" Christ once again commands the devils to open their gates, but Lucifer cheekily urges Jesus to go to His Kingdom, "There is plenty of room in heaven . . . rule there" (ll. 569–570).

Christ warns of His imminent coming, and foretells the joyous welcome He will receive. On the other side of the gates, Abraham urges Christ to come, free them all, and lead them to His heavenly kingdom. Adam upbraids the devils, and greets the arrival of the Lord. Finally, Christ enters hell and, taking the chains, binds Lucifer as He rebukes him for joking with God as if he were an equal.

Lucifer's cry of "Biada, biada, biada, gorze!" (l. 637) when Christ ties him up is much like Hades' cry of "Gvalt, gvalt" [literally, "Rape, rape"] in *Slovo*. Rather than having Christ pacifying Lucifer and Hades, the Polish play has Cerberus comforting Lucifer by telling him that they will travel to taverns, cloisters and hospitals, and will gather afresh the souls of popes and peasants, alewives and virgins (a scene which also recalls earlier German plays. See above.) Christ adds that Lucifer should not complain; he still has unbelievers with him, whereupon the Prince of Darkness is pushed into hell. Christ then turns to the righteous, who greet Him with great joy, singing *"Advenisti desiderabilis."* Christ urges them not to fear these evil creatures anymore, but to follow Him and Michael to heaven. Isaiah begs Christ to send someone to His Mother, in order to let her hear of His Resurrection. Adam, then Abel, Noah, John the Baptist, and the Good Thief all request that they be sent as messengers, but Christ refuses each one, citing various "comic" reasons (e.g. the Good Thief is lame). Finally, an angel is summoned to bear the news. Mary is greeted by *"Regina celi, letare,"* and Christ is presented to His Mother, who falls at His feet. A song concludes the scene: "Ukazał się napierwiej Maryjej" ("He First Appeared to Mary").

In his study of *Historyja*, Julian Lewański refers to a Ukrainian seventeenth century "adaptation"[102]—apparently a cryptic reference to *Slovo o zbureniu pekla*. However, even a cursory view of the play reveals that the Polish play is substantially different from the Ukrainian in construction, tonality, and character. A few verbal parallels suggest some similarities. For instance, Cerberus' question "Is there perhaps not enough *kvass*, / Or potions or tar / Or fires of sulphur?"[103] is reminiscent of Lucifer's remarks in *Slovo* when he taunts St. John the Baptist with hellish *kvass* and tar in quite another context (see *Slovo* l. 261). And the Polish play's Lucifer urges the newly-arrived Christ to "Go to [His] Kingdom: There is plenty of room in heaven . . . rule there," very like *Slovo*'s Lucifer, who remarks: "Let him sit in heaven . . . He doesn't have any business with us" (ll. 420, 424) and also, "If You are God, stay there in paradise" (l. 473). These may suggest that the *Slovo* writer knew the Polish play, but it seems scant evidence.

Beyond these verbal echoes, the humourous, at times farcical, but certainly human spirit of *Historyja* resembles *Slovo*. The familiarity with which St. John or Solomon are treated are absent in the Polish play, although something like it is found in the characterization of Adam, who is called Mr. Jadamek (a diminutive of Adam), recalling the diminutives of Ivanashko (Johnny) in reference to St. John the Baptist in *Slovo*. The Polish play is, however, more thoroughly comic. Even Christ jokes with the other characters. *Slovo*, on the other hand, confines the comedy to the devils; Christ's dignity is kept intact, and His speaking role is both brief and, for the most part, formulaic.

Most significantly, the overall structure of *Slovo* and *Historyja* differ. The compact Ukrainian play builds to the climax of Christ's entry and harrowing of hell. The Polish harrowing scene (only a small part of a long Passion play) begins with Christ and has Him almost comically waiting on the other side of the gates for half of the play. The comic repartee seems to disperse the sense of awe and wonder at the harrowing and, instead, focuses on the real delight of the souls' liberation and of the Resurrection of the Lord.

The *dramatis personae* are also quite different in both plays. The Polish has Lucifer and Cerberus, the Ukrainian Lucifer and Hades; both of the latter have much larger, more interesting roles, as does John the Baptist and Solomon (who does not figure in Polish plays). Conversely, Adam, as well as Noah, Isaiah, Abraham, Abel and the Good Thief have no speaking parts in *Slovo*.

Despite the differences between the two plays, we cannot rule out the possibility that the *Slovo* writer knew the Polish play. And a comparison of the two may be useful in explaining some cryptic moments in the Ukrainian text. The tying up of Lucifer, the actual harrowing, is shown in the Polish play, while in the Ukrainian fragment there is a lacuna. Lucifer's odd comment (l. 446) about fearing "another's fire" is justified in the Polish text, when Christ pushes Lucifer into the fires of hell towards the end of the play.[104]

Another brief harrowing occurs in *Dialog o Zmartwychwstaniu Pana Naszego Jezusa Chrystusa*, also called *Dialogus de Resurrectione Domini Nostri Jesu Christi*,[105] from the sixteenth century. A true Resurrection play, *Dialog* begins with a Prologue in rhyming couplets which announces the events of Easter and reveals Mary Magdalene approaching the empty sepulchre. The harrowing is not shown but, curiously, is narrated by Satan, who mournfully relates his loss, binding and beating at the hands of Christ. An angel rebukes Satan, and reminds him that all of the recent events were foretold long ago by

God. But Satan continues to complain about the injustice of God in taking all—even money—from him just because of what Eve started in the garden. When the angel is unable to convince Satan of God's goodness, Satan laughs and promises to continue in his evil, citing his new version of the ten commandments in which virtue leads to disaster. If one won't steal, one won't eat; if one doesn't commit adultery, one won't multiply; and so forth. Confirmed in his evil, Satan goes off to see Judas with whom he'll drink some tar. The play suddenly concludes with Mary Magdalene, who, in a parallel action, goes to seek her Master, happy in the news of His Resurrection.

NOTES

1 See Sandro Sticca, ed., *The Medieval Drama* (Albany: State University of New York Press, 1972), especially his article "The Literary Genesis of the Latin Passion Play and the *Planctus Mariae*: A New Christocentric and Marian Theology," pp. 39–68. Kurt Weitzmann, "Das Evangelion im Shevophylakion zu Lawra," *Seminarium Kondakovianum*, 8 (1936), p. 87, draws attention to an earlier change in art. At the end of the tenth century, new aspects of the *Anastasis* were portrayed, the most important of which was Christ's centrality in a symmetrical grouping.

2 While this shift in sensibility applies to Western Europe, it is not true of the East, which long ago evolved a more emotional approach to these events. As Sticca points out, p. 56, the oldest extant lamentation of the Virgin stems from the apocryphal Greek *Acts of Pilate* (*Gospel of Nicodemus*), dated approximately the fourth (and certainly no later than the fifth) century.

3 The only book to survey the use of the apocryphal story in vernacular drama, Richard Paul Wülker, *Das Evangelium Nicodemi in der abend-ländischen Literatur* (Paderhorn: Ferdinand Schöningh, 1872), suffers from its brevity and absence of literary analysis; it also makes no reference to harrowing plays in Eastern and Central Europe.

4 Jörg O. Fichte, *Expository Voices in Medieval Drama* (Nurnberg: Verlag Hans Carl Nurnberg, 1975), p. 118.

5 For example, D.D.R. Owen, *The Vision of Hell; Infernal Journeys in Medieval French Literature* (Edinburgh and London: Scottish Academic Press, 1970), p. 230.

6 John Fox, *A Literary History of France: The Middle Ages* (London: Ernest Benn, Ltd., 1974), p. 244, and more especially Kenneth Urwin, "The Mystère d'Adam: Two Problems," *Modern Language Review*, 34 (1939), 70–72.

7 Richard Axton and John Stevens, ed. and trans., *Medieval French Plays* (Oxford: Basil Blackwell, 1971), p. xiv.

8 Carl H. Odenkirchen, *The Play of Adam (Ordo Representacionis Ade)* (Brookline, Mass. and Leyden: Classical Folia Editions, 1976), p. 133. These lines roughly translate as: "Have pity on poor Adam, / Deliver him from sin."

9 L. Petit de Julleville, *Les Mystères* (Paris: Librairie Hachette, 1880), I, p. 92. The prologue tells us that we may expect thirteen distinct scenes, including heaven, hell, Calvary, the sepulchre, a "jail," Galilee, and Emmaus.

10 Owen, p. 231.

11 This date is unusual and appears only in the *Passion des Jongleurs*, but not in traditional sources. See Owen, p. 233.

12 Owen, p. 231, and also Henri Rey-Flaud, *Le Cercle magique; Essai sur le*

théâtre en rond à la fin du Moyen Age (Paris: Gallimard, 1973), pp. 27–36 discusses the acting *vs.* lecteur theories. Walter Becker, *Die Sage von der Höllenfahrt Christi in der altfranzösischen Literatur* (Göttingen: n.p., 1912), p. 37, puts the date of *Autun* at the end of the thirteenth century.

13 Peter Meredith and John E. Tailby, eds., *The Staging of Religious Drama in Europe in the Late Middle Ages: Texts and Documents in English Translation*, trans. Raffaella Ferrari *et al.* (Kalamazoo: Medieval Institute Publications, 1983), p. 6.

14 Achille Jubinal, *Mystères inédits du quinzième siècle*, II (Paris: Téchener, 1837). Text pp. 290–297.

15 Meredith and Tailby, p. 162.

16 For the text see Omer Jodogne, ed., *Le Mystère de la Passion d'Arnoul Gréban*, I (Brussels: Palais des Académies, 1965).

17 "That which is lost is lost, / but let us think on that which remains, / to better save that which we can." (Translation mine.)

18 Although a text has not survived from the Mons *Mystère de la Passion* performed in 1501, mention must be made of the *Livre de Conduite du Régisseur* and the list of expenditures which give a lively portrayal of an elaborate harrowing scene. Gustave Cohen's detailed study has shown that the Mons play was probably a combination or a "contamination" of the *Passion* of Gréban and of Jehan Michel. See Gustave Cohen, *Le Livre de Conduite du Régisseur et Le Compte des Dépenses pour Le Mystère de la Passion joué à Mons en 1501* (Strasbourg: Publications de la Faculté des Lettres, 1924), p. xxxi.

19 Owen, p. 243. This point is reinforced by Harold C. Gardiner, *Mysteries' End; An Investigation of the Last Days of the Medieval Religious Stage* (New Haven: Archon Books, Yale University Press, 1967), p. 102, who notes that French drama was "in increasing danger of being discredited because of their generous admixture of comic and unbecoming elements, a danger much more acute in them than in English or German plays."

20 William Henry Hulme, ed., *The Middle-English Harrowing of Hell and Gospel of Nicodemus* (London, N.Y., Toronto: Oxford University Press, Early English Text Society, 1907; rpt. 1961), p. lxvii. Unfortunately, space does not permit a study of this important poem, which provides a useful vernacular base for comparison with the English cycles. Hulme's introduction provides an excellent summary of the various English versions of the *Gospel of Nicodemus*. Ian Lancashire, *Dramatic Texts and Records of Britain* (Toronto: University of Toronto Press, 1984), includes a number of tantalizing references to English harrowing plays no longer extant. The very first item in his chronological account is a reference in 721/24–40? to a fragmentary harrowing of hell dialogue in the *Book of Cerne*.

21 This "Abuse of Power" theory is studied by Timothy Fry, "The Unity of

the Ludus Coventriae," *Studies in Philology*, 48 (1951), 527–568, and by Peter Stuart Macaulay, "The Play of the Harrowing of Hell as a Climax in the English Mystery Cycles," *Studia Germanica Gandensia*, 8 (1966), 115–134.

22 Macaulay examines the use of simultaneous and backward-forward movement of time in his article. See especially pp. 124–126.

23 Peter W. Travis, *Dramatic Design in the Chester Cycle* (Chicago and London: The University of Chicago Press, 1982), p. 194.

24 Travis, p. 194.

25 For the text see K.S. Block, *Ludus Coventriae or The Plaie Called Corpus Christi* (London: Oxford University Press, Early English Text Society, Extra Series 120, 1922; rpt. 1960). See above, Iconography, note 9 for the chronology of the Descent.

26 A.M. Nagler, *The Medieval Religious Stage: Shapes and Phantoms* (New Haven and London: Yale University Press, 1976), p. 9.

27 Nagler, p. 10.

28 Rosemary Woolf, *The English Mystery Plays* (London: Routledge and Kegan Paul, 1972), p. 272, suggests that N-Town may have been influenced by the *Palatinus Passion*, which places the harrowing between the Crucifixion and the Burial.

29 Woolf, p. 273, argues that the harrowing of the prophets "seems merely a formal tribute" in N-Town because the episode of the prophets' anticipatory joy at Christ's coming has been excluded from the play.

30 F.M. Salter, *Medieval Drama in Chester* (Toronto: University of Toronto Press, 1955), pp. 40–42. For the play text see ed. R.M. Lumiansky and David Mills, *The Chester Mystery Cycle* (London, N.Y., Toronto: Oxford University Press for the Early English Text Society, 553, 1974), I, pp. 325–339. See vol. II (1986) for commentary and a detailed examination of parallels between the *Gospel of Nicodemus* and the Chester harrowing, pp. 262–276.

31 Hardin Craig, in *English Religious Drama of the Middle Ages* (Oxford: Clarendon Press, 1955), p. 255 believes that the origin of the Chester cycle is continental, and that it follows the pattern of the Benediktbeuern plays, the oldest known examples of Passion plays.

32 Travis, pp. 67–68.

33 See R.M. Lumiansky, "Comedy and Theme in the Chester *Harrowing of Hell*," *Tulane Studies in English*, 10 (1960), 5–12 for a thematic argument on behalf of the inclusion of the scene. Travis, pp. 67–68, argues the opposite case.

34 Walter Earl Meyers, *A Study of the Middle English Wakefield Cycle Plays* (Ann Arbor, Michigan: University Microfilms, 1967), later revised and published as *A Figure Given: Typology in the Wakefield Plays* (Pittsburgh: Duquesne University Press, 1970).

35 For the text see Richard Beadle, ed., *The York Plays* (London: Edward Arnold, 1982), pp. 333–343.

36 Peter Happé, ed., *English Mystery Plays* (Harmondsworth: Penguin, 1975), p. 688, note 35, remarks that Michael's inclusion is probably the result of a later revision, since he does not appear in the Towneley play, nor is he mentioned in Richard Burton's 1415 list of plays.

37 Woolf, pp. 271–272, observes that "Christ's verbal defeat of the devil is a far more impressive symbol of the victory of the redemption than his token destruction of the gates of hell."

38 Beadle, p. 453.

39 For the text see G.A. England and A. Pollard, ed., *The Towneley Plays* (London: Oxford University Press, Early English Text Society, 1897; rpt. 1907, 1925, Extra Series 71, 1897).

40 See W.A. Craigie, "The Gospel of Nicodemus and the York Mystery Plays," in *Furnivall Miscellany* (Oxford: n.p., 1901), p. 54 for a list of verbal parallels, and John Gardner, *The Construction of the Wakefield Cycle* (Carbondale and Edwardsville: Southern Illinois Press, 1974), pp. 120–124 for an analysis of the similarities and differences between the York and the Towneley.

41 Gardner, p. 121.

42 Gardner, p. 123, develops the idea of Christ as magician in this play.

43 Meyers, p. 113.

44 Meyers, pp. 114–116.

45 For the text see E. Norris, ed., *Ordinalia; The Ancient Cornish Drama*, 2 vols. (Oxford: Oxford University Press, 1859), II, pp. 173–179, or for a more recent text see *The Cornish Ordinalia; A Medieval Dramatic Trilogy*, trans. Markham Harris (Washington: The Catholic University of America Press, 1969).

46 Jane A. Bakere, *The Cornish Ordinalia; A Critical Study* (Cardiff: University of Wales Press, 1980), p. 1.

47 Bakere, p. 109.

48 Bakere, p. 95.

49 Bakere, p. 95.

50 See Bakere's chapter on "Staging," pp. 151–169, as well as Harris' introductory remarks, pp. xix–xxiv.

51 J.P.W. Crawford, *Spanish Drama Before Lope de Vega* (Philadelphia: University of Pennsylvania Press, 1967), p. 3. The same may be said of Portuguese drama. Gil Vicente (c. 1465–1537?), a bilingual Portuguese-Spanish writer, is the author of *Auto da Historia de Deus*, 1527, which includes many typical figures from the harrowing plays (such as Lucifer, Belial, Satan, Adam, Eve, David), but also allegorical figures such as Time (Tempo) and the World (Mundo). The actual harrowing occurs only in the stage direction. See *Obras completas*, I, ed. Marques Braga

(Lisbon: Livraria Sá da Costa, 1955–58), pp. 171–215. No other harrowings occur in Portuguese drama.

52 Ronald E. Surtz, *The Birth of a Theater: Dramatic Convention in the Spanish Theatre from Juan del Encina to Lope de Vega* (Madrid: Editorial Castalia, 1979), p. 34. There is evidence, however, of an early harrowing play in Toledo. In the list of expenditures of the Corpus Christi play of 1493, payment is recorded for eight patriarchs (3 *rreales*), for the man playing Christ (4 *rreales*), and for the man whose job it was to set off rockets in hell (1 *rreal*). It seems that this was truly a spectacular performance. See Peter Meredith and John E. Tailby, ed., p. 257.

53 Crawford, p. 46. The word "*auto*" is difficult to translate, but perhaps can be designated as any religious play.

54 J.P.W. Crawford, in "The Pastor and Bobo in the Spanish Religious Drama of the Sixteenth Century," *The Romanic Review*, 2 (1911), 401 argues that "the chief comic figure of the Spanish religious drama of the sixteenth century is the logical outgrowth of the shepherds' plays which were performed in the churches on Christmas day."

55 Joseph E. Gillet, "An Easter Play by Juan de Pedraza (1549)," *Revue Hispanique*, 81 (1933), Part I, 550–607.

56 Gillet, p. 552, and Crawford, *Spanish Drama*, p. 142.

57 The original reads:

     ay de mi si ciertamente
     es este que esta llamando
     el que gran tiempo esperando
     esta me cautiua gente (ll. 232–235)

58 N.D. Shergold, *A History of the Spanish Stage; From Medieval Times Until the End of the Sixteenth Century* (Oxford: Clarendon Press, 1967), pp. 37–39.

59 Shergold, p. 39.

60 Léo Rouanet, ed., *Colección de autos, farsas y coloquios del siglo XVI* (Madrid, Barcelona, Macon: 1901; rpt. Hildesheim and N.Y.: Georg Olms Verlag, 1979).

61 Crawford, *Spanish Drama*, p. 142.

62 Cited in J.L. Klein, *Geschichte des Italienischen Drama's* [sic], 3 vols., (Leipzig: T.O. Weigel, 1866–1868), I, p. 153.

63 For the text see Vincenzo de Bartholomaeis, *Laude Drammatiche e Rappresentazioni Sacre*, 3 vols. (Florence: Le Monnier, 1943), I, pp. 243–258, reprinted by Emilio Faccioli, *Il Teatro Italiano* (Turin: Einaudi, 1975), I, pp. 90–112.

64 Mario Apollonio, *Storia del Teatro Italiano*, I (Florence: Sansoni, 1981), p. 173.

65 Mario Bonfantini, *Le Sacre Rappresentazioni Italiane* (Milan: Bompiani, 1942), p. 69. Translation mine.

66 Bonfantini, p. 69.

67 Joseph Spencer Kennard, *The Italian Theatre: From Its Beginnings to the Close of the Seventeenth Century* (N.Y.: Benjamin Bloom, 1932), I, p. 20. This is apparently also true of a play not available to me, *La Passione di Revello*, ed. A. Cornagliotti (Turin, 1976), which was performed in 1489, and shows strong French influence on both the text and the staging. See Meredith and Tailby, p. 10.

68 Giuseppe Galli, *Laudi inedite dei Disciplinati Umbri* (Bergamo: Istituto Italiano d'Arti Grafiche, 1910).

69 Kennard, p. 30.

70 Orville K. Larson, "Bishop Abraham of Souzdal's Description of 'Sacre Rappresentazioni,'" *Educational Theatre Journal*, 9 (1957), 381–426.

71 For the text see Luigi Banfi, ed., *Sacre Rappresentazioni del Quattrocento* (Turin: Unione Tipografico-Editrice Torinese, 1968), pp. 381–426.

72 For the text see Bartholomaeis, III, pp. 243–262.

73 For the text see Bartholomaeis, II, pp. 183–196.

74 For the text see Edward Hartl, ed., *Das Drama des Mittelalters*: *Osterspiele* (Leipzig: Philipp Reclam, 1937), pp. 281–284.

75 Larry E. West, ed. and trans., *The Saint Gall Passion Play* (Brookline, Mass. and Leyden: Classical Folia Editions, 1976), p. 20.

76 For the text see Wolfgang F. Michael, *Das Deutsche Drama des Mittelalters* (Berlin, N.Y.: Walter de Gruyter, 1971), pp. 145–151.

77 West, p. 38.

78 West, p. 38.

79 For the text see Edward Hartl, *Das Drama des Mittelalters: Passionsspiele II* (Darmstadt: Wissenschaftliche Buchgesellschaft, 1966), or West for an English translation of the play.

80 A.E. Zucker, ed. and trans., *The Redentin Easter Play* (Columbia University Press, 1941; rpt. N.Y.: Octagon Books, 1966), p. 18.

81 For the text see Hartl, *Passionsspiele*, pp. 143–155.

82 The unhappy soul (*anima infelix*) scene may be the germ of the Solomon episode in *Slovo*. It is not improbable that the *Slovo* writer may have studied in Germany, or perhaps may have known clerics who did so. Hryhoryi Nud'ha, "Pershi mahistry i doktory; ukrains'ki studenty v universytetakh Evropy XIV-XVIII stolit' [The First Magisters and Doctors; Ukrainian Students in the Universities of Europe 14–18 Centuries]," *Zhovten'*, No. 3 (1982), 89–101 has revealed the fact that many Ukrainians studied in German universities, as well as those of Prague, Padua, Milan, Paris, and even Oxford between the fourteenth and eighteenth centuries (although the largest number comes from the sixteenth century). By the time the *Slovo* writer was composing his play, the tale of the unhappy soul probably passed into Ukrainian popular lore and became attached, along with other stories, to the well-beloved figure of Solomon.

The development of the figure of the devil in German Easter, Christmas, cycle and miracle plays is thoroughly studied by Luis Schuldes in his
published dissertation, *Die Teufelsszenen im Deutschen Geistlichen Drama
des Mittelalters*, Göppinger Arbeiten zur Germanistik, 116 (Göppingen:
Verlag Alfred Kümmerle, 1974). See especially Schuldes' idea that the
development (and consequent humanizing) of the devil causes him to lose
his eschatological form; he becomes a mere buffoon. For an unpublished
dissertation on a similar topic see E. Kunstein, "Die Höllenfahrtszene im
geistlichen Spiel des deutschen Mittelalters; Ein Beitrag zur mittelalter-
lichen und frühzeitlichen Frömmigkeitsgeschichte," Diss. Cologne, 1972.
Unfortunately, the latter work was unavailable to me.

83 For the text see Hartl, *Passionsspiele*, pp. 90–258.

84 Hans Rueff, ed., *Das rheinische Osterspiel der Berliner Handschrift Ms.
Germ. Fol. 1219*; *mit Untersuchungen zur Textgeschichte des deutschen
Osterspiels* (Berlin: Weidmannsche Buchhandlung, 1925). In addition to
the play text, Rueff presents a comparative study of German Easter plays.
For his comments on the harrowing sequence see pp. 91–92.

85 For the text see Hans Blosen, ed., *Das Wiener Osterspiel* (Berlin: Erich
Schmidt Verlag, 1979).

86 Zucker, p. 7.

87 For the text see Froning, pp. 123–198, and Zucker, pp. 41–113.

88 For the text see Froning, pp. 567–860.

89 Josef Truhlář, "O staročeských dramatech velikonočnich [About Old
Czech Easter Plays]," *Časopis Musea Královstvi Českého*, 65 (1891),
191. But also see Filip Kalan, "Le jeu de la Passion à Škofja Loka,"
Le Livre Slovène, No. 3 (1966), 24–32 for a description of the procession
of the Passion in the sixteenth century. The text, according to Kalan, was
probably in German, or partially in Latin.

90 Josef Hrabák, ed., *Staročeské drama [Old Czech Drama]* (Prague: Československý Spisovatel, 1950), p. 247. For the text, see pp. 43–70.

91 Hrabák, p. 64.

92 Zbigniew Raszewski, *Krótka historia teatru polskiego [A Short History of
the Polish Theatre]* (Warsaw: Państwowy Instytut Wydawniczy, 1977),
p. 14.

93 Raszewski, p. 9.

94 *Teatr ludowy w dawnej Polsce [Popular Theatre in Ancient Poland]* (Cracow: Biblioteka Pisarzów Polskich, 25, Drukarnia Universytetu Jagiel-
lonskiego, 1893), p. 3.

95 Windakiewicz, p. 3. Julian Lewański, *Dramat i teatr średniowiecza i
renesansu [Drama and Theatre of the Middle Ages and the Renaissance]*
(Warsaw: Państwowe Wydawnictwo Naukove, 1981), p. 143 notes that
the Vienna Passion Play was performed in Silesia in the fifteenth century.

96 Lewański, p. 150.

97 Jerzy Ziomek, *Renesans* [*Renaissance*] (Warsaw: Państwowe Wydawnictwo Naukove, 1977), p. 115.

98 Ziomek, pp. 116–117.

99 Ziomek, p. 136. Surprisingly, Ziomek does not make any connections between its appearance and that of the Passion play. He studies apocrypha in a separate chapter.

100 Ziomek, p. 113.

101 Mikołaj z Wilkowiecka, *Historyja o Chwalebnym Zmartwychwsaniu Pańskim*, in Julian Lewański, ed., *Dramaty staropolskie* [*Ancient Polish Drama*], II (Warsaw: Państwowy Instytut Wydawniczy, 1959), p. 288. The play influenced Ukrainian homilies. See M. Vozniak "Znadibky do ukrains'koi velykodnoi dramy [Findings Towards a Ukrainian Easter Drama]," *ZNTSh*, 146 (1927), 119–153. For a more recent edition of the text see Jan Okoń, ed., *Historyja o Chwalebnym Zmartwychwstaniu Pańskim* (Wroclaw: Zakład Narodowy im. Ossolińskich, 1971).

102 Julian Lewański, *Studia nad dramatem polskiego odrodzenia* [*Studies in the Drama of the Polish Renaissance*], IV (Wroclaw: Wydawnictwo Polskiej Akademii Nauk, 1956), p. 120. Although approaching the issue of comparison between *Slovo* and *Historyja* from a slightly different angle, Paulina Lewin also argues that the two plays are substantially different. Paulina Lewin, "The Ukrainian Popular Religious Stage of the Seventeenth and Eighteenth Centuries on the Territory of the Polish Commonwealth," *Harvard Ukrainian Studies*, 1, No. 3 (1977), 308–329.

103 The Polish reads:
   Aboć nie dostaje kwasu,
   Czyli trunku smolanego
   Albo ognia siarczanego? (ll. 544–546)

104 I have avoided reference to the rich tradition of Latin poetry about the harrowing of hell, since such an enormous task would be outside the scope of this volume. However, a comparison of *Sapphicon de inferorum vastatione et triumpho Christi* (1512) by the Ukrainian writer Paulus Crosnensis, who lived in Poland and wrote in Latin, and *Slovo o zbureniu pekla* is a useful test case, for it shows how far removed *Slovo* is from academic, regularized poetry, peopled with mythological beings such as Sisyphus, Ixion, Cerberus, Orcus, and Thalia. For the text of this poem see Bronislavus Kruczkiewicz, ed., *Pauli Crosnensis Rutheni atque Ioannis Vislicensis, Carmina* (Cracow: Jagellonian University, 1887), pp. 135–144.

105 Reprinted by Lewański in *Dramaty staropolskie*, II, pp. 355–369.

Conclusion

Occupying a unique position among the plethora of plays on this same subject, *Slovo o zbureniu pekla* is a fully contained, independent harrowing play of approximately 500 lines (a playing time of perhaps one hour), not preceded by scenes of Christ's Passion.

The play begins in a leisurely fashion with Lucifer's monologue on the history of creation occupying the first ninety-seven lines. Although the speech is ostensibly addressed to Hades, it is really directed at the audience. This introductory address acts as a type of cosmic frame for the action of the play since it reminds the observers of the Providential plan (which will also encompass all actions in the play). Reviewing the mortality of all men, the monologue reaches back to the beginning of time, and then moves forward to the present by alluding to tsars and knights. Two falls are narrated, that of Lucifer from heaven, and of Adam from paradise. Both prepare us for Lucifer's second "fall": his proud boasts in capturing Christ will lead to his own captivity. The audience's superior knowledge makes Lucifer's speech full of dramatic ironies which also underlie the whole play up until the moment of Christ's entry. The frame also reveals that the devil is only a posturer and a braggart, but not a real adversary of God.

Besides being the evil manipulator who causes Judas to betray Christ, Lucifer is the jealous overreacher who wished to equal God. Just as Christ-God is all-knowing and all-seeing, so Lucifer believes that he knows all, and sees all that Christ does. Moreover, he seems to be able to penetrate Christ's thoughts, as he tells us: "In every hour I will know / What that Christ will be thinking and what he will be doing" (ll. 140–141). Yet despite these powers of mental telepathy, Lucifer finds a certain opacity in Christ; the devil cannot comprehend exactly who Christ is and where he comes from. For, as Paulina Lewin has pointed out, Lucifer's repeated statement, "I know" (six times in the opening speech) ironically points out what he does not know, and what he cannot comprehend with pure reason: the invincible strength of Christ. "The power—faith—is contrasted with verbose reason." [1]

Slovo o zbureniu pekla is structured as a series of many such contrasts, and reflects the central agon of the play, the conflict between good and evil.[2] St. John the Baptist, the most recent arrival in hell, takes on the main role of spokesman of the righteous and opposition to the devils. Other harrowing plays have each of the prophets speak in turn, a device which, while recalling past prophecies of the coming of Christ, results in repetitiousness and in a slackening of the play's tempo. The decision of the playwright of *Slovo o zbureniu pekla* to limit speaking roles has the effect of condensing and sharpening the conflict between good and evil.

The first crisis occurs approximately one-third of the way into the play (l. 226f), and concerns the disturbances which St. John the Baptist is causing in hell by his prophesying and preaching. Lucifer attempts to undercut the seriousness of the Baptist's words by treating him like a naughty child. "Johnny," unlike the other "children"—inhabitants of hell—refuses to sit quietly (ll. 250–251), but instead foretells the doom of the infernal princes. Lucifer's serio-comic conflict with the Baptist prefigures the final confrontation with Christ. While the devil is able to ignore the apocalytic notes of the Baptist's prophecies and makes fun of St. John, Hades is not so sanguine. The threat of Christ's imminent arrival and the rumours of His intended destruction of hell frighten Hades who proposes that Lucifer strengthen hell's fortifications. Unlike Hades, however, Lucifer appears to be unafraid of the son of a mortal woman.

A lack of complete knowledge does not prevent Lucifer from planning Christ's demise. Feeling slighted by the prophets and ignored by Adam and the angels who praise their Creator, Lucifer is delineated psychologically as a type of empire builder who is jealous of God. The Prince of Darkness finds it unjust that even though people have the devil's name on their lips more often than they do the name of the Creator, all glory is God's. Lucifer's plan to capture Christ's soul is thus not merely a plan to defeat a rival, but also is another bid for world power (and hence attention and glory): "But if we caught His soul, / Then we would be safe and not fear anyone in the world, / And I would be the lord of the whole world" (ll. 174–176). This notion is further underscored by Lucifer's explanation that it took him over 5,000 years to build up hell; like a proud feudal lord, he now refuses to bow to the might of one man and to give him tribute money.

Lucifer's clear recollection of his days in heaven, living in luxury, is then seen as a motive for regaining power by defeating the Son, rather than by equalling the Father—his past action for which he was thrown from heaven. In this bid for power is implicit the notion that the Father and the Son are one and the same, a notion not explored in the same way by other harrowing plays.

In the course of the play, Lucifer acts in part as field commander, readying his army, sending out his commanders, and awaiting dispatches from his scouts. His exchanges with Hades are long and reassuring. But as Hades' fear rises, and the tension increases, Lucifer appears to be less confident. The characterizaiton of Lucifer and Hades recalls the puppet theatre's (vertep) familiar stereotypes. Lucifer is the youngblood, the ambitious braggart who confidently asserts that his clever plan will destroy his rival, Christ. Hades is the senex, the old man who, it turns out, is not so foolish, since his fearful quakings are justified; hell is finally harrowed. Described as a rich village elder who has seen much in his time, and who has, like any careful landowner, watched over his hospodarstvo (holdings), Hades wishes to lose no particle of his holdings. Appearing to be almost as old as God himself, Hades' caution stems from experience. Recently, he has found that even a dead man, Lazarus, may be snatched from his realm. Old, cautious, and fearful of change, Hades is hence perhaps easily browbeaten by a more aggressive newcomer, Lucifer, the provincial governor, who has grand plans for hell. But Hades is also a figure personifying Death (another stock vertep type), who mows man down to increase his kingdom. These detailed psychological portraits have no precedent in other harrowing plays.

News from the upper-realm, the earth—and hence information about Christ's trial, crucifixion, and death—is conveyed by messengers who punctuate and increase the tension of the play by relating Christ's fortunes. This intelligence at first appears to be working toward fulfilling Lucifer's plan of ensnaring Christ's soul. The First, Second and Third Messengers follow each other in quick succession, all bringing reassuring news about the successful implementation of Lucifer's plan: Christ is now in chains, now on the cross, now awaiting imminent death. Lucifer begins to gloat, but Hades, hearing the prophets rejoicing, urges Lucifer to refuse to accept custody of Christ's soul. Thus, almost in Senecan fashion, the messengers of hell reveal that another action, the action of Holy Week is going on at the same time as the action we observe on stage: the confusion and mounting fear of the devils, and in particular of Hades and Lucifer.

In fact, the tribulations and nervous sufferings of Hades are referred to as his *strasty* or his passions (l. 203). We have, then, a mental picture of a type of diptych, only one half of which we actually see: the comic, earthly action which takes place on the lower or subterranean level, and the religious, spiritual action (which we hear about), and which takes place apparently literally above the stage action. The devil's "passion" is thus a type of dark parody of the serious, unseen action of the play.

The Fourth Messenger (l. 335) turns the tide by bearing frightening news of the angelic and natural world's response to the death of Christ. The messenger also has heard the angel's prophecy about the harrowing and Resurrection. The "terrifying" (l. 159) commanders Venera and Trubai reveal the disarray of the devilish forces when they return to hell, seeking advice about the awful calamity. Yet Lucifer continues to brazen it out. His speech (ll. 381–400) "Take to your arms, all my soldiers," is a traditional pep talk addressed to the troops, urging them not to fear, and to stand firm. A certain chivalry is apparent when the Prince of Darkness promises that he will fight "manfully . . . / Even if I were to lose the field" (ll. 379–380). Lucifer once again bases his arguments on logic, reminding the devils of their past successes in conquering all kings and queens.

Finally, the Last Messenger reports that Christ is proceeding to hell with a multitude of angels. Despite the news, Lucifer urges his devils to stand their ground. At the same time, he wonders what business this man, who might be the Son of God, has with them in hell. The servants' news of great miracles precede the coming of the Lord, who announces His presence with the words from Psalm 24. Lucifer's pleadings go unheeded, and Christ, after thrice reciting from the Psalm, proceeds to harrow hell. The gates and chains disintegrate and Christ enters as both warrior and priest, spoiling hell and exorcizing the evil spirits.

After Christ harrows hell and depopulates it, Hades and Lucifer weep. As a parting shot, Christ's voice is heard promising to fill the chasm of hell once more, a reminder both that the powers of hell have not been completely vanquished, and a warning to sinners to beware. The reference thus serves to bring us back to the cosmic frame of the opening speech. While Lucifer's opening speech of the play led us from the creation to the present, the ending of the play looks forward to the Apocalypse and to our part in it. The concluding song (which takes the place of the usual procession of the saints to heaven in other harrowing plays) joyfully celebrates the Resurrection. The play has thus moved through a threefold pattern of crisis, judgement, and salvation, and looks forward to a repetition of this same pattern with the Apocalypse.

NOTES

1 Paulina Lewin, "The Ukrainian Popular Religious Stage of the Seventeenth and Eighteenth Centuries on the Territory of the Polish Commonwealth," *Harvard Ukrainian Studies*, 1, No. 3 (1977), 310.

2 L.A. Sofronova, *Poetika slavianskogo teatra* [*Poetics of the Slavic Theatre*] (Moscow: Nauka, 1981), p. 12f, emphasizes the importance of the pattern of contrasts in baroque works.

About the Harrowing of Hell

(Slovo o zbureniu pekla)

a seventeenth-century Ukrainian verse play

[Dramatis personae

Lucifer
Hades
St. John the Baptist
First Messenger
Second Messenger
Third Messenger
Fourth Messenger
Last (fifth) Messenger
Commander Venera
Commander Trubai
Christ
Solomon
Servants to Lucifer
A multitude of angels]

Lucifer (to Hades):

Hades, I know many things about that Christ,
That He comes from the seed of David, that He is Mary's son,
Who calls Himself the Son of God
And also a man.
5 The prophets long since prophesy about that.
But they propagate this story only in vain.
From half six thousand years they assure us, and believe
That he is God and man,
But us they take for nothing.
10 Yet I have servants for my well-skilled matters,
Not only on earth, but also on bright clouds.
I also know what's happening at the ends of the world,
When God created earth and placed temporal existence on it.
In a single hour through my servants I have much news,
15 Thus I know what's happening under the heavens and in the sea
and under the earth.
About that Christ I have heard nothing at this time,
But still await reassuring news.
It would be a strange thing if God's Son were on earth.
20 I can't with my mind understand
From what causes
He could come about.
I know the Creator from time immemorial,
Living in heaven and with men,
25 I know the angels who serve God in heaven,
But Him who calls Himself the Son of God I cannot know.
Still from my servants on earth I have much news,
And thus I still await reassuring intelligence.
And those things that God created, I know them all,
But what it could be that calls itself the Son of God, that
30 I don't understand.
I, too, was a shining angel and lived in the clouds,
And while there, I carefully looked into everything;
I know what is happening there in the palaces of Eden,
But I greatly wonder at these things [happening now].
35 And I know that God created Adam from the earth,
And everything living that is on the earth,
And in paradise in the east He placed him,
So that he would praise God and his Creator on earth.

But I was very envious of that.
40 With a serpent I drove Adam and Eve out of their reason.
So that they transgressed the Lord's command—
To this did I lead them: that they sinned.
And when they sinned, they knew that they were naked,
And God did not want to suffer their sin.
45 He sent His angel and threw them from the bliss of paradise,
A bliss which cannot be comprehended with the mind.
And although Adam does have that comprehension,
From that time he works the earth
And in the sweat of his face he eats his bread.
50 This here is what they say,
But he doesn't know the end of the world.
At that time I rejoiced and laughed at him,
Because I led him to this. It serves him right,
Since he was punished this way.
55 And I waited for it [his punishment] a long time.
Moreover, I also know this:
That God has nine choirs of angels,
From whom in heaven He receives praise.
But I only thought to equal Him.
60 And for this I was presently thrown from heaven,
And there He placed me
Where I had been needed long before.
So also Adam sinned,
Who from the cursed tree ate the fruit,
65 From which tree the angel commanded him
That he not take [anything] into his hands.
But all this came about because of my intervention,
That he ate the fruit from the forbidden tree.
And I also strove to have
70 Adam bequeath me himself and his descendants.
And I incited Adam's own sons to this,
That Cain his brother Abel packed from the world.
And from that time I began to build hell
And to collect sinful souls from this earth.
75 And no one from his descendants obstructed me:
Adam, the first-created, I led into hell,
And having thus betrayed Adam,
I also led Abraham,

Isaac and Jacob and all twelve patriarchs,
80 I myself had no other troubles about them.
And tsars without number
And knights very mighty,
I gathered from the entire world,
Almost to this time.
85 Samson very strong
And King Alexander the mighty of the world.
Hell, my wonderful, my only joy,
Devoured sinners up to the narrow summit,
[Including] David the King, from whose tribe [is descended]
90 Jesus Christ, they say,
About which all the prophets teach the people.
But they debase my Lord Hades and all of us in hell,
Of whom [evil spirits] in my pits there are many,
And I always have many of them in my place.
95 But whoever will yet be with me,
He to the end of time won't forget me.
Johnny is here, and therefore so will be Christ himself.

Hades (to Lucifer):

Master Lucifer, Master Elder,
Even though you have a hundred thousand servants,
100 For some reason great thoughts trouble my mind,
And no small sufferings disturb me.
Let us take my advice, ignore that Christ,
And summon your servants,
And we will tell them to leave that Christ in peace,
105 That they don't bother Him, so that we, too, will have peace.
Because when we had Lazarus with us for four days,
And when He called him with one word only,
He chose him for a secret participant,
And pulled him from my sharp teeth,
110 And dulled my very sharp tools,
Which I had from time immemorial,
Although I didn't fight with Him.
And now I worry my head about this:
I'm afraid that I will be in bondage with you.

Lucifer (*to Hades*):

115 Don't alarm yourself, my Hades, my Benefactor,
You only are my first hope.
Who won't be at your place?
You will have Christ at your place.
Is He so terrifying, this Mary's son?
120 Look here, I will try to get an army
And I'll have a good fight with Him,
And I will try to find something against Him.
Now → Already I have set the Jews on Him, and they are in council,
So that they might invent false treason against Him.
125 To that we persuaded our delight, Judas,
So that he would betray Christ to a false court.
If He wants to be taken for a God,
Who is it that stands before Him [to defend Him]?
At this moment not a single apostle is seen with Him,
130 And even Mary is afraid to petition for Him.
I don't see Him, because He is afraid of me as well.
So about those twelve apostles of His
We won't be afraid,
Even if there were twenty thousand or so.
135 Soon the Jews will take the accusing side against Him,
And will ask help of us.
And I will dispatch my servants,
From whom I have well-disposed friendship.
And at any time we will have exact intelligence.
140 In every hour I will know
What that Christ will be thinking and what He will be doing.

Hades (*to Lucifer*):

Lucifer, O Elder, my good friend,
I beg you, keep a careful watch about my household.
Watch carefully! You know what you've gotten yourself into,
Because John the First Comer frightened our menials very
145 much.
But better let us not provoke this Christ!
From whence He is, we don't well know.
All my veins begin to shake,—
What is happening near us is not a joke!
For some reason I'm afraid that there may be some troubles

150 awaiting us,
    That we may lose our hellish structures.

Lucifer (*to Hades*):

    My Lord Hades, why are you so timid?
    Don't you see an army before you? But yet so fearful!
    Don't alarm me and my faithful servants,
155 Whom I also have in foreign lands,
    [And] with whom I have lived [these] many years.
    But, Hades, I have good hope that
    The soul of Christ I'll capture for myself.
    Presently, I will send with the army the terrifying commander
    Trubai,
160 And a second Venera; there let them run
    To the city of Jerusalem, to the great grove.
    May they carefully guard Christ,
    So that the angels don't take His soul to heaven.

Lucifer (*to his servants*):

    Hey, sirs, commanders! You, Lord Trubai,
165 And you, Venera, for this I summon you:
    That we will take some counsel,
    So that the angels don't betray us by taking Christ's soul.
    And so that we may now take counsel well
    And the soul of that Jesus not let into heaven.
170 Because the Jews certainly mean to crucify Him,
    For which they are diligently striving.
    And we must also try to do this diligently,
    So that we can capture His soul for ourselves.
    But if we caught His soul,
175 Then we would be safe and not fear anyone in the world,
    And I would be lord of the whole world.
    Now run carefully,
    But guard His soul with vigilance.
    Wherever that Jesus should turn, we must know about it;
180 Because He says that for us they are just a joke.
    May you catch that Jesus,
    And quickly let me know about it.

Lucifer (to Hades):

> Already, Hades, I've sent after Jesus my faithful servants
> Venera and Trubai, by no means weak commanders.
> 185 And when they drum,
> At that time they will lead His soul.
> And we won't allow angels in here.
> Let us not give them a free hand,
> So that they won't betray us
> 190 And lead His soul on to heaven.
> Don't fear, Hades, my dear lord!
> Why are you so very downcast?
> I haven't yet been negligent in your household,
> In all the time I passed, not a little time in cheer.
> 195 Don't be afraid of Mary's son! (If He's a man,
> He won't do anything to us, ever.
> And I'm always, to the end, with you,
> Ready even to the field of battle;
> And Hell, that is my capital,
> 200 Where my right hand will take care of Him.
> If He were God's Son, He wouldn't suffer torments,
> He wouldn't give Himself up to the hands of the Jews.

Hades (to Lucifer):

> I already see my sufferings and lament,
> Although I don't hear any attack.
> 205 My stomach is tight,
> And my vision is hazy.
> My stomach feels something, but it says naught—
> Probably, once that Jesus arrives, He will tie us all up.

Lucifer (to Hades):

> What, Hades, why are you crying so and growling,
> 210 Why do you curse all the days that you have lived?

Hades (to Lucifer):

> O Elder Lucifer, close hell with a guard
> So no soul will escape from it.
> And there from all sides put up brazen gates,
> And lock them with strong iron chains
> 215 Pulled tightly.

And with very hard locks
Close them well!
I have a thousand thousand forces under arms;
Perhaps so many don't accompany Christ.

Lucifer (to Hades):

220 Don't fear, my lord!
I will fight as well as I can with Him,
Until the bones in one of us break into ten pieces. ✓
And I won't allow Him to approach.
I am only waiting for messengers—
225 And await the first news.

St. John the Baptist (to Hades):

Be sorrowful, Hades, cry and lament for eternity,
When God and man comes to us!
You prepared hell, a prison, for us. } irony
This time it is [meant] for you.
230 Together with your servants
You will be under God's feet.
Rise, David, and strike on your strings,   icon?- of David.
And praise God and your Creator!
He will surely be with us,
235 And will not go forth without us.

Lucifer (to St. John the Baptist):

Wait a bit, John, don't praise your Christ just yet,
And don't glorify that Jesus.
Both you and your Jesus will be here with us,
And he who is stronger, he will win from amongst us.
And you won't be allowed to wriggle out of it, no matter
240 how you play pranks
With Him, for Whom I prepared the way.
For you are John, you are called the preacher of penitence,
But you are Jesus' own adulator.
You are something of family to Him,
245 Which is why you interrupt us about Him.
Why did you trouble my prisoners,
Vainly repeating this tale to them?
Would God were with you when you were born,

So that you wouldn't spread such news!
250 Why do the other saints sit quietly?
Where did you find trouble here?
What do you mean, Jesus is going to come into hell
And take all my prisoners from me?
You will never live to see that,
255 You are just spreading that glory in vain.
And will you stand here a long time yet,
And each time will you speak of Christ?
And until when will you, John, be preaching,
And each time be prophesing about that Christ?
260 O, why do you prophesy so much, my little brother?
Give him some tar to drink and infernal *kvass*!
So come on over here, don't preach any more,
Don't give my friends or me any more dread!
Because we don't even fear His sign,
265 And don't pay attention to His Godhead.
I know that God is in heaven,
For whom the angels sing "Glory to you!"
But here on earth you don't have God in the flesh,
But you prophesy about Him, yet you yourself don't know Him,
270 [You] only call upon Him for help.
God rules in heaven with the angels,
But my glory spreads over the whole world,
And all people have my name on their tongues,
And solicit me more often than God.
275 And I will, upon request, carry these [things] out,
And will love him who will do my deeds.
And for that I will show him my rich grace.
More than one will I place in the infernal fire,
And will show them for this my rich grace.
280 More than one beaker of infernal *kvass* will I give them.
And you, John, go on to hell, don't cry any more,
Don't help your friends in their sorrow.
I see that you are making mischief,
And understand that you are getting ready to flee from here.
285 Oh, you won't escape from me, my knight, my little bird!
We're not afraid of that, Johnny.
It seems that Jesus will be with us, and so will you—
In this our pit. (*John withdraws*)

First Messenger (*runs in and says*):

    Master Hades, and you our Master Elder—
290 And where is there a greater than you?
    The commanders Venera and Trubai sent me:
    Don't be afraid for a minute.
    All that you wanted, and requested, was carried out,
    And they dressed that Christ in chains.
295 The Jews lead Him from council to council.
    Not once does anyone tell Him the truth.
    I heard from the Jews that He will be led out of the city,
    And I know well that they are preparing a loving place for
    Him.

Second Messenger (*runs in and says*):

    Thus already, our Master Hades, the Jews have nailed Christ
    to the cross,
300 Pierced His hands and feet with iron nails.
    He won't live, that is certain truth,
    But we will live forever safe with you.
    The commanders sent me to tell you this,
    So that your joy would immediately be augmented.

Third Messenger (*runs up and says*):

305 So, our Master Hades, Christ is now dying.
    He bows His head to the cross.
    The Jews scourged His whole body,
    And pierced His side with a spear.
    They gave Him vinegar with gall to drink,
310 And treated Him with [such] spices, seasonings.
    Our commanders remained behind there,
    So that they could take His soul and bring it here,
    According to our agreement.

Lucifer (*to Hades*):

    You see, Hades, what news I have,
315 To what shame Mary's son has been put?
    Already the Jews have nailed Him to the cross,
    And pierced His side with a spear,
    And placed a wreath of thorns upon His head.
    But we need to apply diligent efforts concerning His soul,

320 So that we will catch His soul in our nets.

Hades (*to Lucifer*):

      My advice—look at my old head—
      Is this:
      Don't take the soul of Christ,
      Don't even take custody of it,
325 So that for one
      Much is not lost.
      Let His soul go to heaven,
      We don't need it here.
      For all the prophets have risen and are rejoicing,
330 They hear of His arrival from the Holy Spirit.
      This must be the true God.
      For a single soul we will have to spew up all,
      For I see our end is near,
      And the leadership which we have now will be gone tomorrow.

Fourth Messenger (*runs up and says*):

335 So, Christ has surely died,
      And I saw Him not long ago, but just now.
      But when His soul left His body,
      More than one body fainted there,
      And we were all frightened,
340 And fled far away from it.
      We wanted to catch His soul,
      But we saw that it was frightening to approach it closely.
      Angelic armies encircled it,
      And didn't admit us to it.
345 The earth trembled, so much so that cliffs crumbled.
      There was, and is still, a great dismay.
      The sun and moon turned to blood.
      And many of the dead rose from their graves;
      And these, out of great fright, fell to the ground,
350 And lay [there] for three hours;
      They didn't get up quickly.
      And we, already filled with fear,
      Are returning to hell, taking up arms.
      And we heard a voice from the angels, which said
      That on the third day Christ will be resurrected, and He

355 will come to us,
And is certain to take all prisoners from us.

Commanders Venera and Trubai (say):

Our great Master Hades, and you, Master Elder Lucifer,
It is certain that Christ comes directly to us.
We wanted to take His soul,
360 But God's powers wouldn't allow us to approach it.
Oh, what calamity! We saw unbearable horror,
Lightning and great thunder.
It seems indeed that Christ is the true and the same Christ
Lord,
For no one could work such miracles but He.
365 We came here into hell to take counsel:
What to do with this Christ and how do we live through this?
For He will certainly come here to us,
And is supposed to take all saints, beginning with Adam,
from us.

Lucifer (says to his servants):

Well, I will defend myself as best as I can,
370 Because it doesn't please me to flee from my dominion.
If He is God's Son, let Him rule in heaven,
Let Him not battle with us and with hell.
For I would be ashamed if I had to bow to Him,
And give tribute when I raised myself.
375 I endured for five thousand years, almost to the end of time,
And now I'm to give myself up to the power of one man?
I will await Him on the field of battle, with you, Hades,
And if He's a man, then I don't fear Him.
And I will fight manfully with Him,
380 Even if I were to lose the field.
Take to your arms, all my soldiers,
And, should fear come upon you, don't be disheartened;
Stand bravely against Him,
And I will stand boldly behind you with yet another army.
385 So quickly close the iron gates,
And raise the moat bridge, and strengthen it with chains,
And close them with strong and hard locks!
Because it is certain that Christ will come,

But the stronger one will go forth.

390 As for you, may your hearts not faint from fear,
So that you don't all flee from Christ,
But take to Him boldly,
All stand against Him.
Yet I know that fighting isn't new to you,
And that you have taken on more than such knights on the
395 field of battle,
And fought with them and ruled them all.
And all the kings and queens did not escape our grasp,
But you yourselves see that they are here in hell.
So, don't be anxious,
400 And don't fear that Christ.
I still await the last messenger,
And the arrival of Christ on the battlefield.

The Last Messenger (*runs up and says*):

Master Hades, and you, Master Elder Lucifer,
I report to you that Christ is coming directly to us.
405 A terrifying King and a multitude of angels,
Seraphim are with Him and His Godhead.
We could do nothing against [even] a single angel.
Christ Himself and His speech alone were terrifying to hear.
We ran to hell to let you know.
410 How can we live through this?

(*They see the banners of Christ and become frightened.*)

Lucifer (*has his banners brought to him and says to his servants*):

There He is, coming to us! Watch carefully,
And hold your weapons tightly in your hands.
And when they come to you, reply ferociously,
And strongly hold up the doors with your backs.
415 And if they break, kill the angels.
Don't let Him come here! Don't spare anyone,
Because nothing here
Will be left after Him.
If He is God's Son,
420 Let Him sit in heaven.
And let Him not go do battle with us and with hell.

If He is God's Son,
I don't know for what reasons He comes here.
He doesn't have any business with us.
425 And I cannot understand what King of Glory this is.

St. John (to Lucifer):

Ah, so you haven't heard from us, from my lips,
About the King of Glory, the one about whom I prophesied?
Not only I, but also all the prophets,
Not only the prophets, but also all the patriarchs—all ages
foretell that.

Lucifer (to St. John):

430 I know, John, that God did all this,
Not that King of Glory
About whom you prophesied!
And I know an enthroned God,
And I don't understand about the [one] here on earth:
435 From whence could He come to be on earth?
That I can't comprehend with my reason.

Then *Lucifer (to his servants says):*

Hey, young sirs! Let your hearts not be frightened,
Let not all the army flee from that Christ!
Stand boldly,
440 And let no one flee from the field of battle!
Be fierce with Him, and take to the doors, loudly crying,
With the cry cause Him fear.
Because I understand thusly: if you don't make an uproar,
Then He won't do battle with us.
445 But if He calls, asking for prisoners,
I wouldn't begrudge Him ten.
Gladly would I confer with Him,
But I fear another's fire . . . Because I have not read anywhere,
450 Nor have heard from wise people
Who this King of Glory might be.
That one doesn't have any business with us,
He who is supposed to come fiercely to us
And destroy our hell!

Servants (say to Hades):

455 So, our Lord Hades, already we've seen great miracles.
It's true, our Judas also arranged things [for Him] very
quickly; however,
[Christ] worked miracles not only in Jerusalem, but
everywhere.
The dead were resurrected, the sick were brought to health,
But He drove us far away from Him with His word.

(Then Christ Himself comes in and says):

460 The Lord is mighty in battle!
Lift up your gates, O you princes,
And be lifted up, O eternal gates,
And the King of Glory shall enter in.

Lucifer (to Jesus says):

I ask you in a kind manner, O Christ,
Give me peace, and do not disturb me any more.
465 If you are God, take praise from the apostles
And glory from your angels,
And do not call on me and my gate-keepers any more.

Then *Christ (blesses the gates with a gonfalon and says again):*

The Lord is strong and mighty in battle!
Be lifted up, O eternal gates,
470 And the King of Glory shall enter in.

Lucifer (cries out to Christ):

Once again I ask you, Christ, do not despoil me or my hell,
Because You will not be able to befoul anything!
If You are God, stay there in paradise,
I do not need You here.

*(And a third time Christ says and strikes with a gonfalon; he
strikes so hard that the gates crumble.):*

475 Now the King of Glory enters through you.
The Lord is mighty, He is the King of Glory.
*(And while He makes the sign of the cross three times, then
the gates and the chains disintegrate, and Christ enters
hell, and illuminates it with His bright rays, and blesses*

all *infernal places*, and *He sprinkles holy water* [imbuing
hell] with the Holy Spirit.)

Hades (*cries*):

    Help, help, sirs! They are breaking the gates,
    And sprinkle us with some potent water!

Lucifer (*says to Christ*):

    Why do You wreck my secure gates?
480 It is certain that You want to take my prisoners away.
    Why do You violate me so, O Son of God,
    And why take my prisoners with You,
    Those whom I have gathered for myself from time immemorial?

Hades:

    And now You have harrowed hell and laid waste the capital, ⨯ᵉ⁰
485 And have tied me, Hades, with eternal knots,—
    What am I to do now?
    You have already taken my prisoners, that I know for certain.
    You have spoiled my eternal palaces,
    And laid waste all of my hell,
490 And us you took and trampled underfoot.
    Adam and Eve and all the saints you took with you.

Lucifer (*says*):

    I can barely sit—except for fear alone—
    Yet, as in the old days, I see before me a single righteous
    man.
    I ask you, Solomon, why did you stay behind here?
495 It seems that Christ presented me with you.

Solomon (*to Lucifer says*):

    Christ will come a second time for me; S. left behind
    Terrible was His first coming,
    Even more terrible will be the second.

Lucifer (*says to his servants*):

    My servants, take King Solomon,
500 Lead him out of hell!
    I don't regret [losing] him,

Nor that Christ,
Let Him not come here any more
To alarm us and our hell.

(*At this point the devils take Solomon and lead him out of hell,
and say thus to Christ and Solomon*):

Devils (*say*):

505 Go, go after your Christ, and don't stay here,
And don't stir us or our hell up any more.

(*Solomon, jumping joyfully, begins to sing; Lucifer and Hades cry
and weep.*)

Christ (*says to him*):

Do not weep, Hades, I will fill [hell] with beer on the
last day,
You will have as much as you had.

Solomon (*begins to praise the Trinity and the Virgin Mother of God*):

Most blessed art thou, O Virgin Birth-Giver of God,
510 [For through] Him who became incarnate of thee
Hell is led captive,
Adam is recalled [from the dead],
The curse is made void,
Eve is set free,
515 Death is brought to death,
And we have been endowed with life.
Wherefore let us sing aloud:
Blessed art Thou, O Christ our God,
Who willed this. Glory to Thee.

Slovo o zbureniu pekla

ehda Khrystos ot mertvykh

vstavshy peklo zburyl

(About the Harrowing of Hell,

When Christ, Having Risen

From the Dead, Harrowed Hell)

Ukrainian text as first published by Ivan Franko in *Zapysky Naukovoho Tovarystvo im. T. H. Shevchenka*, 81 (1908), 5–50 (ll. 1–421), and in *Kievskaia starina*, 53 (1896), 380–412 (ll. 398–428). Later reprinted, with minor changes, by V. Rezanov (1926).

СЛОВО О ЗБУРЕНЮ ПЕКЛА,

єгда Хрⷭтосъ Ѿ мртвыхъ вставши пекло збурилъ.

Люциперъ (мовитъ до Яда)

Знаю я, Яде, ѡ томъ Хрⷭтѣ много причинъ,
Ижъ ѡнъ єстъ Ѿ колѣна Давидова Маріинъ синъ,
Который самъ себе синомъ божнимъ йменуетъ
Й человѣкомъ також називаетъ.
Ѻ томъ пророци здавна пророкуютъ
Й повѣстъ тую тилко дармо розмножуютъ,
Ѿ полшости тисящи лѣтъ запевнаютъ,
Єго быти Богомъ и человѣкомъ вызнавают,
Я нашихъ собѣ за ницо мают.
Яле южъ маю слугъ къ справахъ моихъ вѣглихъ
Не тилко на земли, але й на ѡблакахъ свѣтлихъ;
Знаю я, що ся дѣе й на край свѣта,
Коли Богъ ѡсновалъ землю и положилъ на неи дочаснїе лѣта.
Такъ подъ некомъ и в морахъ й под землею що ся дѣе знаю,
В їединой годинѣ през слуги свои много новинъ маю.
Я ѡ томъ Хрⷭтѣ и разъ не знаю,
Но вѣсти певнои еще ѡжидаю.
Дивная би то рѣчъ була, їжъ би билъ на земли Бжїй [сйⷩъ,
Не могу тое изъ свого разуму понати,
С которыхъ би ся причинъ
Ѻнъ моглъ взяти.
Знаю Творца еще пред вѣки
Живого въ небѣ й со человѣки,
Знаю й аⷢгли, йжъ служатъ къ небѣ Бгу,
Я того, що ся йменуетъ сыномъ божимъ, [знати не могу].
Еще й на земли Ѿ слугъ своихъ много новинъ маю,
Я тамъ еще певной вѣдомости ѡжидаю.
Я я тїи справи, що Бгъ сотворилъ, всѣ знаю,
Я що ся йменуетъ Сномъ бжїимъ, того не разумѣваю.
Й я билемъ аⷢгломъ свѣтлимъ й на ѡблацехъ жилъ,
Й до всего ся тамъ приглядѣлъ;

Знаю,   що ся дѣетъ и во едемскихъ палацахъ,
Але барзо дивѹю ся ѿ тихъ рѣчахъ.
И знаю, що Бг҃ъ Адама создалъ   ѿ землѣ
И все живое,   еже ест наверхъ   землѣ;
И в рай на востоцѣ его посадилъ,
Абы на землѣ Бг҃а и Творца своего хвалилъ.
Але ѧ́   томѹ барзо   позавидѣлъ,
Адама и Евѹ оурежемъ из розѹмѹ извѣлъ,
Ижъ божню заповѣдъ прест̓ѹпили, —
На тое-мъ привѣлъ, что изгрѣшили.
А гди згрѣшили, познали ся нагими.
И Бг҃ъ имъ   не хотѣлъ того грѣха терпѣти,
Послалъ аг҃гла своего и вигналъ ихъ из райской роскоши,
Которои роскоши и розѹмомъ не понѧти.
[И хочъ Адамъ]   розѹмъ тотъ маетъ,
А   ѿ того часѹ землю дѣлаетъ
И въ потѣ лица свой хлѣбъ снѣдаетъ.
Тѹю то ѿповѣдаютъ вѣсть,
Но ѡнъ скончены свѣта не вѣсть.
В той часъ возрадовалемъ ся и смѣꙗлемся з него,
Жемъ го привѣлъ на тое   — барзо добре на него,
Скоро ѡнъ тое ѿтримⷶлъ,
А ѧ̀ того давно ѡжидалъ.
Албо тижъ   и тое знаю,
Ижъ девꙗть хоровъ аг҃гловъ   Бг҃ъ маетъ,
Ѿ которихъ на небѣ   хвалѹ приймаетъ.
А ꙗ тїлко помислилъ ровнати ся з нимъ,
И за тое заразъ стрѹченъ есмь изъ неба,
И тамъ мꙗ посадилъ.
Где мнѣ давно было потреба.
Такъ тижъ и Адамъ согрѣшилъ,
Же ѿ древа заказаного ѿвоцѹ ѣлъ,
Ѿ которого древа ангелъ емѹ заповѣлъ,
[Абы] ани въ рѹки свои не бралъ.
Але то ся все стало з моеи причини,
Ижъ ѿ древа заповѣданнаго ѿвоцѹ ѣли.
И ещемъ ся ѡ то стаⷬⷶлъ,
Абы ся мнѣ Адамъ с потомствомъ   записⷶлъ.
А ꙗ то Адамовѣ синни родние повадилъ,
Же Каинъ Авелꙗ брата своего изъ свѣта изгладилъ.

Й ѿ того часꙋ зачаѧемъ пекло   бꙋдовати
Й дꙋши грѣшнїи из сего свѣта ꙗзбирати.
Изъ всѣхъ потомковъ нѣхто мнѣ не завадилъ:
Ꙗдама первозданна [ш в пекло] спровадилъ,

Й [зрадившꙑ]   такь Ꙗдама,
Запровадилъ и Ꙗврама,
Исаака й Іꙗкова и всѣхъ дванадесꙗтъ патрїарховъ,
Тамъ мнѣ не било ѿ нихъ иншихъ страховъ.

Й царей незличонихъ
Й рицеровъ барзо моцнихъ
Назбиралемъ ѿ всего свѣта
Не мало ажъ до сего лѣта.

Самсона барзо дꙋжаго
И цра Ꙗлександра всего свѣта можнаго.
Пекло, моꙗ слѣчнаꙗ потѣха едина
Грѣшниковъ ажъ до верхꙋ оузкаго пожерла.

И Двда цра, с которого племꙗ Исꙋса Хрта повидлютъ,
О чемъ вси пророци людъ наꙋчаютъ,
Ꙗ пана моего Ꙗда й насъ всѣхъ въ пеклѣ понижаютъ.
Которыхъ во ѿхланꙗхъ моихъ повно,
Й завше оу мене ихъ есть много.
Ꙗ хтожъ оу мене еще бꙋдетъ,
Той до скончаниꙗ вѣка мене не забꙋдетъ.
Іѡанко [есть], а потомꙋ и самъ Христосъ оу мене бꙋдетъ.

Ꙗдъ до Люципера мовитъ:

Пане Люциперꙋ, пане старосто,
Хочъ оу тебе самого слꙋгъ тисꙗщъ [зо] сто,
Чемꙋсь мнѣ гадки великие головꙋ здоймлютъ
Й фрасꙋнки не малие мене стросклютъ.
Зажиймо ми поради, а Хрта того занихаймо,
Й слꙋгъ своихъ к себѣ заволаймо.
Й скажемо ми йм, аби томꙋ Хртꙋ дали покой,
Жеби его не зачипали, жеби и намъ билъ оупокой.
Бо гди мѣлемъ Лазара четвероднєвнаго оу себе,
Ꙗ гди ѡнъ его еднимъ словомъ своимъ заволалъ,
[Собѣ его] за таемника [ꙋбобралъ],
Й оу мене из зꙋбовъ ѡстрихъ вирвалъ,
Й мое барзо ѡстрое ѡрꙋжїе притꙋпилъ,
Котороє ꙗ себѣ ѿ вѣка мѣлъ,

Хоча ємъ ся изъ нимъ не билъ.
Й теперъ ла тимъ клопочу голову свою:
Бою ся, жеби   мнѣ не бути в неволи с тобою.

Люциперъ до Яда мовитъ:

Не трекожъ ся, Яде мой   й добродѣю!
Тилко ти оу мене першла надѣла.
Хто вже не буде оу тебе?
Ти будешъ мѣти Христа оу себе.
Єслижъ то такъ страшенъ   Марїинъ сынъ?
Ово й ла ш воиско постараю ся
Й добре вибю ся зъ нимъ,
Й буду шукати на него лакихъ причинъ.
Оуже напустилъ ла   на него жидовъ, и воишли оу радъ,
Яби на него найшли фальшивую зраду.
Й до того подмовилемъ своего оутѣшителла Иоудъ,
Яби видалъ Исуса   до фалшиваго суду.
Бо гдижъ чинитъ ся Богомъ бити,
Я хтожъ передъ нимъ стоитъ [его воронити]?
Теперъ при немъ не видно и жадного апостола,
Й Марїла боит ся за нимъ причинити.
Не вижу ла его, бо ся шнъ и мене боитъ.
Й ш тихъ апостоловъ его дванадцлать
Не будемо волазливими,
Хочъ би било йхъ тислщъ килка-двадцать.
Ш заразъ будутъ на него жиди сторону ймѣти
Й насъ ш помощъ барзо просити.
Н попущлю ла слугъ своихъ,
Ш которихъ маю прилазнь прихилную,
Й въ кождой годинѣ будемъ мати вѣдомость вѣрную.
Б каждой годинѣ буду знати,
Що той Ісъ будетъ оумѣти й що будетъ дѣлати.

Ядъ до Люципера мовитъ:

Люциперу,   старосто, мой добрий друже,
Прошу тла, коло господарства моего пилнуй дуже!

Пилнуй добре! Знаеш, на що-с ся поднялъ,
Бо Іwанъ Предитеча слугъ нашихъ дуже полыкалъ.
Яле радше того Хр҃ста не зачѣпаймо!
ЮкудУ есть, того добре не знаемо.
Бо мой оусѣ жили починають дрижати,
Либой коло насъ не жарти!
Я чемУсь вою ся, абы мнѣ не было якихъ страховъ,
Якисмо не оутратили пекелнихъ нашихъ гмаховъ.

Люципер до Яда мовитъ:

Пане мой Яде, чемУ еси такъ барзо боязливый?
Не вачишъ передъ собою войска? Я такъ лыкавый!
Не тривожъ мене и моихъ слугъ вѣрнихъ,
Которихъ маю й оу сторонахъ чУжихъ.
Якъ-ймъ из ними лѣта долгіи прожилъ.
Яле Яде, добрУ я надѣю маю,
Дш҃У Хр҃стовУ сѣѣ понимаю.
Заразъ пошлю з войскомъ старшого воеводу Трувам,
Й другаго Венеру, тамъ нехай вѣгаютъ
Под мѣсто Єрусалимъ до великаго гаю,
Яби Хр҃ста пилно стрегли,
Жеби аггли дш҃ѣ его до неба не взяли.

Люциперъ до слугъ своихъ мовитъ:

Гей панове воеводи, ти пане Трувaю,
Й ти Венеро, wто я дла того васъ до себе воллю,
Жебисмо зажили яковой порадн,
Щобъ з Хр҃стовою дш҃ею аггли не оучинили зради.
Й щовисмо ся теперъ добре порадили,
Й того Іс҃а дш҃ѣ до неба не пустили.
Бо его жиди конечне разпяти мають
Й w тое ся пилно стараютъ.
Й намъ ся w тое пилно треба старати,
Яби смо до себе дш҃У его могли поймати.
Я гди бисмо его душу до себе поймали,

То бисмо били безпечни и нѣкого на свѣтѣ сıа не бояли,
Й ıа билъ би паномъ всего свѣта.

Теперъ же безпечне вѣжѣте,
Я дшꙋ его пилно стережѣте;
Кꙋди сıа той Іс҃ повернетъ, треба намъ ѿ томъ знати;
Вѣкнъ во кажетъ, що из ними и намъ жарти.
Явисте того Іс҃а поймали,
Й мнѣ ѿ томъ рихло   знати дали.

Люциперъ мовитъ до Яда:

Южемъ, Яде, послалъ по Іс҃а слꙋгъ своихъ вѣрнихъ,
Венерꙋ и Трꙋбла, воеводъ немалихъ.
Я гди бꙋдꙋтъ бꙋкнити,
В той часъ дꙋшꙋ его бꙋдꙋтъ провадити.
Я ми сюди аг҃гловъ не допꙋскаймо,
Потꙋхи ймъ не даваймо,
Яби насъ не зрадили
Й дшꙋѣ его до неба не запровадили.
Не бой сıа, Яде, пане мой милий!
Чемꙋ   естес такъ барзо ꙋнилий?
Еще ıа к господарствѣ твоемъ не ѿспалый
Й весь вѣкъ въ радости пробꙋвъ часъ немалий.
Не бой сıа Марїина сина! Гди ѿнъ   человѣкъ,
Не вчинитъ намъ нѣчого во вѣкъ.
Я ıа завше до конца   с токою
Готовъ хочъ на плацъ до бою;
Я пекло, то моıа столица,
Где рачитъ   его моıа правица.
Гди би ѿнъ билъ бж҃їй сн҃ъ, не терпѣлъ би ѿнъ   мꙋки,
Не видавалъ   би ѿнъ себе въ жидовскїе рꙋки.

Ядъ до Люципера мовитъ:

Южъ ıа бачꙋ страсть свою   й ламентꙋю.
Хочъ еще жаднон навалности   не чꙋю.
Животъ мон древнѣе
Й в очахъ моихъ мрїе;
Животъ   чꙋетъ, тилко не скажетъ,
Подобно той Іс҃ъ   пришедши всѣхъ насъ повıажетъ.

Люциперъ до Яда мовитъ:

Що, Яде, по томъ, що такъ плачешъ и проницлешъ?

Що еси прожикъ, то всѣ днѣ свои проклинаешъ.

Ѧдъ до Люципера мовитъ:

О старосто Люциперꙋ, стражею затвори пекло,
Живи жадной душѣ з него не втекло.
Ѧ тамъ изо всѣхъ сторонъ мѣдѧнне ворота поставми,
И заткори желѣзними ланцухами
Моцними стигни,
И твердими колодками
Барзо замкни!
И тисѧцꙋ тисѧцъ маю войска збройного,
Може й с Хрⷭ҇томъ не ходитъ такъ много.

Люциперъ до Ѧда мовитъ:

Не ꙋжаслй сѧ, Ѧде, пане мой!
Буду сѧ такъ мога изъ нимъ бити,
Поки едному [з насъ] кости на десать сѧ не розпадутъ,
И не дамъ до себе приступити.
Тилко пословъ ѡчѣккую
И вѣсти перкой ѡжидаю.

Стⷯй Іѡанъ Креститель мовитъ до Ѧда:

Смути сѧ, Ѧде, плачъ й лѧментуй ко вѣкъ,
Гди йдетъ до насъ Богъ и человѣкъ!
Готовалъ еси на насъ пекло, виѧзенѧ,
Которое тобѣ будетъ въ сіе времѧ.
Веспол изъ слугами твоими
Будете под ногами божими.
Востани, Давиде, й к струни вдарай,
Ѧ Творца своего й Бга вихвалѧй!
Ото будетъ запевне по насъ
И не пойдетъ ѡсюду безъ насъ.

Люциперъ мовитъ до стго Іѡана Хрⷭ҇телѧ:

Постой, Іѡане, еще сѧ своимъ [Іⷭ҇омъ] не вихвалѧй
И того Іса не прославлѧй.
И ти тутъ будешъ и твой Іⷭ҇ будетъ ꙋ насъ,
Ѧ хто дужшїй, той сѧ виграетъ з мижи насъ.
И ти сѧ не вифиглюешъ, хоч кнс ѧкъ фиглокалъ
С тимъ, которому ѧ дорогу готовалъ.
Бо еси Іѡанъ, зовутъ тѧ покаѧнию проповѣдникъ,

Але ти власній Ісусовъ похлѣбникъ.
Ти естесь   ему щось за родина,
Що така твоя ш . немъ зъ нами перепина.
Для чогожъ ти вязневъ моихъ потривоживъ,
Же имъ еси повѣсть тую   дармо розможивъ?
Щобъ бу тебе Бгъ кувъ, коли би ти сѧ народивъ,
Щобись намъ тїи вѣсти не множилъ!
Чому инши стїии сидатъ тихо?
Гдесь й тобѣ оу насъ прийшло лихо.
Якъ, то, тутъ маетъ Іс̃ъ до пекла буступлати
И всѣхъ моихъ вязневъ ѿ мене взяти?
Ти того   нѣс'ди не дочекаешь,
Тилко славу тую дурно розможляешъ.
Я долго ще ти тутъ будешъ стояти,
Я щоразъ то болш ш Хрⷭ̃тѣ повѣдати?
Я докиж ти, Іwане, будешъ практиковати,
Я щоразъ то болше ш томъ Хрⷭ̃тѣ пророковати?
О, що ти такъ богато пророкуешъ, [пташку]?
Дайте ему смоли напити сѧ й пекелного кваску!
Я ходи но ти сюда, болше не проповѣдай,
Товаришу моему й мнѣ   страху не задавай!
Бо ми сѧ и знаку его не боимо
И на божество его не глядимо.
Знаю я, же естъ Богъ въ небѣ,
Которому спѣвлютъ аг̃гли: „Слава тебѣ!"
Але тутъ на земли въ тѣлѣ Бога не маешъ,
Я ти ш немъ пророкуешъ и самъ его не знаешь,
Тилко его на помощъ признвлешъ.
Бо Богъ к небѣ со аг̃гли   панѣетъ,
Я моя слава по всемъ свѣту   роскошуетъ;
И мене люде всѣ на язицѣ носятъ
И колше нижли   Бога ш що просятъ.
Я я ведлугъ прозби ихъ буду   чинити,
Я хто мои бучинки чинитъ, буду его любити.
Я за тое имъ шбфитую ласку покажу:
Не едного к wгонь пекелнїй бусажу,
И покажу имъ за тое шбфитую ласку.
Не единъ бо им дам киляя пекелного кваску.
Я ти, Іwане. пойди въ адъ,   болше не волай,
Товариству своему въ смутку   не помагай.
Вижу я, же ти то   фиґлюешъ

И розумѣю, же ти ѿтоль ѹтекти сѧ готуешъ.
Ой не ѹвойдешъ ѿ мене, рицерѹ Пашкѹ!
Ми того не ѹбоймо сѧ, Иваншкѹ.
Подобно ѹ насъ той Їсъ будє, и ти будешъ из нами
Въ той нашой тамѣ. (Іван відходить.)

О т о ж ъ   п о с е л ъ   п е р в ы й   в и ж и т ъ   и   м о в и т ъ :

Панє Ѧде и ти панє старосто нашъ,
Ѧ гдижъ над тебе волшого немашъ!
Послали мене воєводи Венера й Трубай:
Ничого сѧ ни разъ не лѧкай!
Ѧ що еси хотѣлъ их просилъ, то все поѡрѹдовали
И Хр̃ста того ѹ ланцухи поѹбирали;
Водѧтъ его жиди ѿ ради до ради,
Нихто ему не дастъ и разъ правди.
Чулємъ ѿ жидовъ, ижъ ведєнъ будетъ за мѣсто,
И знаю добре, ижъ готуютъ на него лобное мѣсто.

П о с е л ъ   в т о р і й   п р и в ѣ г л е   й   м о в и т ъ :

Ото южъ, панє Ѧде нашъ, жиди Хр̃ста на крестѣ при-
И желѣзними звоздами рѹци и нози пробили.   [били
Южъ не будетъ живъ, то правда конечне,
Ѧ ми будемо с тобою жити на вѣки безпечне.
Послали мене воєводи повидати,
Ѧби токѣ заразъ радостъ тую примножати.

П о с е л ъ   т р е т й   п р и б и г л е   й   м о в и т ъ :

Отожъ, панє нашъ Ѧде, южъ Хр̃тосъ оумираетъ,
На хрестѣ главу свою прикланяетъ.
Жиди все тѣло его бичами избили
И копнемъ бокъ его пробили;
Ѡцтомъ со жолчію [его] напоили
И приправами, присѣками его частовали.
Остали сѧ тамъ нашѣ воєводи,
Ѧби дiйѹ его взѧвши принесли сюди
На нашие оугоди.

Л ю ц и п е р ъ   д о   Ѧ д а   м о в и т ь :

Видишъ, Ѧде, такую маю новину,
Що сѧ стало презрѣне Мариину сн̃у.

Южъ жиди на крестѣ его прибили
И бокъ ему копнемъ пробили ,
И терновий винецъ на главу вложили.
Я намъ потреба ѿ душѣ его пилное старанѭ мѣти,
Яки дшу его поймати во свою сѣти.

Идѣ до Люципера мовитъ:

Моѭ рада такаѭ
И голова стараѭ:
Дшѣ Христовой не вѣрѣте
Янѣ ей стережѣте,
Цобъ для едного
Не ѹтратити много.
Нехай дша его идетъ до неба,
Я намъ ей тутъ не треба.
Бо всѣ пророци поднесли сѧ и радуютъ,
Приходъ его духомъ стымъ чуютъ.
Муситъ то правдивый Богъ бути,
Я [намъ] для едной душѣ всѣми треба ригнути.
Бо ѹже ѩ вачу близко конець нашъ,
И наше старшинство теперь естъ, а завтра немашъ.

Поселъ четвертй прѣбѣгъ и мовитъ:

Отожъ Хрстосъ запевне ѹмеръ,
Я ѩ [бачив його] не давно, [а] теперъ.
Але гди душа его вишла с тѣла,
Тогди не едина тамъ плоть изимълѣла.
И мы всѣ сѧ били полѩкали
И далеко ѿ ней повтѣккали.
Хотѣли-смо его дшу поймати,
Але гди-смо ѡбачили, страшно было к ней приступати.
Яггелскіе войска ѡколо ѡступили,
Я насъ до ней не допустили.
Дрижала землѩ, же ажъ ламали сѧ ѡпоки,
Бувъ страхъ великий и естъ и доки.
Сѣнце й мѣсѩцъ во кровъ сѧ премѣнѩли,
И много ѿ мертвихъ ѿ гробовъ повставали;
И тие ѿ страха великаго ажъ на землю падали
И черезъ три годнни лежали,

Яжъ не хꙋдко встали.
И ми сѧ страха оуже набравши
Идемо   до пекла зброю побравши.
И чꙋлисмо ѿ агглcovъ гласъ,
Же во третїй днⷩъ Хрⷭ҇тосъ воскреснетъ и приде до насъ,
И млетъ взѧти всѣхъ вꙗзнєвъ конечне ꙋ насъ.

Воеводи Кенера и Трꙋвлй мовⷶтъ:

Великий нашъ пане Ꙗде й ти пане Люциперꙋ   старосте,
Запевне   Хрⷭ҇тосъ идетъ до насъ просто.
Мы хотѣли дꙋшꙋ его собѣ   взѧти,
Яле вжⷩїй   сили не дали к ней пристꙋпати.
Ѡхъ лихо наше, вѣдѣлисмо страхъ незносный,
Блискавицѣ и громи великие;
Подобно правдивꙋй й власний естъ Хрⷭ҇тосъ Бгⷩъ,
Бо нѣхто такихъ чꙋдесъ кромѣ него чинити не могъ.
Оустꙋпилисмо тоу до пекла поради зажити,
Що въ ис тимъ Хрⷭ҇томъ чинити и ꙗкъ прожити?
Бо бꙋдетъ тꙋтъ запевне до насъ,
Я почавши ѿ Ꙗдама, й всѣхъ стыхъ млетъ ꙋзѧти ѿ насъ.

Люциперъ мовитъ до слꙋгъ своихъ:

Ѡва, бꙋдꙋ сѧ коронити ꙗкъ могꙋчи,
Бо не подоблетъ ми   из своего панства ꙋтечи.
Если ѡнъ вжⷩїй сⷩъ, нехай собѣ в неби панꙋетъ,
Я з нами й пекломъ нехай сѧ не воюетъ.
Бо вило ви мнѣ завстидъ, гди бимъ сѧ емꙋ кланꙗлъ
И данѣ давати гди бимъ сѧ поднѣмалъ.
Тревалемъ пꙗтъ тисꙗцъ лѣтъ, мало не до вѣкꙋ,
Я теперъ бимъ сѧ в моци далъ едномꙋ человѣкꙋ?
Бꙋдꙋ его чекати ажъ на плацъ, Ꙗде, с тобою,
Я гдижъ ѡнъ человѣкъ, то сѧ ꙗ его не вою.
И бꙋдꙋ сѧ з нимъ менжне   воевати,
Хочъ бимъ мѣлъ и поле програти.
До бронѣ всѣ мои жолнѣре берѣтъ сѧ,
Я гди ꙗкїй страхъ прїйшолъ, то ви не смꙋтѣтъ сѧ;
Ставте сѧ противко его менжне,
Я ꙗ за вами з дрꙋгимъ войскомъ потенжне.
Я ви ворота желѣзние   рихло зачинꙗйте,
И зводи звѣвши ланцꙋхами заволѣкайте,

И колодками моцними и твердими замикайте!
Бо дужє зипєвнє той Хс̃тосъ придєтъ,
Алє хто дужший, той внидєтъ.
А вамъ нєхай срдцє ѿ страху нє умликаєтъ,
Ижъ ѿ Хс̃та того всє повтѣкаєтъ;
Алє бєрѣтє ся до нєго смѣлє,
Ставайтє з нимъ цѣлє.
Алє я знаю, жє нє новина вамъ воєвати,
И нє такихъ рицєровъ в полю и на плацу имати,
И з ними воєвати и всѣмъ кролювати.
И всѣ кролєвє й царѣ нашихъ рукъ нє втєкли,
Алє й сами бачитє, жє єстъ они оу пєкли.
Прєзто ви нє тривожтє ся
И Хс̃та того нє бойтє ся.
Єщє ѡжидаю посла ѡстатного
И на плацъ присты Хс̃тового.

    П о с є л ъ ѡ с т а т н и й п р и б и г а є и   м о в и т ъ:

Панє Адє й ти, панє Люципєру старосто,
Ознаймую вамъ, ижъ Хс̃тосъ йдєтъ до насъ просто.
Цр̃ъ грознїй й агг̃ловъ множєство,
Сєрафимъ з нимъ и єго бжєство.
Нѣчого ми противо єдного аг̃гла нє могли скурати,
А самого Ис̃а й мови єго страшно було й слухати.
Повѣглисмо до пєкла даючи знати вамъ,
Акъ би прожити намъ. (Зобачили короговъ Хс̃товъ
и полякали ся).

Л ю ц и п є р ъ д о с л у г ъ м о в и т и к о р о г о в с о б ѣ в є л и т
д а т и:

Ѡножъ йдєтъ къ намъ! Пилно стрєжѣтє,
И в рукахъ своихъ ѡружиє моцно дєржѣтє,
А акъ до васъ придутъ, грозно ѡповѣдайтє,
И плєчима двєрѣ моцно подпирайтє,
И єсли би ся ламалъ, аг̃гловъ забивайтє.
Нєхай они тутъ нє идєтъ! Никому нє фолгуйтє,
Бо нѣчого тутъ
По нєму нє будтъ.
Коли они бж̃ий сн̃ъ,
Нєхай собѣ в нєби сидитъ,
А воєвати ся з нами и пєкломъ нєхай нє идєтъ.

Коли ѡнъ естъ Бжїй снъ,
Ӣ не знаю, для такихъ идетъ сюда причинъ.
Не маетъ ѡнъ до насъ жадной справи.

И не можу разумѣти, що то за царъ слави.

Святий Іоанъ до Люципера мовитъ:

А, то ти отъ насъ царя слави не чувалъ
Изъ устъ моихъ, о которомъ (я) пророковалъ?
Не тилько я, али и всѣ пророки;
Не тилько (пророки), али и всѣ патриархи (о) тымъ пред-
сказуютъ усѣ роки.

Люциперъ до Іоана мовитъ:

Знаю и Іоане, же то Богъ все тое справилъ,
Не той царъ слави,
О которомъ ти пророковалъ!
А я Бога сѣдящаго знаю,
А тутъ на земли о томъ не розумѣю:
Отколь би то онъ мѣлъ (ся) на земли взяти,
То не могу з розуму моего понятн.

Втеди Люциперъ до слугъ мовитъ:

Гей, панове молодцѣ! Нехай вамъ серце ся не лякаетъ,
(Же) отъ того Христа восько все повтѣкаетъ!
Потужне си ставте,
А зъ пляцу я жаденъ не утѣкайте!
Грозне ся до него ставте, а за дверѣ берѣте и голосно
волайте,
Крикомъ страху ему завдавайте.
Бо якъ розумѣю: якъ жи гвалту не будетя чинити,
То онъ не схочетъ з нами войни точити.
А если би кликавъ, вязний просилъ,
Не билбимъ ему и десяти боронилъ.
Радъ би я з нимъ поради зажити,

Але боюся иншого огни...
Бо я апѣ письма не читалъ,
Анѣ отъ людий мудрихъ не чувалъ,
Що би (то) билъ за царъ слави?
То той не маетъ до насъ справи,
Же маетъ грозно до насъ прийти
И пекло наше розпошити.

Слуги мовятъ до Ада:

Отожъ пане нашъ Аде, що-смо видѣли уже виликія чуда.
Правда, исправилъ емъ худо бирзо и нашъ Іюда.
Не тилько чинилъ чудо во Ерусалимѣ, але и всюда:
Мертвихъ воскресилъ, хорихъ уздоровилъ,
А насъ словомъ своимъ далеко прогонилъ.

Потомъ самъ Христосъ приходитъ и мовитъ:

Гдъ силенъ во брани!
Возмѣте врата, князи, ваша,
И возмѣте ся врата вѣчная,
Внидетъ въ васъ цръ слави.

Люциперъ до Іса мовитъ:
Прошу тя Хрⷭте в добрій ѡбичай,
Дай мнѣ покой й болше ми не докучай.
Я хтожъ ест за царъ слави?
Коли ти Бгъ, приймни ѿ апслъ хвалу
И ѿ аггловъ своихъ славу,
И на воротаровъ моихъ болше и на мене не колай.

Потомъ Христосъ другій разъ рече и благословитъ короговъю:
Гдъ крѣпокъ и силенъ во брани!
Возмѣте ся, врата вѣчная,
Вныйдетъ во васъ царъ слави.

Люциперъ до Іса мовитъ крикомъ:
Повторне прошу тя, Ісе, не напастуй пекла [мого],

Ѩнѣ мене, бо не виналастуешъ нѣкчого.
Коли ти Бг҃ъ, тамъ собѣ сиди к раю,
Ѩ ꙗ тебе тутъ не потребую.

И третїй разъ Хр҃стосъ рече и быетъ корогвою,
и быстъ тако, сокрушиша сꙗ врата:

Ѡто воходитъ во власъ цар҃ слави!
Гд҃ѣ силенъ, той естъ цр҃ъ слави.

И перехрестивши на три части, в той часъ ворота и ланцухи сокрушиша сꙗ и входитъ Хр҃стосъ во пекло и wсвѣщаетъ ꙗснымъ
своимъ променемъ и wсвѣщаетъ всѣ мѣстца пекелнїи и кропитъ
водою и Д҃хомъ ст҃им.

Ѩдъ кричитъ:

Гвалтъ, гвалтъ, панови! Врата ломатъ,
И водою ꙗкоюсь wстрою насъ кропатъ.
Що ти ломишъ мои врата безпечне?
Гдесь вазней моихъ хочешъ взати конечне.
И для чого мꙗ такъ, сн҃у божий, гвалтуешъ
И вазневъ моихъ из собою приймуешъ,
Которихъ ꙗ билъ собѣ ѿ вѣка назбиралъ,
Ѩ [ти] теперъ пекло збурилъ и столицу сплюндровалъ,
Ѩ мене Ѩда вѣчними узами звꙗзалъ.
Щожъ ꙗ теперъ чинити маю?
Южъ вазней моихъ побралъ, запевне знаю.
Вѣчний палаци мои попсовалъ
И все мое пекло сплюндровалъ
И насъ подъ ноги свои бралъ и потопталъ.
И слуги мои милїи всагди порозганꙗлъ,
Ѩдама и Еву и всѣхъ сватихъ с собою забралъ.

Люциперъ мовитъ:

Тилко з еднаго страху ледво сижу,
Ѩ по старому передъ собою едного праведника вижу.
Питаю сꙗ ꙗ тебе, Соломоне, чему ти сꙗ тутъ зосталъ?
Подобно мнѣ тебе Хр҃стосъ даровалъ.

Соломонъ до Люципера мовитъ:

Южъ повторне Хр҃стосъ по мене прїйде;
Страшний его билъ приходъ первїй,
Еще другїй страшнѣйшїй буде.

Люциперъ мовитъ до слугъ свихъ:

Слуги мои, юзмѣте,
Цр҃а Соломона изъ пекла випровад[ѣ]те!
На жа[лу]ю его,
Янѣ Хр҃ста того,
Нехай сюди болше не приходитъ,
Пекломъ нашимъ и нами не тривожитъ.
(К той часъ бѣси взявши Соломона и випровадили ис пекла й
мовятъ такъ бѣси на Хр҃ста и на Соломона)

Бѣси мовятъ:

Идижъ, иди за своимъ Хр҃стомъ, а тутъ не букай,
И пекломъ нашимъ й нами болше не колатай!
(Соломонъ скачучи началъ спѣвати,
Люциперъ из Ядомъ плакати й ридати).

Христосъ до него рече:

Не ридай мене, Яде, наполню пива во ѿстатнїи день,
Будешъ мѣти, якось мѣлъ.

Соломонъ началъ Бг҃а во тройци вихвалѧти и пре-
чистую Богородицу:

Преблг҃ословена еси Бц҃е дѣво,
Воплотивий во ся ис тебе [Божое слово].
Ядъ плѣненъ бистъ, Ядамъ призва ся,
Клятва потреби ся,
Ева свободи ся.
Смертъ оумертви ся,
И ми ѿжихомъ!
Тѣмъ покще воспоемъ:
Благословенъ Хр҃стосъ Бг҃ъ нашъ
Изволивый й такля. Слава тебѣ.

Textual Notes and Annotations

For a detailed examination of the textual variants of *Slovo o zbureniu pekla*, see Franko's (1908), Vozniak's (1927), and Rezanov's (1926) editions.

l. 1 In the *Gospel of Nicodemus*, and in the related homilies, the devil is referred to as Satan, the Devil, or Beelzebub; he is always paired with Hades. The name Lucifer, "brilliant star," invented by St. Jerome, appears in the apocryphal *Questions* of St. Bartholomew and in the *Life of Adam and Eve*. See Émile Turdeanu, *Apocryphes slaves et roumains de l'Ancient Testament* (Leiden: E.J. Brill, 1981), p. 25.

ll. 1–97 The technique of a self-revelatory soliloquy by a villain is much developed in English morality plays, and influences the devices of Renaissance drama. For example, Shakespeare's "Now is the winter of our discontent" (*Richard III*, I.i.) is obviously dependent upon this tradition. It is not, however, a technique commonly found in Slavic drama.

l. 7 A not unusual Slavonic method of referring to 5,500 years. The calculation of 5,500 years is noted in both the Latin A and the Greek versions of the *Gospel of Nicodemus*. *Cf* Latin A *Gospel of Nicodemus*: "Michael the archangel declared before unto Seth the third son of Adam, that after five thousand and a half *thousand* years Christ the Son of God hath (? should) come." And also the *Questions* of St. Bartholomew (Slavonic text, v. 17): "And Hades said: which of the prophets is it? Show me: Is it Enoch the scribe of righteousness? But God hath not suffered him to come down upon the earth before the end of the six thousand years." See M.R. James, *The Apocryphal New Testament* (Oxford: Clarendon, 1924), p. 145 and p. 168.

J.A. MacCulloch, *The Harrowing of Hell: A Comparative Study of an Early Christian Doctrine* (Edinburgh: T. and T. Clark, 1930), p. 332, and J. Finegan, *Handbook of Biblical Chronology* (Princeton: Princeton University Press, 1964), p. 139, note that the chronological system popular in the early centuries was explained by the fact that the Creation was accomplished in six days. Since "one day is with the Lord as a thousand years" (2 Pet 3:8; Ps 90:40), and since in 6,000 years all things will be consummated, therefore the Incarnation took place in the middle of the last age (i.e. 5,500 years ago). This date is found in Hippolytus, Julius Africanus, Theophilus, the Epistle of Barnabas, and others. But N.K. Gudzy, *History of Early Russian Literature*, trans. Susan Wilbur Jones (N.Y.: Macmillan, 1949), p. 40 observes that the period of creation to the birth of Christ was 5508, according to ancient calculation.

ll. 23–26 In one opinion adopted by many of the Church Fathers, Satan acquired full rights over mankind through Adam's sin. God hid Christ's divinity in the flesh of man; therefore the devil, who saw the miracles performed by Christ and was aware of His great powers, believed that He was merely a prophet. Wishing to obtain Christ's soul, Satan helped bring about His death (cf *Slovo* ll. 123–124, 133–134). However, since Satan had no rights over the Son of God, who was not subject to the law of sin, Satan also forfeited his rights over man for overstepping his authority. God therefore delivered humanity from his grasp and put him into the trap the Devil created for Christ. A central belief of the Bogomils (a Bulgarian sect which arose in the tenth century and preached dualism), it also appears in Bulgarian legend, as well as in a popular Ukrainian variant which deals with the dual creation of the earth by God and the Devil. This idea of Satan's deception is thoroughly studied by MacCulloch, especially p. 199f.

ll. 45–46 Literally, "the luxuries of paradise / Luxuries which cannot be comprehended with the reason." The idea of the envy of Lucifer (l. 39), and of the Lord sending His angel (Michael) to drive out Adam and Eve appears in Eve's story of the Fall and its consequences in the *Life of Adam and Eve* (22, 27). See the English translation of this apocrypha in H.F.D. Sparks, *The Apocryphal Old Testament* (Oxford: Clarendon Press, 1984). The apocrypha is extant in Latin, Greek, Slavonic, and Armenian, among others. See V. Jagič, *Slavische Beiträge zu den biblischen Apocryphen* (Vienna: Denkschriften der Kaiserlichen Akademie der Wissenschaften, 1893), I, pp. 17–99 for the Slavic text.

l. 50 The contemporary English slang expression "this here" reflects the Ukrainian original. Lucifer's language encompasses both the colloquial and the formal.

l. 57 Dionysius the Areopàgite (5th c.) constructed the celestial hierarchy (*De hierarchia celesti*), which consisted of nine choirs of angels, based on the political organization of the Byzantine empire. The nine choirs include thrones, cherubim, seraphim; powers, virtues, dominions; principalities, angels, and archangels. See J.C.J. Metford, *Dictionary of Christian Lore and Legend* (London: Thames and Hudson, 1983), p. 26.

ll. 76–79 Cf. Edward Kennard Rand, "*Sermo de Confusione Diaboli*," *Modern Philology*, 2 (1904–1905), 14: "Abraham, Isaac et Iacob et omnes prophetas. . . ."

l. 97 "Johnny" refers to St. John the Baptist, who figures in all versions of the Nicodemus Gospel. The notion of John the Baptist as Christ's precursor in the underworld, as well as on earth, is first found in St. Hippolytus, *Adv. haer.* 3, 20; 4; 4, 22, I (*Patrologia Graeca* 7: 945; 1046f). The Baptist plays a prominent role in the pseudo-Eusebian homily, while the pseudo-Epiphanian homily for Easter eve particularly emphasizes the role of John the Baptist as

twofold forerunner to the living and the dead. For a good discussion of the
Baptist's role as precursor of Christ in hell see Daniel Sheerin,"St. John the
Baptist in the Lower World," *Vigiliae Christianae* (1976), 1–22.

l. 98 One of the difficulties in translating this play is in conveying English
equivalents of terms of address. Hades accords Lucifer the title of Elder
(*starosta*), which refers to his administrative position, rather than to his age;
Lucifer reciprocates by calling Hades his Benefactor (*dobrodii*), a polite form of
address. Venera and Trubai are called *voievody*. The references are to specific
administrative positions in the Polish-Lithuanian Commonwealth. Ukrainian
lands in the Commonwealth were divided into several *voievodstvos* (provinces),
and these, in turn, into counties or lands. The county chief official or governor
was the *starosta*.

ll. 106–107 *Cf. Gospel of Nicodemus*, Latin B: "If it be he that by the word
of his command alone made Lazarus, which was four days dead, to fly out of
my bosom like an eagle, then is he not a man in his manhood, but God in his
majesty." (James, p. 126) And Greek: "And is he indeed so mighty that he
can do such things with a word only?" (James, p. 129) Latin A: "Who is this
Jesus which by his own word without prayer hath drawn dead men from me?"
(James, p. 131). Also, see the pseudo-Eusebian homily in I. Porfirev, *Apokrificheskiia skazaniia o Novozavetnykh litsakh i sobitiiakh [Apocryphal Legends
about New Testament Characters and Events]* (St. Petersburg: n.p., 1890), 52,
No. 4, p. 44.

ll. 113–114 In Vozniak's edition Hades is worried that he will be in trouble.

ll. 120–121 *Cf. Sermo*, p. 14: "Potentes habeo ministros meos et non timeo
pugnare cum eo."

ll. 123–124 *Cf. Gospel of Nicodemus*, Latin A: Satan says, "I have stirred
up mine ancient people of the Jews with envy and wrath against him." And
Greek: "I feared him not, but I did set on the Jews, and they crucified him . . ."
(James, p. 130). The complicity of the Jews is a regular feature of harrowing
plays in all countries, and appears to stem from this apocryphal gospel. See,
for example, the York play "The Council of the Jews" in which the Jews agree
to "seek a means of bringing blame on him [i.e. Christ]."

l. 130 Unlike the Western Church's tradition which portrays Mary as patiently
enduring Christ's death for the salvation of mankind, the Eastern Church's
tradition emphasizes Mary's maternal, human response to the Passion: her
lamentations and fear. See, for example, Sandro Sticca, "The Literary Genesis
of the Latin Passion Play and the *Planctus Mariae*: A New Christocentric and
Marian Theology," in Sandro Sticca, ed., *The Medieval Drama* (Albany: State
University of New York Press, 1972), pp. 39–68.

ll. 135–136 The Vozniak edition makes no mention of the Jews about to ask help of the devils.

ll. 142–143 The Slavonic version of the *Questions* has Hades say, "Allow me, do not oppose me, for I was created before you," suggesting as the *Slovo* play does, that Hades was created before Satan. See James, p. 168. W. Schneemelcher, *New Testament Apocrypha* (Philadelphia: The Westminster Press, 1963) finds this a surprising belief, and attributes this piece of dialogue to Christ. The *Slovo* writer appears to follow the *Questions* in characterizing Hades as an old man and Satan as a relative newcomer to Hell. The friendship of Hades and Lucifer has precedent in the Eusebian homilies, as well as in the *Gospel of Nicodemus*, and Ephraim Syrus.

l. 145 The Vozniak edition makes no mention of the fright sustained by the menials because of John the Baptist.

l. 148 Line missing in Vozniak.

l. 152 The Lucifer-Hades opposition is already established in the Nicodemus Gospel, where Satan appears to be more assured than Hades is.

l. 156 Line missing in Vozniak.

ll. 157–158 There was a mediaeval iconographic tradition which represented the devil sitting on the arm of the cross and waiting to capture Christ's soul. See C.M. Marx and M.A. Skey, "Aspects of the Iconography of the Devil at the Crucifixion," *Journal of the Warburg and Courtauld Institutes*, 42 (1979), 233–35. This image may be related to a passage in the Ukrainian version of the pseudo-Eusebian homily (see above, p. 65f), where the devil flies up to Christ while He is on the cross.

ll. 159–160 Venera appears as Benera in Vozniak's edition. Venera is (still) the Ukrainian name for Venus. An appropriately infernal connection is made between the goddess of love, associated with lasciviousness, and the inhabitants of hell. More particularly, the name of Venera may indicate the Orthodoxy of the author of *Slovo*, and his contempt for Catholic Renaissance art. When the Lutsk Uniate Bishop Kyrilo Terlets'kyi brought back Renaissance engravings from Rome to his native Ukraine, Orthodox clerics reacted with horror at the "shameless books." In one sermon, Fabian Birkovs'kyi castigated the "heretics" who replaced images of Christ and Mary in their homes with those of "fauns . . . Veneras, and Fortunas, summoning the shameless goddess from hell. . . ." See P.M. Zholtovs'kyi, *Ukrains'kyi zhyvopys XVII-XVIII st.* [*Ukrainian Painting, XVII-XVIII Centuries*] (Kiev: Naukova Dumka, 1978), pp. 16–17.

See Ernst Curtius, *European Literature and the Latin Middle Ages*, trans. W.R. Trask (London: Routledge and Kegan Paul, 1953), p. 406 for another possibility. He notes that there are many mediaeval misunderstandings of antiquity, and cites as one example an eighth-century Anglo-Saxon who makes Venus a man out of "sheer ignorance."

The second commander is named Lord or Master Trubai ("One who blows a trumpet"). His devilish actions in the play do not appear to suggest an allusion to the Western idea of "fame" or *fama*, as seen, for example, in the numerous models suggested in Samuel Chew, *The Pilgrimage of Life* (New Haven and London: Yale University Press, 1962), pp. 22, and 82, except insofar as they are (as Venera is) a parody of those Western images.

Also, *Cf. Sermo*, p. 16, where the devils are referred to as "Tricapite et Beelzebub."

l. 161 Literally, "under the city," in the sense of outside the city proper.

l. 164 The Ukrainian word for commanders used here is *voievody*. Throughout the play, the social strata of the Polish-Lithuanian Commonwealth are being satirized.

l. 167 That is, steal Christ's soul for themselves.

ll. 178–180 Missing in Vozniak.

l. 180 Garbled sentence, meaning obscure.

l. 188 Possibly *potuha*, not *potukha*, in which case the line would be best translated as "Let us not give them might. . . ."

l. 200 Literally, "Where my right hand will favour Him."

l. 203 Literally, "I already see my passion and lament." Hades' "passion" is a black parody of Christ's. In Vozniak's edition Hades experiences "cries" and "lamentations." Hades' intuition of the actions of Christ are, of course, accurate, and they dovetail with Hades' speech at the end of the play (especially l. 485), where Hades, not Lucifer (as in the *Gospel of Nicodemus*), claims to be tied up. The suggestion here, however, seems to be that both Hades and Lucifer will be tied up.

ll. 205–208 *Cf. Questions*: (v. 19): Hades: "These be no good words that I hear from thee: my belly is rent, and mine inward parts are pained: it cannot be but that God cometh hither." James, p. 168.

ll. 213–218 *Cf. Gospel of Nicodemus*, Latin A: "Shut ye the hard gates of brass and put on them the bars of iron and withstand stoutly, lest we that hold captivity be taken captive." James, p. 133. Also, *cf* Idiomela, Eighth Tone (Blessing of the New Light), in Most Rev. Joseph Raya and Baron José de Vinck, *Byzantine Daily Worship* (Combermere, Ont: Allelluia Press, 1969), p. 835: "O Lord, the gates of death opened to You out of fear, and when the gate-keepers of Hades saw you, they trembled. They trembled again when you crushed its gates of bronze and its iron bars and delivered us from the shadow and gloom of death and broke our fetters." Unless otherwise noted, all references to the Eastern Divine Liturgy are taken from Raya and de Vinck.

l. 219 Literally, "don't walk with Christ."

l. 220 In Vozniak's edition St. John enters after Hades expresses his fears; Lucifer's speech to Hades, calming and assuring him of the devils' victory, is missing.

ll. 221–223 Cf. *Questions* (v. 16–17) in which the devil tries to comfort Hades, and believes that a prophet, and not God, descends into hell. James, p. 168.

l. 232 Cf. *Sermo*, p. 17: "Primus David percutiebat cytharu[m] et dicebat. . . ." Perhaps David sings verses from Psalm 148 (First tone) from Easter Lauds: "Praise Him with the blast of the horn, praise Him with the harp and the zither. . . . Praise Him with timbrel and chorus, praise Him with strings and pipes." Raya and de Vinck, p. 856.

l. 234 Literally, "He will certainly be after us." The general sense is clear: Christ comes for the righteous and will not leave hell without them.

l. 240 Here Lucifer subverts Scripture and usurps the place of the Baptist when he claims to have prepared the way for Christ.

ll. 243–244 Vozniak's edition makes no mention of St. John's relationship to Christ.

ll. 248–249 Vozniak's edition makes no mention of this ironic idea of Lucifer's that it is too bad God wasn't present when St. John was born; God would then have supposedly controlled the Baptist's "spurious" prophecies.

l. 260 In Vozniak, the Baptist is referred to as "My knight, my little bird."

ll. 261 *Kvass* is rye-beer. Compare this torture of hellish *kvass* to the heavenly drink offered in the Easter Canon, Third Ode: "Come, O faithful: let us drink a new drink, produced miraculously not from a barren rock, but springing from the tomb which is a fountain of immortality: the tomb of Christ by which we are strengthened." Raya, p. 849. There is no mention of *kvass* in Vozniak.

l. 281 Here Lucifer makes clear that hell proper with its torments is found in another, lower region.

l. 289 In Vozniak's edition, the First Messenger addresses Hades only.

ll. 299–304 In Vozniak, the Second Messenger's speech is slightly different, and is not directly addressed to Lucifer. The Jews, he says, will never have such a council again.

ll. 305–311 In Vozniak, although the Third Messenger says nothing of vinegar and gall, he remarks that Christ was beaten by his captors.

ll. 319–320 The collaboration of the Devil, Sin, and Death is found in the reference to Lucifer's net, by which he hopes to catch Christ's soul. Death's

ensnaring of the soul is a common image which appears in many emblem
books. See, for example, the illustrations of the snare in Francis Quarles, ✓
Emblemes (London: 1635), reprinted as illustration 10 in Samuel C.
Chew, *The Pilgrimage of Life*. The snare intended for Christ becomes the snare which
entraps Lucifer and his devils. Luke 21:35 (which may be one source here)
compares the suddenness of the Lord's coming to the springing of a trap. Other
plays also make use of this image. In the York play "The Council of the Jews,"
Lucifer speaks of "new engines" (l. 50) he will devise to entrap Christ. Once
he realizes who Christ is, however, he attempts to stop the events he has put
in motion by causing Pilate's wife to dream and to attempt to intervene in her
husband's decision. The snare appears as a mousetrap in Peter Lombard, and
as a hook in Gregory of Nazianzus. See MacCulloch, p. 199f for a thorough
discussion of this idea.

ll. 325–326 Missing in Vozniak.

ll. 345–353 In Vozniak, the Fourth Messenger lacks specificity in his speech.
He remarks that the sun and moon were transformed (*cf Slovo*'s "turned into
blood"), and that those who rose from the dead fell down. Angels, rather than
a single angel's voice, informed the devils of Christ's coming.

ll. 348–349 *Cf.* Matt. 27:51–53.

l. 360 *Cf.* Jean Daniélou, *The Angels and Their Mission*, trans. David Heimann
(Westminster, Maryland: The Newman Press, 1957), p. 99: angels "help the
soul escape the sufferings of death; the guardian angel accompanies it and
assures it a peaceful journey; he defends it against the demons who want to
stop it; the angels sit in charge of the gate of heaven and welcome it."

l. 362 The voice of Christ is described as "a voice of thunder" in all versions
of the *Gospel of Nicodemus*.

ll. 371–378 *Cf.* Ephraim of Syrus' Hymn 36: "If thou be God show thy
power; and if thou be man, feel our power." See John Gwynn, ed., "Selections
Translated into English from the Hymns and Homilies of Ephraim the Syrian,
and from the Demonstrations of Aphrahat the Persian Sage," in *Nicene and
Post-Nicene Fathers*, 13, Series 2 (Oxford: James Parker and Co., 1898),
pp. 196–198.

l. 389 Literally, "the stronger one will walk forth."

l. 404 For a summary of the controversy about Christ's physical presence in
hell, see J. Turmel, chap. X, "Comment a eu lieu la descente," in *La Descente
du Christ aux Enfers* (Paris: Bloud, 1908).

ll. 405f The image of the multitude of angels may have some iconographic
basis (See above, p. 91), but it is also an idea found in the Divine Liturgy.
For example, the First Tone of the Holy Saturday Office: "The host of angels

X (surround Him and glorify Him while He is counted with the dead in Hades: for He is the Lord!" Raya, p. 832. The host of angels is also present in Eusebius' Easter homily. See above, p. 66.

l. 408 In Vozniak: "He alone was terrifying to hear."

ll. 410f (stage direction) "Banners" refers to Christ's resurrection banner, a red cross on a white field; it is a symbol of Christ's victory. Only one is usual, the banner carried by Christ. Perhaps the dramatist wished to emphasize the spectacle of the battle scene by using many. In some icons, Christ carries a cross, instead of a banner. (See above, *Iconography and Symbolism*.) The cross also appears in the *Gospel of Nicodemus*, Latin A and B, and is referred to in the Greek version. In Vozniak, there are no stage directions concerning the banners.

l. 414 Line missing in Vozniak.

ll. 418–419 Lucifer now seems to intuit the harrowing and emptying of hell.

ll. 426–427 *Cf. Sermo*, p. 17: "Et Johannes dicebat, 'Nonne dixi uobis quia ueniet et aperiet nos?'"

ll. 426–464 Franko omits this section in his reconstruction.

l. 438 Vozniak's Lucifer refers to "this Spirit," rather than to "this Christ."

l. 443–444 Line garbled. The double negative and the sentence appear to be illogical.

l. 448 Line missing in Vozniak; garbled speech. *Cf. Sermo*, p. 17: "Tunc adprehendit Dominus Diabolum et ligauit eum indissolutis uinculis et deposuit eum in inferiora terrae et substernit eum ignem inextinguibilem, et uermes non moriuntur: et clausus plorans et suspirans." *Gospel of Nicodemus*, Latin B: "To-day do I deliver thee unto eternal fire." James, p. 136.

l. 454 *Cf.* Vozniak: "He who is supposed to come in fierceness and will break our pates."

ll. 455–459 In Vozniak the servant's speech is presented in a slightly different version: "Our Mr. Hades, all that we have seen up to this time / Will we tell." (My translation.)

l. 456 Line missing in Vozniak.

 ll. 460–463 Christ probably sings Psalm 24 at this point in the play.

ll. 465, 471 *Cf.* the more dignified, and more rhythmical questions of the pseudo-Augustine homily: "Si Deus, utquid venit? Si homo, quid praesumptsit? Si Deus, quid in sepulchro facit?" Migne, *Patrologia Latina*, 39:2060.

l. 476f (stage direction) Literally, this stage direction notes that Christ sanctifies hell with water and with the Holy Spirit. The sprinkling of holy water symbolizes purification and the expulsion of evil. See George Ferguson, *Signs and Symbols in Christian Art* (N.Y.: Oxford University Press, 1961), p. 98. The play's syntax is problematic here and perhaps the playwright actually meant "imbues with the Holy Spirit," for otherwise it is difficult to envisage the way this direction could be carried out. If *Slovo* were performed in church with the actor playing Christ dressed in priestly robes, he could suggest the presence of the Holy Spirit by his dress, as well as by his action. As Vladimir Lossky, *The Mystical Theology of the Eastern Church* (London: James Clark and Co. Ltd., 1957), p. 242 observes, in the Eastern Church Christ is only known in the Holy Spirit.

It is also interesting to note that in the litany of the Offertory, just before the reading of the Creed, the priest exclaims, "The doors, the doors! With wisdom let us attend!" Originally, this command was directed at doorkeepers who were to shut the doors lest an heretic or unbeliever should enter. The parodic application to *Slovo* is obvious. Later, the practical application of this meaning was lost and the phrase has now come to mean almost the very opposite of its original intention: that is, open the door of your hearts to the Lord. See Raya for a brief discussion of the litany.

l. 477 *Cf.* the crumbling of the gates to the Resurrection Canon, Fifth Tone, Kontakion: "O Saviour, You went down to Hades, and being almighty, shattered its gates. As the Creator, you raised the dead and destroyed the sting of death: Adam was relieved of the curse. . . ."

ll. 479–492 *Cf. Gospel of Nicodemus*, Latin Form A: "When Hell and Death and their wicked ministers saw that, they were stricken with fear. . . ." James, p. 135. And the Greek version, "Hades cried out straightway: 'We are overcome, woe unto us'." James, p. 135. Also, *cf.* the Resurrection Homily attributed to St. John Chrysostom: "Hades is angered because frustrated, it is angered because it has been mocked, it is angered because it has been destroyed, it is angered because it has been reduced to naught, it is angered because it is now captive. . . ."

ll. 484–485 Curiously, Christ Himself seems to have tied up Lucifer. Michael, the chief emissary of God in Orthodox Slavic visions, and the angel usually given the function of leading out the saints in harrowing plays, is conspicuously absent here. In a brief note (p. 202), however, Jean Monnier, *La Descent aux enfers* (Paris: Librairie Fischbacher, 1905), notes that in a Byzantine ivory fragment at the Louvre John the Baptist leads out the saints.

ll. 485–491 Lucifer-Satan is traditionally tied up. Satan is fettered in Latin B, and cast into Tartarus. In Latin A Satan is delivered into the power of Hell, while in the Greek, he is delivered to the angels who proceed to bind his hands, feet, neck, and mouth with irons.

l. 492 *Cf.* Second Tone, Oktoekhos (Hymns in Honour of the Resurrection of Christ), Kontakion: "Almighty Saviour, You are risen from the tomb! At the sight of this miracle, Hades is filled with fear, the dead rise up, the whole creation rejoices with You, Adam exults, and the universe exalts You forever, O Saviour!"

ll. 494–504 *Cf.* Speranskii's recording of an oral legend about Solomon in *Russkaia ustnaia slovestnost'* [*Russian Oral Literature*] (Moscow: 1917; rpt. The Hague, Paris: Mouton, 1969), p. 435. Solomon, by means of his cleverness, escapes from hell and later tells what he found there—vodka and tobacco, which are not found in heaven. N.K. Gudzy, pp. 40–41, remarks that Solomon "was the biblical personage to whom apocryphal literature paid the most attention." In many Slavic apocrypha he distinguishes himself as a solver of riddles.

ll. 507–508 The text is problematic here, probably corrupt, although the meaning is quite clear. B reads: "I will fill with beer." Christ promises to fill the "cellar" of hell (which He has just emptied) once more with souls on Judgement Day. The reference to a "cellar" both reflects the subterranean location of the play, and seems to underscore Hades' position as a householder-tavern-keeper.

ll. 509–519 Holy Saturday Office, the Great Doxology: "Most blessed art thou, O Virgin Birth-Giver of God: through Him who became incarnate of thee Hades is led captive, Adam is recalled from the dead, the curse is made void, Eve is set free, Death is slain, and we have been endowed with life. Wherefore we cry aloud, extolling in song: 'Blessed art thou, O Christ Our God, in whose sight it is thus well-pleasing. Glory to Thee!'" See Isabel Florence Hapgood, *Service Book of the Holy Orthodox-Catholic Apostolic Church* (Englewood, N.J.: Antiochian Orthodox Christian Archdiocese, 1975), p. 34. A version very close to this one is found in Raya and de Vinck.

Compare this concluding song with the conclusion of other mediaeval Slavic texts, for example, the Slavic apocryphon *Khozhdenie Bogoroditsi po mukam* (roughly translated as *The Journey of the Birth-Giver of God Through the Torments of Hell*): "Glory to Thy goodness. Glory to the Father and the Son and the Holy Ghost, now and forever, unto ages and ages. Amen." See the English translation of this apocryphon, entitled "The Holy Virgin's Descent into Hell," trans. Leo Weiner, *Anthology of Russian Literature* (N.Y.: Benjamin Bloom, 1967), I, p. 100. In both cases (that is, in *Slovo* and in *Khozdenie*), the conclusion has a paraliturgical function, and serves to end the work on a jubilant note.

Selected Bibliography

Sources, Analogues: Apocryphal, Biblical, Patristic

Altaner, Berthold. *Patrology*. Trans. Hilda C. Graef. N.Y.: Herder and Herder, 1960.

Andrieu, M. *Les Ordines romani du haut Moyen Age*. Vol. IV. Louvain: Spicilegium Sacrum Lovaniense, 1951.

St. Augustine. *Letters*. Trans. Sister Wilfrid Parsons. N.Y.: Fathers of the Church, 20, 1953.

––––––. *Sermons on the Liturgical Seasons*. Trans. Sister Mary Sarah Muldowney. N.Y.: Fathers of the Church, 38, 1959.

Bernard, J.H. *Texts and Studies*. Vol. 8: *The Odes of Solomon*. Ed. J. Armitage Robinson. Cambridge: Cambridge University Press, 1912.

Bohahlasnyk; Pesni Blahohoveiniia Prazdnykom . . . Lviv: Institut Stavropihiisky, 1886.

Burstein, S.R. "The Harrowing of Hell." *Folklore*, 39 (1928), 113–132.

Cabaniss, Allen. "The Harrowing of Hell, Psalm 24, and Pliny the Younger: A Note." In *Liturgy and Literature; Selected Essays*. University, Alabama: University of Alabama Press, 1970, pp. 62–71.

Campbell, Jackson J. "To Hell and Back: Latin Tradition and Literary Use of the 'Descensus ad Inferos' in Old English." *Viator*, 13 (1982), 107–158.

Charlesworth, James H. *The Old Testament Pseudepigrapha*. Vol. II. N.Y.: Doubleday and Company, 1985.

Chubatyi, Mykola. *Istoriia Khrystianstva na Rusy-Ukraini*. Vol. I (to 1353). Rome-N.Y.: Logos, 1965.

Cross, F.L., ed. *St. Cyril of Jerusalem's Lectures on the Christian Sacraments*. London: S.P.C.K., 1951.

Daniélou, Jean. *From Shadows to Reality: Studies in the Biblical Typology of the Fathers*. Trans. Wulstan Hibberd. London: Burns and Oates, 1960.

––––––. *The Bible and the Liturgy*. London: Darton, Longman and Todd, 1964.

Dorozhyns'kyi, Dionisii. *Prazdnychyi kartyny hreko-kadolytskoi Tserkvy* [*sic*]. Lviv: Gustav Brake, 1908.

Dumville, D.N. "Liturgical Drama and Panegyric Responsory from the Eighth Century? A Re-Examination of the Origin and Contents of the Ninth-Century Section of the Book of Cerne." *The Journal of Theological Studies*, 23 (1972), 374–406.

Emerton, J.A. *The Apocryphal Old Testament*. Oxford: Clarendon Press, 1984.

Eusebius Pamphili. *Ecclesiastical History*. Trans. Roy J. Deferrari. N.Y.: Fathers of the Church, 19, 1953.

Ferrar, W.J., ed. *The Proof of the Gospel Being the Demonstratio of Eusebius of Caesarea*. Translations of Christian Literature, Series I, Greek texts, Vol. II. N.Y.: Macmillan, 1920.

Finegan, J. *Handbook of Biblical Chronology*. Princeton, N.J.: Princeton University Press, 1964.

Franko, I. "Apokryfy i lehendy z ukrains'kykh rukopysiv." In *Pamiatnyky ukrains'ko-rus'koi movy i literatury* [Monuments of the Ukrainian-Rutherian Language and Literature]. Ed. Stepan Komarevs'kyi. Vol. II. Lviv: n.p., 1899.

Geerard, Mavritius, ed. *Clavis Patrum Graecorum*. Turnhout: Brepols, 1974.

Grillmeier, Alois. *Mit ihm und in ihm; Christologische Forschungen und Perspectiven*. Freiburg: Herder, 1975.

Gwynn, John, ed. "Selections Translated into English from the Hymns and Homilies of Ephraim the Syrian, and from the Demonstrations of Aphrahat the Persian Sage." In *Nicene and Post-Nicene Fathers*. 2nd ser. Vol. 13. Oxford: James Parker and Co., 1898.

Hardison, O.B. *Christian Rite and Christian Drama in the Middle Ages*. Baltimore: Johns Hopkins, 1965.

Harnack, Adolf. *Geschichte der altchristlichen Literatur bis Eusebius*. Leipzig: J.C. Hinrichs Verlag, 1958.

Harris, Rendel and Alphonse Mingana. *The Odes and Psalms of Solomon*. Vol. II. Manchester, N.Y., London: Longmans, Green and Quaritch, 1920.

Hemmerdinger-Iliadou (Montmorency), Démocratie. "L'Ephrem Slave et sa tradition manuscrite." *Geschichte der Ost- und Westkirche in Ihren Wechselseitigen Beziehungen*. Annales Instituti Slavici. Vol. I/13 (1967). Wiesbaden: Otto Harrassowitz, 1967.

Hennecke, Edgar – Wilhelm Schneemelcher. *New Testament Apocrypha*. Vol. I. Trans. R.L. McL. Wilson. Philadelphia: Westminster Press, 1963.

Hitchcock, Donald Raymond. *The Appeal of Adam to Lazarus in Hell*. The Hague, Paris, N.Y.: Mouton, 1979.

Hulme, William Henry, ed. *The Middle-English Harrowing of Hell and the Gospel of Nicodemus*. London, N.Y., Toronto: Oxford University Press, Early English Text Society, 1907. Rpt. 1961.

Ivanova-Mircheva, Dora, ed. *Khomiliiata na Epifanii za Slizaneto v Ada*. Sofia: Akademiia na Naukime, 1975.

James, M.R. *The Apocryphal New Testament*. Oxford: Clarendon Press, 1924.

Kaeppeli, Thomas. *Scriptores ordinis praedicatorum medii aevi*. Vol. II. Rome: Ad. S. Sabinae, 1970.

Kelly, J.N.D. *Early Christian Creeds*. London, N.Y., Toronto: Longmans, Green and Company, 1950.

Kim, H.C., ed. *The Gospel of Nicodemus.* Toronto: Centre for Medieval Studies, Pontifical Institute, 1973.

King, Archdale A. *The Rites of Eastern Christendom.* Rome: Catholic Book Agency, 1948.

✓ Kretzmann, Paul Edward. "A Few Notes on the 'Harrowing of Hell'." *Modern Philology*, 13 (1915–1916), 49–51.

———. *The Liturgical Element in the Earliest Forms of the Medieval Drama.* Minneapolis: Bulletin of the University of Minnesota, 1916.

Laba, Vasyl'. *Patrologia.* Rome: Editiones Universitatis Catholicae Ucrainorum S. Clementis Papae, vol. 36, 1974.

Leff, G. *Medieval Thought: St. Augustine to Ockham.* Harmondsworth, England: Penguin, 1958.

Lossky, Vladimir. *The Mystical Theology of the Eastern Church.* London: James Clarke and Co. Ltd., 1957.

Lundberg, Per. *La typologie baptismale dans l'ancienne Eglise.* Uppsala: A.B. Lundequist, 1942.

MacCulloch, J.A. *The Harrowing of Hell: A Comparative Study of an Early Christian Doctrine.* Edinburgh: T. and T. Clark, 1930.

McCown, Chester Charlton, ed. *The Testament of Solomon.* Leipzig: J.C. Hinrichs'sche Buchhandlung, 1922.

Metford, J.C.J. *Dictionary of Christian Lore and Legend.* London: Thames and Hudson, 1983.

Migne, J.-P. *Patrologiae cursus completus.* Paris: Lutetia, 1857–1912.

Michaelis, Wilhelm, trans. and commentary. *Die Apokryphen Schriften zum Neuen Testament.* Bremen: Carl Schunemann Verlag, 1956.

Monnier, Jean. *La Descente aux enfers.* Paris: Librairie Fischbacher, 1905.

Naumow, Aleksander E. *Apokryfy w systemie literatury cerkiewnosłowiańskiej.* Prace komisji Słowianoznawstwa, No. 36. Wroclaw, Warsaw, Cracow, Gdansk: Polska Akademia Nauk, 1976.

O'Ceallaigh, G.C. "Dating the Commentaries of Nicodemus." *Harvard Theological Review*, 56 (1963), 21–58.

Owst, G.R. *Literature and Pulpit in Medieval England.* New York: Barnes and Noble, 1961.

Pelikan, Jaroslav. *The Christian Tradition: A History of the Development of Doctrine.* Vol. II: *The Spirit of Eastern Christendom* (600–1700). Chicago: University of Chicago Press, 1974, 1977 (Phoenix edition).

Polivka, Jiři. "Evangelium Nikodemovo literaturách slovanských." *Časopis Musea Královstvi Českého*, 65 (1891), 94–101, 155–160, 440–460.

Porfir'ev, I. Ia. *Apokrificheskaia skazaniia o Novozavetnykh litsakh i sobytiiakh po rukopysakh Solovetskoi biblioteki.* St. Petersburg: Tipografia Imp. Akademii Nauk, 1890.

Quasten, Johannes. *Patrology.* 3 vols. Utrecht-Antwerp: Spectrum, 1950–1960.

Rand, Edward Kennard. *"Sermo de Confusione Diaboli."* *Modern Philology*, 2 (1904–1905), 261–278.

Raya, Most Rev. Joseph and Baron José de Vinck. *Byzantine Daily Worship*. Combermere, Ont.: Alleluia Press, 1969.

Rose, A. " 'Attolite Portas, Principes, Vestras . . .': Aperçus sur la lecture chrétienne du Ps. 24 (23) B." In *Miscellanea liturgica in onore di Sua Eminenza il Cardinale Giacomo Lercaro, arcivescovo di Bologna . . .* Vol. I. Rome: Desclée, 1966, pp. 453–478.

Reicke, Bo. *The Disobedient Spirits and Christian Baptism*. Copenhagen: E. Munksgaard, 1946.

Saint Cyrille de Jerusalem. *Cathéchèses baptismales et mystagogiques*. Trans. J. Bouvet. Ecrits des Saints, 14. Namur, Belgium: Le Soleil Levant, 1961.

Saint Gregoire le Grand. *Homélies pour les dimanches du cycle de Paques*. Trans. René Wasselynck. Intro. Philippe Delhaye. Ecrits des Saints, 44. Namur, Belgium: Le Soleil Levant, 1962.

Saint Jean Chrysostome. *Oeuvres complètes*. Trans. M. L'Abbé Joly. Vol. I. Paris: Bordes, 1864.

Saint Jean Damascène. *La foi orthodoxe suivie de Défense des icônes*. Trans. E. Ponsoye. Préface Jean Kovalevsky. Paris: Saint-Denys, Institut orthodoxe français de théologie, 1966.

Sally, Antoinette. "Le thème de la descente aux enfers dans le 'credo' épique." *Travaux de linguistique et de littérature*, 7, No. 2 (1969), 47–63.

Santos Otero, Aurelio de. *Die Handschriftliche Überlieferung der Altslavischen Apokryphen*. Vol. II. Patristische Texte und Studien, 23. Berlin, N.Y.: W. de Gruyter, 1981.

Saward, John. *Perfect Fools: Folly for Christ's Sake in Catholic and Orthodox Spirituality*. Oxford: Oxford University Press, 1980.

Schulz, Hans-Joachim. "Die 'Höllenfahrt' als 'Anastasis': Eine Untersuchung über Eigenart und dogmen-geschichtliche Voraussetzungen byzantinischer Osterfrömmigkeit." *Zeitschrift für Katholische Theologie*, 81 (1959), 1–66.

Severjanov, S., ed. *Codex Suprasliensis*. Vol. I. St. Petersburg, 1904. Rpt. Graz: Akademische Druck-U. Verlagsamstalt, 1956.

Sheerin, Daniel. "Signum uictoriae in inferno." The Twentieth International Congress in Medieval Studies. Kalamazoo, Michigan. 8 May, 1986.

Skubiszewski, Piotr. "La place de la Descente aux Limbes dans les cycles christologiques préromans et romans." *Romanico padano, Romanico europeo*. Modena-Parma: Università degli Studi di Parma, 1982, pp. 314–321.

Solovey, Meletius Michael. *Eastern Liturgical Theology*. Toronto: The Ukrainian Catholic Religion and Culture Society *et al.*, 1970.

Speranskii, M. *Slavianskiia apokrificheskiia Evangeliia*. Trudy vos'mogo arkheologicheskogo s'iezda v Moskvy 1890. Vol. II. Moscow: 1895.

Sticca, Sandro. "The Literary Genesis of the Latin Passion Play and the *Planctus Mariae*: An New Christocentric and Marian Theology." In *The Medieval Drama*. Albany: State University of New York Press, 1972.

Taft, Robert. *The Great Entrance*. Orientalia Christiana Analecta, 200. Rome: Pont. Institutum Studiorum Orientalium, 1975.

Thomson, Francis J. "The Nature of the Reception of Christian Byzantine Culture in Russia in the Tenth to Thirteenth Centuries and Its Implications for Russian Culture." In *Belgian Contributions to the Eighth International Congress of Slavists*. Zagreb, 1978. Slavica Gandensia, 5. Ghent: Department of Slavonic Philology, Ghent State University, le Centre Belges d'Etudes Slaves, 1978, pp. 107–130.

Tischendorf, C. von, ed. *Evangelia Apocrypha*. Leipzig: Avenarius and Mendelssohn, 1853.

Turmel, J. *La Descente du Christ aux enfers*. Science et Religion, No. 342. Paris: Bloud, 1908.

Vaillant, André. *L'Evangile de Nicodème*. Geneva, Paris: Librairie Droz, 1968.

———. "L'Homélie d'Epiphane sur l'ensevelissement de Christ." *Radovi Staroslavenskog Instituta*, 3 (Zagreb, 1958), 5–101.

Wellesz, Egon. *A History of Byzantine Music and Hymnography*. Oxford: Clarendon Press, 1949.

Young, Karl. *The Drama of the Medieval Church*. 2 vols. Oxford: Clarendon Press, 1933.

———. "The Harrowing of Hell." *Transactions of the Wisconsin Academy of Sciences, Arts, and Letters*, 16, No. 2 (1910), 889–947.

Symbolism, Iconography

Barida, Michael N. "Iconography and Its Meaning." In *The Iconography of St. Nicholas Church*. Toronto: St. Nicholas Ukrainian Catholic Parish, 1977.

Chew, Samuel C. *The Pilgrimage of Life*. New Haven, London: Yale University Press, 1962.

Daniel, Howard. *Encyclopedia of Themes and Subjects in Painting*. London: Thames and Hudson, 1971.

Davidson, C. "From *Tristia* to *Gaudium*: Iconography and the York-Towneley *Harrowing of Hell*." *American Benedictine Review*, 28 (1977), 260–275.

Evdokimov, Paul. *L'Art de l'icône; Théologie de la beauté*. Brussels: Desclée De Brouwer, 1970.

Ferguson, George. *Signs and Symbols in Christian Art*. N.Y.: Oxford University Press, 1961.

Grabar, André. *Christian Iconography: A Study of Its Origins*. Trans. Terry Grabar. Princeton: Princeton University Press, 1968.

Hall, James. *Dictionary of Subjects and Symbols in Art*. London: John Murray, 1974.

Hordyns'kyi, Sviatoslav. *Ukrains'ka ikona 12–18 storichchia*. Philadelphia: Provydinnia, 1973.

Hughes, Robert. *Heaven and Hell in Western Art*. London: Weidenfeld and Nicholson, 1968.

Hulme, Edward. *Symbolism in Christian Art*. Poole, Dorset: Blandferd Press, 1976.

Kirschbaum, Engelbert, *et al*. *Lexikon der christlichen Iconographie*. Vols. II, IV. Rome, Freiburg, Basel, Vienna: Herder, 1970.

Kroll, Josef. *Gott und Hölle; der Mythos vom Descensuskampfe*. Leipzig, Berlin: B.G. Teubner, 1932.

Lohvyn, Hryhorii, Lada Miliaeva, Vira Sventsits'ka. *Ukrains'kyi seredn'ovichnyi zhyvopys*. Kiev: Mystetstvo, 1976.

Onasch, Konrad. *Ikonen*. Gütersloh: Gütersloher Verlagshaus Gerd Mohn, 1961.

Ouspensky, Leonide. *La Théologie de l'icône dans l'Eglise orthodoxe*. Paris: Cerf, 1980.

Ouspensky, Leonid and Vladimir Lossky. *The Meaning of Icons*. Trans. G.E.H. Palmer and E. Kadloubovsky. Olten, Switzerland: Urs Graf-Verlag, 1952.

Pelc, Janusz. *Obraz-Słowo-Znak; Studium o emblematach w literaturze staropolskiej*. Wroclaw: Polska Akademia Nauk, 1973.

Réau, Louis. *Iconographie de l'art chrétien*. Vol. II. Paris: Presses Universitaires de France, 1957.

Rushforth, G.M. "The Descent into Hell in Byzantine Art." *Papers of the British School at Rome*, 1 (London: 1902), 114–119.

Schiller, Gertrud. *Ikonographie der christlichen Kunst*. Vol. III: Die Auferstehung und Erhöhung Christi. Gütersloh: Gütersloher Verlagshaus Gerd Mohn. 1971.

Skorobucha, H. "Zur Ikonogr. des Jungsten Gerichts in der russ. Ikonenmal." *Kirche im Osten*, 5 (1962), 51–74.

Still, Gertrude Grace. *A Handbook of Symbols in Christian Art*. N.Y.: Macmillan, 1975.

Stuart, Donald Clive. "The Stage Setting and the Iconography of the Middle Ages." *The Romanic Review*, 4 (1913), 330–342.

Treeck, Carl van and Aloysius Croft. *Symbols in the Church*. Milwaukee: The Bruce Publishing Co., 1960.

Weitzmann, Kurt. "Das Evangelion im Shevophylakion zu Lawra." *Seminarium Kondakovianum*, 8 (1936), 83–98.

———. *The Icon: Holy Images Sixth to Fourteenth Century*. London: Chatto and Windus, 1978.

Weitzmann, Kurt *et al*. *The Icon*. London: Evans Brothers Ltd., 1982.

The Drama: France

Editions of Harrowing Plays

Axton, Richard and John Stevens, trans. *Medieval French Plays*. Oxford: Basil Blackwell, 1971.

Cohen, Gustave, ed. *Le Livre de Conduite du Regisseur et Le Compte des Dépenses pour le Mystère de la Passion joué à Mons en 1501*. Strasbourg: Publications de la Faculté des Lettres de Strasbourg, 1924.

Jodogne, Omer, ed. *Le Mystère de la Passion d'Arnoul Gréban*. Vol. I. Brussels: Palais des Académies, 1965.

Jubinal, Achille, ed. *Mystères inédits du quinzième siècle*. Vol. II. Paris: Téchener, 1837.

Odenkirchen, Carl J., ed. *The Play of Adam (Ordo Representacionis Ade)*. Brookline, Mass. and Leyden: Classical Folia Editions, 1976.

Secondary Sources

Becker, Walter. *Die Sage von der Höllenfahrt Christi in der altfranzösischen Literatur*. Göttingen: n.p., 1912.

Berger, Blandine-Dominique. *Le Drame liturgique de Pâques du Xe au XIIIe siècle: Liturgie et Théâtre*. Théologie Hist., 37. Paris: Beauchesne, 1976.

Clédat, L. *Le Théâtre en France au Moyen Age*. Paris: Lecène et Oudet, 1896.

Cohen, Gustave. *Histoire de la mise en scène dans le théâtre religieux français du Moyen-Age*. Paris: n.p., 1926.

_____. *Le Théâtre en France au Moyen-Age*. Paris: Les Presses Universitaires, 1948.

Crossland, Jessie. *Medieval French Drama*. Oxford: Basil Blackwell, 1956.

Fox, John. *A Literary History of France: The Middle Ages*. London: Ernest Benn, Ltd., 1974.

Frank, Grace. *The Medieval French Drama*. Oxford: Clarendon Press, 1954.

_____. "Popular Iconography of the Passion." *PMLA*, 46 (1931), 333–340.

Gardiner, Harold C. *Mysteries' End; An Investigation of the Last Days of the Medieval Religious Stage*. New Haven: Yale University Press, 1967.

Jasinski, René. *Histoire de la littérature française*. Vol. I. Paris: A.G. Nizet, 1977.

Jauss, Hans Robert. "Littérature médiévale et théorie des genres." *Poétique*, 1 (1970), 79–101.

Jeanroy, Alfred, ed. *Le Théâtre religieux en langue française jusqu'à la fin du XIVe siècle*. Paris: Imprimerie Nationale, 1959.

Knight, Alan E. *Aspects of Genre in Late Medieval French Drama*. Manchester: Manchester University Press, 1983.

Petit de Julleville, L. *Les Mystères*. Vol. II. Paris: Librairie Hachette, 1880.

Owen, D.D.R. *The Vision of Hell; Infernal Journeys in Medieval French Literature*. Edinburgh and London: Scottish Academic Press, 1970.

Rey-Flaud, Henri. *Le Cercle magique: Essai sur le théâtre en rond à la fin du Moyen Age.* Paris: Gallimard, 1973.

Roy, Emile. *Le Mystère de la Passion en France du XIVe au XVIe siecle.* Paris: H. Champion, 1904.

Sepet, M. *Le Drame Chrétien au Moyen Age.* Paris: Didier et Co., 1878.

Stone, Edward N. *Adam: A Religious Play of the Twelfth Century.* University of Washington Publications in Language and Literature, 4, No. 2, 1926. Rpt. Seattle, Wash.: University of Washington Press, 1928.

Urwin, Kenneth. "The *Mystère d'Adam*: Two Problems." *Modern Language Review*, 34 (1939), 70–72.

England

Editions

Block, K.S., ed. *Ludus Coventriae or the Plai called Corpus Christi.* Early English Text Society, Extra Series 120, 1922. Rpt. London: Oxford University Press, 1960.

Cawley, A.C., ed. "The Chester Harrowing of Hell." In *Everyman and Medieval Miracle Plays.* N.Y.: Dutton, 1959.

Deimling, H., ed. *The Chester Plays.* Early English Text Society, Extra Series 62, 115. London: Kegan Paul, Trench, Trubner, 1916.

England, G.A. and Pollard, A., eds. *The Towneley Plays.* Early English Text Society, 1897. Rpt. London: Oxford University Press, 1907, 1925.

Foster, F.A., ed. *A Study of . . . The Northern Passion.* London: R. Clay and Sons, 1914.

Happé, Peter, ed. "The York Harrowing of Hell." *English Mystery Plays.* Harmondsworth: Penguin, 1975.

Harris, Markham, trans. *The Cornish Ordinalia; A Medieval Dramatic Trilogy.* Washington: The Catholic University of America Press, 1969.

Lumiansky, R.M. and David Mills, eds. *The Chester Mystery Cycle.* Vol. I. London: Oxford University Press for the Early English Text Society, 1974.

————. *The Chester Mystery Cycle: Essays and Documents.* Chapel Hill and London: The University of North Carolina Press, 1983.

Norris, E., ed. *Ordinalia; The Ancient Cornish Drama.* 2 vols. Oxford: Oxford University Press, 1859.

Pollard, A.W., ed. *English Miracle Plays, Moralities, and Interludes.* Oxford: Clarendon Press, 1909.

Rose, M., ed. *The Wakefield Mystery Plays.* London: Evans, 1961.

Secondary Sources

Adolph, H. "On Medieval Laughter." *Speculum*, 22 (1947), 251–253.

Axton, Richard. *European Drama of the Early Middle Ages*. London: Hutchinson University Library, 1974.

Bakere, Jane A. *The Cornish Ordinalia; A Critical Study*. Cardiff: University of Wales Press, 1980. Denny, Neville

B̶r̶a̶d̶b̶u̶r̶y̶,̶ ̶M̶a̶l̶c̶o̶l̶m̶,̶ ̶a̶n̶d̶ ̶D̶a̶v̶i̶d̶ ̶P̶a̶l̶m̶e̶r̶, eds. *Medieval Drama*. Stratford-Upon-Avon Studies, 16. London: Edward Arnold, 1973.

Clark, Eleanor Grace. "The York Plays and the Gospel of Nichodemus [*sic*]." *PMLA*, 43 (1928), 153–161.

Collier, Richard J. *Poetry and Drama in the York Corpus Christi Play*. Hamden, Connecticut: Archon, 1977.

Craddock, L.G. "Franciscan Influences on Early English Drama." *Franciscan Studies*, 10 (1950), 383–417.

Craig, Hardin E. *English Religious Drama of the Middle Ages*. Oxford: Clarendon Press, 1955.

Craigie, W.A. "The Gospel of Nicodemus and the York Mystery Play." In *Furnivall Miscellany*. Oxford: n.p., 1901, pp. 56–61.

Curtius, E.R. *European Literature and the Latin Middle Ages*. Trans. W.R. Trask. London: Routledge and Kegan Paul, 1953.

Fichte, J.O. *Expository Voices in Medieval Drama*. Nurnberg: Verlag Hans Carl, 1975.

Frye, Timothy. "The Unity of the *Ludus Coventriae*." *Studies in Philology*, 48 (1951), 527–568.

Gardiner, Harold C. *Mysteries' End: An Investigation of the Last Days of the Medieval Religious Stage*. New Haven: Yale University Press, 1967.

Gardner, John. *The Construction of the Wakefield Cycle*. Carbondale: South Illinois University Press, 1974.

Kahrl, S.J. *Traditions of Medieval English Drama*. Pittsburgh: University of Pittsburgh Press, 1975.

Kolve, V.A. *The Play Called Corpus Christi*. Stanford: Stanford University Press, 1966.

Lumiansky, R.M. "Comedy and Theme in the Chester *Harrowing of Hell*." *Tulane Studies in English*, 10, (1960), 5–12.

Macauley, Peter Stuart. "The Play of the Harrowing of Hell as a Climax in the English Mystery Cycles." *Studia Germanica Gandensia*, 8 (1966), 115–134.

McAlindon, T. "Comedy and Terror in Middle English Literature: The Diabolical Game." *Modern Language Review*, 60 (1965), 323–332.

Meredith, Peter and John E. Tailby, eds. *The Staging of Religious Drama in Europe in the Later Middle Ages: Texts and Documents*. Trans. Raffaella Ferrari *et al*. Early Drama, Art, and Music. Monograph Series, 4. Kalamazoo: Medieval Institute Publications, 1983.

Meyers, Walter Earl. *A Study of the Middle English Wakefield Cycle Plays*. Ann Arbor: University Microfilms, 1967.

Nagler, A.M. *The Medieval Religious Stage: Shapes and Phantoms.* New Haven and London: Yale University Press, 1976.

Nelson, A.H. *The Medieval English Stage.* Chicago: University of Chicago Press, 1974.

Peter, Thurstan C. *The Old Cornish Drama.* London: Elliot Stock, 1906.

Prosser, Eleanor. *Drama and Religion in the English Mystery Plays.* Stanford: Stanford University Press, 1961.

Travis, Peter W. *Dramatic Design in the Chester Cycle.* Chicago and London: The University of Chicago Press, 1982.

Tydeman, W. *The Theatre in the Early Middle Ages.* Cambridge: Cambridge University Press, 1978.

Woolf, Rosemary. *The English Mystery Plays.* London: Routledge and Kegan Paul, 1972.

Spain

Editions

Gillet, Joseph E., ed. "An Easter Play by Juan de Pedraza (1549)." *Revue Hispanique*, 81 (1933), Pt. I, 550–607.

———. "Tres pasos de la Pasión y una égloga de la Resurrección (Burgos, 1520)." *PMLA*, 47 (1932), 949–980.

Rouanet, Léo, ed. *Colección de autos, farsas y coloquios del siglo XVI.* 4 vols. Madrid, Barcelona: Macon, 1901. Rpt. Hildesheim and New York: Georg Olms Verlag, 1979.

Secondary Sources

✓Arias, Ricardo. *The Spanish Sacramental Plays.* Boston: Twayne Publishers, 1980.

✓ Crawford, J.P.W. "The Devil as a Dramatic Figure in the Spanish Religious Drama Before Lope de Vega." *The Romanic Review*, 1 (1910), 302–312.

———. "The Pastor and Bobo in the Spanish Religious Drama of the Sixteenth Century." *The Romanic Review*, 2 (1911), 376–401.

———. *Spanish Drama Before Lope de Vega.* 3rd ed. Philadelphia: University of Pennsylvania Press, 1967.

Flecniakoska, Jean-Louis. *La Formation de l'"Auto" religieux en Espagne avant Calderon (1550–1635).* Montpellier: Impr. P. Déhan, 1961.

———. "Les Rôles de Satan dans les Pièces du Codice de Autos Viejos." *Revue des Langues Romanes*, 75 (1963), 195–207.

Maravall, José Antonio. *Culture of the Baroque: Analysis of a Historical Structure.* Trans. Terry Cochran. Theory and History of Literature, 25. Minneapolis: University of Minnesota, 1986.

Parker, Alexander A. "Notes on the Religious Drama in Medieval Spain and the Origins of the 'Auto Sacramental.'" *Modern Language Review*, 30 (1935), 170–182.

Shergold, N.D. *A History of the Spanish Stage; From Medieval Times Until the End of the Sixteenth Century*. Oxford: Clarendon Press, 1967.

Stern, Charlotte. "The Early Spanish Drama: From Medieval Ritual to Renaissance Art." *Renaissance Drama*, 6 (1973), 177–201.

Surtz, Ronald E. *The Birth of a Theater: Dramatic Convention in the Spanish Theater from Juan del Encina to Lope de Vega*. Madrid: Editorial Castalia, Princeton University Department of Romance Languages and Literatures, 1979.

Wardropper, B.W. *Introducción al teatro religioso de Siglo de Oro*. 2nd ed. Madrid, Barcelona, Caracas: Anaya, 1967.

Wilson, Edward M. and Duncan Moir. *A Literary History of Spain, The Golden Age: Drama 1492–1700*. London: Ernest Benn, 1971.

Italy

Editions

Ancona, Alessandro d', ed. *Sacre Rappresentazioni dei secoli XIV, XV e XVI*. 3 vols. Florence: Successori Le Monnier, 1872.

Banfi, Luigi, ed. *Sacre Rappresentazioni del Quattorcento*. Turin: Unione Tipografico – Editrice Torinese, 1968.

Bartholomaeis, Vincenzo de, ed. *Laude Drammatiche e Rappresentazioni Sacre*. 3 vols. Florence: Le Monnier, 1943.

———, ed. *Il Teatro Abruzzese del Medio Evo*. Bologna: Arnaldo Forni Editore, 1924.

Bonfantini, Mario, ed. *Le Sacre Rappresentazioni Italiane*. Milan: [Bompiani], 1942.

Faccioli, Emilio, ed. *Il Teatro Italiano*. Vol. I. Turin: Einaudi, 1975.

Galli, Giuseppe. *Laudi inedite dei Disciplinati Umbri*. Bergamo: Istituto Italiano d'Arti Grafiche, 1910.

Secondary Sources

Amico, Silvio d'. *Storia del Teatro Drammatico*. n.p.: Garzanti, 1950.

Ancona, Alessandro d'. *Origini del Teatro Italiano*. 2 vols. Turin: Ermanno Loescher, 1891.

Apollonio, Mario. *Storia del Teatro Italiano*. Vol. 1. Florence: Sansoni, 1891.

Cioni, Alfredo. *Bibliografia delle Sacre Rappresentazioni*. Florence: Sansoni Antiquariato, 1961.

Jackson, W.T.H. *The Literature of the Middle Ages*. N.Y. and London: Columbia University Press, 1960.

Kennard, Joseph Spencer. *The Italian Theatre: From Its Beginning to the Close of the Seventeenth Century.* N.Y.: Benjamin Bloom, 1932.

Klein, J.L. *Geschichte des Italianischen Drama's* [*sic*]. 3 vols. Leipzig: T.O. Weigel, 1866–1868.

Larson, Orville K. "Bishop Abraham of Souzdal's Description of 'Sacre Rappresentazioni.'" *Educational Theatre Journal*, 9 (1957), 208–213.

Lees, Dorothy Nevile. "The 'Sacre Rappresentazioni' of Florence." *The Mask*, 4 (1911–1912), 219–249.

Tonelli, Luigi. *Il Teatro Italiano; dalle Origini al Giorni Nostri.* Milan: Modernissima, 1924.

Germany and Austria

Editions

Blosen, Hans, ed. *Das Wiener Osterspiel.* Berlin: Erich Schmidt Verlag, 1979.

Froning, Richard, ed. *Das Drama des Mittelalters.* 3 vols., 1891–1892. Rpt. Darmstadt: Wissenschaftliche Buchgesellschaft, 1964.

Hartl, Eduard, ed. *Das Drama des Mittelalters: Osterspiele.* Leipzig: Verlag von Philipp Reclam, 1937.

————. *Das Drama des Mittelalters: Passionsspiele II.* Darmstadt: Wissenschaftliche Buchgesellschaft, 1966.

Rueff, Hans, ed. *Das rheinische Osterspiel der Berliner Handschrift Ms. Germ. Fol. 1219, mit Untersuchungen zur Textgeschichte des deutschen Osterspiels.* Berlin: Weidmannsche Buchhandlung, 1925.

Schutzeichel, Rudolf, ed. *Das Mittelrheinische Passionsspiel der Galler Handschrift 919.* Tubingen: Max Niemeyer Verlag, 1978.

West, Larry E., ed. *The Saint Gall Passion Play.* Brookline, Mass. and Leyden: Classical Folia Editions, 1976.

Zucker, A.E., ed. *The Redentin Easter Play.* N.Y.: Octagon Books, 1966.

Secondary Sources

Abbey, Everett Lucius. *The Religious Drama of the Tyrol.* Cleveland: n.p., [c. 1900].

Bartsch, Karl. "Das alteste Deutsche Passionspiel." *Germania*, 8 (1863), 273–297.

Bergmann, Rolf. *Studien zu Entstehung und Geschichte der Deutschen Passionsspiele des 13. und 14. Jahrhunderts.* Munich: Wilhelm Fink Verlag, 1972.

Duriez, Georges. *Les Apocryphes dans le drame religieux en Allemagne au moyen âge.* Lille, Paris: n.p., 1914.

————. *La Théologie dans le drame religieux en Allemagne au moyen âge.* Diss. University of Lille. Paris: J. Tallandrier, 1914.

Fichte, Jörg O. *Expository Voices in Medieval Drama*. Nurnberg: Hans Carl Nurnberg, 1975.

Gardiner, Harold C. *Mysteries' End: An Investigation of the Last Days of the Medieval Religious Stage*. New Haven: Yale University Press, 1967.

Hase, Karl August von. *Miracle Plays and Sacred Dramas; A Historical Survey*. Trans. A.W. Jackson. Ed. W.W. Jackson. London: Trubner and Co., 1880. ✓

Kroll, Josef. "Zur Geschichte des Spieles von Christi Höllenfahrt." *Vortrage der Bibliothek Warburg 1927–1928 zur Geschichte des Dramas*, 6–7, 257–302. London: Kraus reprint, 1967.

Michael, Wolfgang F. "Die Bedeutung des Wortes *Figur* im Geistlichen Drama Deutschlands." *Germanic Review*, 21 (1946), 3–8.

_____. *Das Deutsche Drama des Mittelalters*. Berlin, N.Y.: Walter de Gruyter, 1971.

Rudick, Michael. "Theme, Structure, and Sacred Context in the Benediktbeuern 'Passion' Play." *Speculum*, 49 (1974), 267–286. ✓

Rudwin, M.J. *A Historical and Bibliographical Survey of the German Religious Drama*. Pittsburgh: University of Pittsburgh, 1924.

Schuldes, Luis. *Die Teufelsszenen im Deutschen Geistlichen Drama des Mittelalters*. Göppinger Arbeiten zur Germanistik, 116. Göppingen: Verlag Alfred Kummerle, 1974. ✓

Stammler, Wolfgang. *Das religiöse Drama in deutschen Mittelalter*. Leipzig: Verlag von Quelle and Mener, 1927.

Steinback, Rolf. *Die deutschen Oster- und Passionsspiele des Mittelalters*. Cologne: Böhlau Verlag, 1970.

Tashiro, Tom T. "The Donaueschingen Passion Play: A Study of the Theme and Structure of Spiritual Blindness." *Germanic Review*, 37 (1962), 5–23.

Wackernell, J.E. *Altdeutsche Passionsspiele Aus Tirol*. 1897. Rpt. Weisbaden: Martin Sandig-ottG, 1972.

Wülker, Richard Paul. *Das Evangelium Nicodemi in der abendländischen Literatur*. Paderborn: Ferdinand Schöningh, 1872.

au des p. 141 – Kunstein.

Poland

Editions

Lewański, Julian, ed. *Dramat i teatr średniowiecza i renesansu w Polsce*. Warsaw: Państwowe Wydawnictwo Naukowe, 1981.

_____, ed. *Dramaty staropolskie*. Vol. II. Warsaw: Państwowy Instytut Wydawniczy, 1959.

_____. *Studia nad dramatem polskiego odrodzenie*. Vol. IV. Wroclaw: Wydawnictwo Polskiej Akademii Nauk, 1956.

Okoń, Jan, ed. *Historyja o Chwalebnym Zmartwychwstaniu Pańskim*. Wroclaw: Zakład Narodowy im. Ossolińskich, 1971.

Windakiewicz, Stanislaw, ed. *Teatr ludowy w dawnej Polsce*. Biblioteka Pisarzów Polskich, 25. Cracow: Drukarnia Universytetu Jagiellońskiego, 1893.

Secondary Sources

Balinski, Michał. *Dawna Akademia wileńska*. Petersburg: J. Ohryzko, 1862.

Grabowski, Tadeusz. "Ze studiów nad teatrem jezuickim we Franciji i w Polsce w wiekach XVI-XVIII." *Poznańskie Towarzystwo Przyjaciół Nauk*. Wydział Filologiczno-Filozoficzny. Prace Komisji Filologicznej [Poznań], 21 (1963), No. 3.

Hahn, Wiktor. *Literatura dramatyczna w Polsce XVI wieku*. Lviv: Towarzystwo dla popierania Nauki Polskiej, 1906.

Jurkowski, Henryk. "Teatr lalek w dawnej Polsce; Próba zarysu historycznego." In *O Dawnym Dramacie i teatrze*; *Studia do syntezy*. Wroclaw, Warsaw, Cracow, Gdansk: Wydawnictwo Polskiej Akademii Nauk, 1971, pp. 7–40.

Kridl, Manfred. *A Survey of Polish Literature and Culture*. Trans. Olga Scherer-Virski. Leiden: Mouton and Co., 1956.

Kro'l-Kaczorowska, Barbara. *Teatr dawnej Polski*. Warsaw: Państwowy Instytut, 1971.

Krzyżanowski, Julian. *A History of Polish Literature*. Warsaw: Polish Scientific Publishers, 1978.

Okoń, Jan. *Dramat i teatr szkolny sceny Jezuickie XVII wieku*. Wroclaw, Warsaw, Cracow: Wydawnictwo Polskiej Akademii Nauk, 1970.

Raszewski, Zbigniew. *Krótka historia teatru polskiego*. Warsaw: Państwowy Instytut Wydawniczy, 1977.

Sajkowski, Alojzy. *Barok*. Warsaw: Państwowe Zakłady Wydawnictw Szkolnych, 1972.

Sokołowska, Jadwiga. *Dwie nieskończoności; Szkice o literaturze barokowej Europy*. Warsaw: Państwowy Instytut Wydawniczy, 1978.

Weintraub, W. "Teatr Seneki a struktura 'Odprawy posłów greckich.'" In *Kultura i Literatura Dawnej Polski*. Warsaw: Państwowe Wydawnictwo Naukowe, 1968, pp. 95–106.

Windakiewicz, Stanislaw. *Teatr kollegiow Jezuickich w Dawnej Polsce*. Cracow: Polska Akademja Umiejętnośce, 1922.

Ziomek, Jerzy. *Odrodzenie w Polsce; Historia literatury*. Vol. IV. Warsaw: Państwowy Instytut Wydawniczy, 1956.

———. *Renesans*. Warsaw: Państwowe Wydawnictwo Naukowe, 1977.

Old Rus', Russia, Bohemia

Aseev, B.N. *Russkii dramaticheskii teatr ot ego istokov do kontsa XVIII veka*. Moscow: Iskusstvo, 1977.

Birnbaum, Henrik. *On Medieval and Renaissance Slavic Writing: Selected Essays.* The Hague, Paris: Mouton, 1974.

Birnbaum, Henrik and Michael S. Flier, eds. *Medieval Russian Culture.* California Slavic Studies, 12. Berkeley: University of California Press, 1984.

Derzhavina, O.A., ed. *et al. Pervye p'esy russkogo teatra.* Moscow: Nauka, 1972.

———, ed. *et al. P'esy shkol'nykh teatrov Moskvy.* Moscow: Nauka, 1974.

Eremin, I. "Zhanrovaia priroda 'Slovo o polku Igoreve.' " In *Literatura drevnei Rusi; Etudy i Kharakteristiki.* Ed. D.S. Likhachev. Leningrad: Nauka, 1966.

Florovskii, A.V. *Chekhi i vostochnye slaviane.* Vol. I. Prague: Orbis, 1935.

Gudzy, N.K. *History of Early Russian Literature.* Trans. Susan Wilbur Jones. N.Y.: Macmillan, 1949.

Hrabák, Josef, ed. *Staročeské drama.* Prague: Československý Spisovatel, 1950.

Jelinek, H. *Histoire de la littérature tchèque.* Paris: Editions du Sagittaire, 1930.

Kalan, Filip. "Le Jeu de la Passion à Škofja Loka." *Le Livre Slovène,* No. 3 (1966), 24–32.

Likhachov, Dmitry. *The Great Heritage: The Classical Literature of Old Rus.* Trans. Doris Bradbury. Moscow: Progress Publishers, 1981.

Lotman, L.M., ed. *Istoria russkoi dramaturgii XVII—pervaia polovina XIX veka.* Leningrad: Nauka, 1982.

Peretts, V. *Pamiatniki russkoi dramy epokhi Petra Velikogo.* St. Petersburg: n.p., 1903.

———. *Starinnyi teatr v Rossii XVI-XVIII v.* St. Petersburg: Akademiia, 1923.

Picchio, Riccardo. "The Function of Biblical Thematic Clues in the Literary Code of Slavica Orthodoxa." *Slavica Hierosolymitana,* 1 (1977), 1–31.

———. "Levels of Meaning in Old Russian Literature." In *American Contributions to the Ninth International Congress of Slavists. Kiev, 1983.* Vol. II. Ed. Paul Debreczeny. Columbus, Ohio: Slavica, 1983, pp. 357–370.

———. "Models and Patterns in the Literary Tradition of Medieval Orthodox Slavdom." In *American Contributions to the Seventh International Congress of Slavists. Warsaw, 1973.* Ed. Victor Terras. The Hague, Paris: Mouton, 1973, pp. 439–467.

Picchio, Riccardo and Harvey Goldblatt, eds. *Aspects of the Slavic Language Question.* Vol. I. New Haven: Yale Concilium on International and Area Studies, 1984.

Porfir'ev, I. *Istoria russkoi slovesnosti.* Part I. Kazan: Tipografiia Imperatorskogo Universiteta, 1891.

Sofronova, L.A. *Poetika slavianskogo teatra: XVII—pervoi poloviny XVIII v.* Moscow: Nauka, 1981.

Speranskii, M.N. *Russkaia ustnaia slovestnost'.* Moscow: 1917. Rpt. The

Hague, Paris: Mouton, 1969.

Truhlář, Josef. "O staročeskych dramatech velikonočnich." *Časopis Musea Kralovstvi Českého*, 65 (1891), 3–43, 165–197.

Veselovskii, Aleksii. *Starinnyi teatr v Evropi*. Moscow: n.p., 1870.

Vipper, Iu. B., et al., eds. *XVII vek v mirovom literaturnom razvitii*. Moscow: Nauka, 1969.

Vulović-Stanchfield, Gordana. *Russian Baroque: A.D. Kantemir*. Diss. Florida State University, 1977. Ann Arbor: Xerox University Microfilms, 1972.

Ukraine

Editions of Slovo o zbureniu pekla

Bilets'kyi, O.I., ed. "Slovo o zbureniu pekla." In *Khrestomatiia davnoi ukrains'koi literatury*. Kiev: Radians'ka Shkola, 1967, pp. 220–232. (Taken from Rezanov)

Franko, I., ed. "Iuzhnorusskaia paskhal'naia drama." *Kievskaia starina*, 53 (1896), 380–412.

———. "*Slovo pro zburenie pekla*; ukrains'ka pasiina drama." *Zapysky Naukovoho Tovarystva im. T.H. Shevchenka*, 81 (1908), 5–50.

Haevs'kyi, S., ed. "Do istorii pasiinoi dramy—*Slovo o zbureniu pekla*." *Naukovy zbirnyk* (1926), 73–81. (An excerpt only)

Hordyns'kyi, Ia., ed. "*Slovo pro zburenne pekla* po staruns'komu rukopysu XVIII v.," *Zapysky Naukovoho Tovarystva im. T.H. Shevchenka*, 97 (1910), 155–174.

Myshanych, O.V., ed. "*Slovo o zbureniu pekla*." in *Ukrains'ka literatura XVII st*. Compiled, with introduction and notes, by V.I. Krekoten'. Kiev: Naukova Dumka, 1987, pp. 364–374. (Based on Franko's 1908 version).

Rezanov, V., ed. "Slovo o zbureniu pekla." In *Drama ukrains'ka*. Vol. I. Kiev: Ukrains'ka Akademiia Nauk, 1926.

Vozniak, M., ed. "Znadibky do ukrains'koi velykodnoi dramy." *Zapysky Naukovoho Tovarystva im. T.H. Shevchenka*, 146 (1927), 119–153.

Ukrainian Literature and Culture

Antonovych, D. *Trysta rokiv ukrains'koho teatru 1619–1919*. Prague: Ukrains'-kyi hromads'kyi vydavnychyi fond, 1925.

Barvins'kyi Oleksander. *Istoria ukrains'koi literatury*. Vol. I. Lviv: Naukove Tovarystvo im. T.H. Shevchenka, 1920.

Bida, Constantine. "Vestiges of Antiquity in Ukrainian Baroque Literature." In *Canadian Contributions to the VIII International Congress of Slavists Zagreb-Ljubljana 1978: Tradition and Innovation in Slavic Literatures, Linguistics, and Stylistics*. Ed. Zbigniew Folejewski *et al*. Ottawa: Canadian Association of Slavists, 1978, pp. 25–35.

Bilets'kyi, O., ed. *Istoriia ukrains'koi literatury*. Kiev-Kharkiv: Radians'ka Shkola, 1947.

———. "Perekladna literatura vizantiis'ko-bolhars'koho pokhodzhennia." In *Zibrannia prats' u p'iaty tomakh*. Vol. I. Kiev: Academiia Nauk URSR, 1965, pp. 128–187.

———. *Vid davnyny do suchasnosti*. Vol. I. Kiev: Khudozhna literatura, 1960.

Chyzhevs'kyi, Dmytro. *Comparative History of Slavic Literatures*. Nashville: Vanderbilt University Press, 1971.

———. *A History of Ukrainian Literature*. Trans. Dolly Ferguson, Doreen Gorsline, Ulana Petyk. Ed. George S.N. Luckyj. Littleton, Colorado: Ukrainian Academic Press, 1975.

———. *Ukrains'kyi literaturnyi barok*. Vol. III. Prague: Ukrains'ke istorychno-filologichne tovarystvo v Prazi, 1941.

Fedas, I. Iu. *Ukrains'kyi narodnyi vertep*. Kiev: Naukova Dumka, 1987.

[Franko, I.]. Myron. "Iuzhnorusskaia paskhal'naia drama." *Kievskaia starina*, 53 (1896), 380–342.

Franko, I. "Novi materialy do istorii ukrains'koho vertepa." *Zapysky Naukovoho Tovarystva im. T.H. Shevchenka*. 82 (1908), 30–52.

———. *Pro teatr i dramaturhiiu; vybrani statti, retsenzii ta vyslovliuvannia*. Ed. M.F. Nechytaliuk. Kiev: Akademiia Nauk, 1957.

———. *Tvory*. Vol. 16. Kiev: Derzhavne vydavnytstvo khudozhnoi literatury, 1955.

Grabowicz, George G. *Toward A History of Ukrainian Literature*. Cambridge: Harvard Ukrainian Research Institute, 1981.

Hrytsai, M.S. *Ukrains'ka dramaturhiia XVII–XVIII st*. Kiev: Vyshcha shkola, 1974.

Isaevych, Ia. D. *Bratstva ta ikh rol' v rozvytku ukrains'koi kul'tury XVI–XVIII st*. Kiev: Naukova Dumka, 1966.

Ivan'o, I.V. "Pro ukrains'ke literaturne barokko." *Radians'ke literaturoznavstvo*, 10 (1970), 41–53.

Kharlampovych, Konstantin Vasil'ievich. *Zapadnorusskiia pravoslavniia shkoly XVI i nachala XVII veka. . . .* Kazan: Imperatorskii universitet, 1898.

Kuznetsov, E. *Iz proshlogo russkoi estrady; istoricheskie ocherki*. Moscow: Iskusstvo, 1958.

Kysil, O. *Ukrains'kyi teatr*. Kiev: Mystetstvo, 1968.

Lewin, Paulina. "Early Ukrainian Theatre and Drama." *Nationality Papers*, 8, No. 2 (1980), 219–232.

———. "Polish-Ukrainian-Russian Literary Relations of the Sixteenth-Eighteenth Centuries; New Approaches." *The Slavic and East European Journal*, 24, No. 3 (1980), 256–269.

———. "Ruskie Formy Parateatralne XVI-XVIII w. na Dawnych Ziemiach Rzeczypospolitej." *Slavia Orientalis*, 22 (1973), 287–304.

———. "The Staging of Plays at the Kiev Mohyla Academy in the Seventeenth and Eighteenth Centuries." *Harvard Ukrainian Studies*, 5, No. 3 (1981), 320–334.

————. "Stsenicheskaia struktura *Slovo o zburenia pekla*, p'esy ukrainskogo massovogo teatra pervoi poloviny XVII v. i ee reministsentsii." In *Slovo o Polku Igoreve; Pamiatniki literatury i iskusstva XI-XVII vekov*. Moscow: Nauka, 1978, pp. 287–300.

————. "The Ukrainian Popular Religious Stage of the Seventeenth and Eighteenth Centuries on the Territory of the Polish Commonwealth." *Harvard Ukrainian Studies*, 1, No. 3 (1977), 308–329.

————. "The Ukrainian School Theatre in the Seventeenth and Eighteenth Centuries; An Expression of the Baroque." *Harvard Ukrainian Studies*, 5, No. 1 (1981), 54–65.

————. *Wykłady poetyki w uczelniach Rosyjskich XVIII w. (1722–1774) a tradycje polskie*. Wroclaw: Polska Akademia Nauk, Zakład Narodowy im. Ossolińskich, 1972.

Lewitter, Lucjan Ryszard. "Poland, the Ukraine and Russia in the 17th Century." *Slavonic and East European Review*, 27 (1948), 157–171; 414–429.

Lyzhnyts'kyi, Hryhor. "Istoriia ukrains'koho teatru, I: Stara doba ukrains'koho teatru vid XV st. do 1619 r." *Zapysky Naukovoho Tovarystva im. T.H. Shevchenka*, 171 (1961), 135–190.

Łużny, Ryszard. *Pisarze kręgu Akademiji Kijowsko-Mohylańskiej a literatura polska*. Zeszyty Naukowe Universytetu Jagiellońskiego 142, Prace Historyczno-literackie, Zeszyt II. Cracow: 1966.

Makhnovets, Leonid. *Satyra i humor ukrains'koi prozy XVI-XVIII st.* Kiev: Naukova Dumka, 1964.

————. "Vertepna drama." In *Istoriia ukrains'koi literatury*. Vol. II. Kiev: Naukova Dumka, 1967, pp. 81–88.

Markovs'kyi, Ievhen. *Ukrains'kyi vertep*. Istorychno-filolohichnyi viddil, No. 86. Kiev: Akademia Nauk URSR, 1929.

Masliuk, Vitalii, et al., eds. *Apollonova lutnia; Kyivs'ki poety XVII-XVIII st.* Kiev: Molod', 1982.

Myshanych, O.V., ed. *Literaturna spadshchyna Kyivs'koi Rusi i ukrains'ka literatura XVI-XVIII st.* Kiev: Naukova Dumka, 1981.

————. *Ukrains'ke literaturne barokko*. Kiev: Naukova Dumka, 1987.

Nalivaiko, D.S. "Ukrains'ke barokko v konteksti evropeis'koho literaturnoho prosesu XVII st." *Radians'ke literaturoznavstvo*, 1 (1972), 30–47.

Peretts, Varvara Pavlovna. *Starinnyi spektakl v Rossii; sbornik stattei*. Leningrad: Akademiia, 1928.

Petrov, N. *Ocherki iz istorii ukrainskoi literatury XVII i XVIII vekov*. Kiev: Petr Barskii, 1911.

Rezanov, V. *Drama ukrains'ka*. Vol. I. Kiev: Ukrains'ka Akademiia Nauk, 1926.

————. *Iz istorii russkoi dramy; shkol'nie deistva XVII-XVIII vv. i teatr ezuitov*.

Moscow: n.p. 1910.

Rulin, Petro, ed. *Rannia ukrains'ka drama*. Kiev, Kharkiv: n.p., 1927.

Speranskii, M.N. *Istoria drevnei russkoi literatury*. Moscow: n.p., 1914.

Steshenko, I. "Istoria ukrains'koi dramy." *Ukraina*, 1 (March, 1907), 332–361; 2 (April, 1907), 14–40; 2 (May, 1907), 152–171; 2 (July, 1907), 269–285; 3 (July-August, 1907), 101–143; 3 (Sept., 1907), 311–339; 4 (Oct., 1907), 1–19.

Sulyma, M.M. *Ukrains'ke virshuvannia XVI—pochatku XVII st*. Kiev: Naukova Dumka, 1985.

Syvokin', H.M. *Davni ukrains'ki poetyky*. Kharkiv: Kharkivs'koho ordena Trudovoho chervonoho prapora Derzhavnoho universytetu Im. O.M. Hor' koho, 1960.

Vozniak, Mykhailo. "Dialog Ioanykii Volkovycha z 1613 r." *Zapysky Naukovoho Tovarystva im. T.H. Shevchenka*, 129 (Lviv, 1920), 33–79.

––––––. *Istoria ukrains'koi literatury*. Vol. 3: XVI–XVIII c. Lviv: Prosvita, 1924.

––––––. *Pochatky ukrains'koi komedii (1619–1819)*. Kiev: 1920. Rpt. N.Y.: Hoverlia, 1955.

Zguta, Russell. *Russian Minstrels; A History of the Skomorokhi*. Philadelphia: University of Pennsylvania Press, 1978.

Zholtovs'kyi, P.M. *Ukrains'kyi zhyvopys XVII–XVIII st*. Kiev: Naukova Dumka, 1978.

Zhytets'kyi, P. *Narysy literaturnoi istorii ukrains'koi movy XVII v*. Lviv: Ukrains'ke vydavnytsvo, 1941.